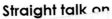

D0686647

ARMED DEFENSE

WHAT THE EXPERTS WANT YOU TO KNOW

EDITED BY
MASSAD AYOOB

Published by

Gun Digest® Books, an imprint of F+W Media, Inc.
Krause Publications • 700 East State Street • Iola, WI 54990-0001
715-445-2214 • 888-457-2873
www.krausebooks.com

To order books or other products call toll-free 1-800-258-0929
or visit us online at www.gundigeststore.com

ISBN-13: 978-1-4402-4754-5
ISBN-10: 1-4402-4754-4

Designed by Dave Hauser
Edited by Corrina Peterson

Printed in the United States of America

10 9 8 7 6 5 4 3 2 1

RELATED TITLES FROM GUN DIGEST BOOKS

Deadly Force: Understanding Your
Right to Self-Defense

Gun Digest Book of Concealed Carry
2nd Edition

Combat Shooting with Massad Ayoob

Defend Yourself:
A Comprehensive Security Plan for
the Armed Homeowner

Handgun Training - Practice Drills
For Defensive Shooting

Concealed Carry for Women

visit gundigest.com

TABLE OF CONTENTS

INTRODUCTION

BY MASSAD AYOOB

This book differs from my previous twenty (counting the occasional updated edition) in that it is a collection. The idea was born not in my office, but in the offices of the publisher when Gun Digest Media's Jim Schlender suggested it to me. While there are excellent books in each of the specialty fields encompassed in this selection, I don't believe this particular approach – a gathering of a dozen SMEs (subject matter experts) each addressing the specific element of threat management for which they are most famous – has been done yet in the self-defense field.

Why this approach? Because threat management, as it encompasses self-defense and defense of other innocent parties, is a multi-dimensional discipline. Each of those dimensions can be a life study in and of itself. Moreover, it's a living discipline in which theory and practice evolve as the threats evolve. Those who do not follow change and absorb it (or fight it when it goes in the wrong direction!) tend to fossilize and become obsolete. Threat management is a classic example of the old saying, "As soon as you think you have all the answers, the bastards change the questions."

In nineteen years as chair of the firearms/deadly force training committee for the American Society of Law Enforcement Trainers, thirteen or so years on the advisory board of the International Law Enforcement Educators and Trainers Association, et cetera, I've taken advantage of the networking that such professional seminars offer. It has allowed me to learn from the best and the brightest…and to invite them to contribute to this book. Happily, they all accepted that invitation.

In the early stages of the collection process, I

considered at first organizing the material into the three stages of crisis management: prevention, intervention, and postvention.

Prevention: We knew the bad thing might happen. We saw it coming. We put bulwarks in place to keep it from happening. If the crisis in question involved human aggression instead of uncontrollable things like hurricanes and tornadoes, we may have created a level of intimidation that made the aggressor realize it was not in his best interest to attack, and thus prevented the attack by deterring the potential attacker. Prevention is always the ideal.

Intervention: For whatever reason, the attack was not prevented. The prevention efforts may have failed, or been in the wrong place at the wrong time, or simply non-existent. It is HAPPENING NOW! At this point, we must intervene: break or at least stall the attack. Prevent further harm to the innocent. Freeze the situation where it is, with no further damage to those who we have determined it is our righteous and lawful need to protect.

Postvention: A term so seldom used most people won't recognize it. (Spellcheck doesn't recognize it either, it turns out.) It's over. All we can do is pick up the pieces. It is in this stage of crisis management that we bury the dead, heal the wounded, and console their loved ones. The legal aftermath of an incident falls into the postvention stage. The Critical Incident Debriefing occurs in the postvention stage, too, and before even that will come the investigation of the matter. Does that fall under postvention, too? Yes, most certainly.

Why, then, is this book not divided into those three sections after all? It is because, sequential as they obviously are, there is too much overlap. For example, the lessons learned from the investigation and the post-incident debriefing will feed back into the next and subsequent cycles of training, planning, and preparation. That improved training, those updated and hopefully better informed policies, will be there to guide the next cop or citizen who faces the next outbreak of deadly criminal violence.

Thus, the triad of prevention/intervention/postvention is not a three-act play. Because successful intervention flows from training that was given at least in part in hopes of prevention; because what was done during the intervention phase will be the focus of the postvention stage; and because the lessons from postvention will feed back into the next cycle of preventative training, the three are more like a continuously moving circle whose three stages are frequently mixed into one another.

PERSPECTIVES

When we discuss emotionally-charged topics that involve people being in mortal fear, we must be able to see the forest for the trees. There's a saying in the world of personal self-defense training: "It's not about the odds, it's about the stakes."

I ask my civilian students, "Do you have fire insurance on your home?" Of course, most raise their hands. My next question is, "Have you had your house burn down?" Occasionally, a student does raise his or her hand. "Damn glad you had the insurance, weren't you?" I ask, and the response is always an enthusiastic "Yes."

Finally, I ask, "Does anyone feel that you were cheated by the insurance company if your house didn't burn down? Is anyone sitting here now thinking 'Damn, my house never burned down, so I lost the bet and I'm a loser?'" They laugh, and shake their heads in the negative.

What we're talking about in this book is a direct allegory to that. If your house doesn't burn down, the premiums you paid on fire insurance were still worth it. Partly for the peace of mind it gave you knowing it was there, and partly because if that horrible thing happened, it could be dealt with.

Being armed and ready to act in self-defense against a lethal threat is much the same. If you are one of the great majority who never needs to pull the trigger, the money you spent on self-defense training and equipment wasn't wasted; it gave you full value in peace of mind. But, if it did happen…well, you were damn glad you were prepared and ready for it.

We're going to start with understanding the mindset of it all, and we'll start with understanding ourselves. Why that, and not begin with understanding "the enemy?" Because not all life-threatening crisis involves a lethally dangerous criminal coming at you and your family. We live finite lives in a dangerous world. Deadly danger is deadly danger. Whether it's a hand-to-hand fight or a gunfight, or a car crash or plane crash or natural disaster or someone we love collapsing from a heart attack before our very eyes, our reactions to lethal danger will be much the same. The shape of what we're facing may change, but what we bring to that "critical incident" will be pretty much the same.

> ## KNOWING AND UNDERSTANDING YOUR LIKELY OPPONENT IS CRITICAL...BUT KNOWING AND UNDERSTANDING YOURSELF MAY WELL BE MORE IMPORTANT.

The years have taught me that knowing and understanding your likely opponent is critical...but knowing and understanding yourself may well be more important.

How our minds and bodies work in crisis is something we must know if we're going to program that mind and body to fight and prevail in a life-or-death situation. I have known John Hearne for many years, and consider him one of the rising stars in the training world. He has spent his adult life studying this topic and correlating it with his deep research into actual gunfights. A champion combat pistol shooter and a career federal law enforcement officer, Hearne has been able to debunk and dispel a great deal of junk science that was formerly applied to this discipline (and still is, by some). His eight-hour presentation on this topic is a highlight of every national Rangemaster Tactical Conference, and his chapter seemed the most logical point at which to start the body of this book.

JOHN HEARNE

"Post-shooting trauma" is a term that has been credited to the great police psychologist Dr. Walter Gorski. I first met him in 1981, at the found-

ing meeting of IALEFI, the International Association of Law Enforcement Firearms Instructors, convened at the Smith & Wesson Academy in Springfield, Massachusetts by that entity's founding director Charlie Smith, who was one of my own mentors early in my career. Gorski was perhaps the first in his field to distinguish the psychological and emotional aftermath of having had to kill a human being, particularly in American society, from generic post-traumatic stress disorder.

Why does that come early in the book, when we're talking about understanding things before the life-threatening crisis occurs? Because when we have to take action, we have to know that we can handle the worst that follows! If we aren't certain of that, we will hesitate at the worst possible time, and become yet another martyr to the truth that "he who hesitates is lost."

DR. ANTHONY SEMONE

Over the decades since Dr. Gorski first trained me in this discipline, for which I will be eternally grateful, I have worked with many psychologists and psychiatrists with extensive experience and research in this field. I could think of none better to write the chapter on this topic than the noted neuro-psychologist Dr. Anthony Semone. Now retired and taking only cases that interest him, Tony over the years has testified as an expert in many death penalty cases and self-defense cases. He has a vast firearms/self-defense training resume that includes fourth level certification in my own system, has dealt with armed violence personally, and has more pieces of the puzzle than most. Dr. Semone's treatise here on managing the aftermath of a lethal force encounter is absolutely priceless. This is why, though dealing with this seems to most a "last stage of everything thing," it needs to come early in the individual's understanding of all the dimensions of a deadly force encounter and how to survive it.

Altered perceptions during – and after – what we euphemistically call "critical incidents" are, well, critical to understand. When everything seems to go into slow motion, you might ask yourself, "Am I losing my mind? Did someone put LSD in my coffee this morning?" and hesitate when you most need to act swiftly and decisively. I've talked with more than one gunfight survivor who, when he realized he wasn't hearing his shots or heard them as muted pops or poofs, thought his gun was malfunctioning. It is vital to be prepared for such altered perceptions beforehand. In the aftermath, one must be equally prepared to explain why the gunfight he won seemed to him to take a full minute, when reconstruction shows that it happened much faster, without those who judge him thinking he is lying about what happened.

DR. ALEXIS ARTWOHL

I have been writing about this sort of thing in police journals and gun magazines since the 1970s, and I am convinced that our leading authority on the topic today is Dr. Alexis Artwohl. Her ascendancy to top expert in the physio-psychological aspects of violent encounters when she was police psychologist for the Portland, Oregon Police Bureau put her on the map. In the years since I've watched her lecture at ASLET, the American Society of Law Enforcement Trainers, and ILEETA, the International Law Enforcement Educators and Trainers Association. A "must read" is her book "Deadly Force Encounters," co-authored with Loren Christensen, a veteran Portland street cop and master martial artist.

DR. WILLIAM APRILL

The face of the enemy is critical to know, for the simple, eternal reason that we cannot expect to defeat an opponent we do not understand. I asked my friend and fourth-level graduate Dr. William Aprill to address that topic for this book, because he is a psychologist who has very deep experience with violent criminals, and likewise with their victims. He knows both sides of that coin, both of which need to be understood if one is going to be successful in self-defense. William also has extensive self-defense training and an extremely high skill level in both firearms and hand-to-hand work. Dr. Aprill has many pieces of the complicated puzzle this book addresses.

Countering the opponent requires knowledge of how he is going to come at you, and what the best and most field-proven tactics for defeating him happen to be. The man I asked to address that here, the master of what he calls ECQC for Extreme Close Quarter Concepts, is Craig Douglas. For many years, the public knew him only by his Internet sobriquet, "SouthNarc." We weren't able to publish his real name until he retired from a more than twenty-year career, most of it in narcotics and a great deal of that in an undercover capacity. Predictably, this earned him a wealth of personal experience in dealing with deadly threat, and his work with various drug task forces put him in contact with other lawmen who'd had similar experiences. Craig combined that with study both deep and wide of hand-to-hand fighting, gunfighting, and the mixture of the two that is known today in the trade as "combatives."

CRAIG "SOUTHNARC" DOUGLAS

I first met Craig circa 1990 when he was an eager young cop, and I took a rattan baton instructor class from him. His eagerness never flagged as his skill, experience, and fame all grew. Today he is a staple at the Rangemaster Tactical Conference hosted every year by Tom Givens. There is simply no one I know of who is better at what he does.

Living it will encompass changes in lifestyle when you carry a loaded weapon virtually everywhere you go. Having carried for several decades, I was in a position to write about that myself.

How important is training? Having intensively studied "officer survival" training and research since 1972, I cannot help but notice how many cops survived attempted murder and when asked what was the key to their survival, answered in one word: "Training!" You see the same in the military. And you see it among armed citizens... at least, the ones who had training in what to do in that type of emergency.

For this book, I've been able to juxtapose two well-credentialed experts to compare how the trained armed citizen fares vis-à-vis the untrained one when violent encounters take place. Each of those experts speaks in this book to incidents that occurred primarily in their major American cities.

TOM GIVENS

Tom Givens is an ex-cop who has made defensive firearms training his life mission, and has done exceedingly well at it. The city where he did most of his work is Memphis, Tennessee – "Mogadishu on the Mississippi" as Tom liked to call it until his recent move to Florida – and being the pre-eminent firearms instructor in the city when he ran his Rangemaster facility there, Tom amassed over sixty case studies of his graduates who were involved in gunfights. I consider Tom one of the leading defensive firearms instructors in America today, whether cop or civilian, and in the many years I've known him I've come to respect him and his training team as a "bullshit-free zone." Givens is also the host of the annual Rangemaster Tactical Conference, a smorgasbord of top instructors each giving two- to four-hour samples of their training to an audience that includes law-abiding armed citizens as well as police officers and military personnel.

In the pages that follow, contrast Tom Givens' study of the truly awesome stats that came out of the gunfights of the students he had trained, versus the stats of those who fought back against violent armed criminals with no training at all. The latter comes from the one contributor to this book who is pseudonymous: "Spencer Blue."

"Spencer Blue" is the nom de plume of a U.S. military war vet and a street cop in a major American city. Political correctness being what it is today, and given that his chapter is supportive of one side of one of America's most politicized and contentious debates, it was decided to not put his career in jeopardy by using his real name or department affiliation. I ran across him on a gun forum frequented by serious professionals in the training world. I later met him and confirmed through sources I know and trust in his city that he is who he says he is. "Spencer" is a robbery/homicide detective, working the former (which often leads to the latter), and in a position to debrief the many people in his city whose cases he investigated after they became the intended victims of sometimes-murderous robbers. Out of personal interest ("Spencer" being a survivor and winner of a fatal line-of-duty gunfight himself), he gathered some remarkably interesting statistics on how things went for people who didn't have training, but did fight back against deadly criminals, with deadly force. The contrasts with his study population and Tom Givens' are most instructive.

Interdicting mass murderers has become a more critical issue today due in part to copycat psychopaths seeking a sick blaze of glory, and jihadists committing wholesale slaughter in the name of radical religious precepts. I have known Ron Borsch for many, many years. After the Columbine atrocity, law enforcement realized that such incidents could not be best handled by waiting for a SWAT team, and went with rapid deployment of first responding officers as an ad hoc team as a better protocol. I can attest that Ron Borsch was the first credible authority in law enforcement to come out and publicly state that entry by even a lone officer first on the scene made even more sense. He was practically burned at the stake at first by other trainers around the country, but the years have proven Ron's approach correct.

RON BORSCH

Borsch notes that a huge number of these incidents have been ended by private citizens who happened to be on the scene and acted courageously, during the achingly long interval between when the attack began and when police could arrive. He has also pointed out that, while armed citizens and off-duty cops have stopped many such potential massacres, many have also been stopped by unarmed citizens who took decisive action.

You'll note that Ron doesn't mention the names of the perpetrators, referring to them generically as "the cowards." This is because he recognizes the undeniable reality that many of these murderers are thwarted losers who see mass murderers on the cover of magazines like TIME and mimic those atrocities to earn their proverbial "fifteen minutes of fame." He, and many other authorities, believe that burying the names of these butchers in contemptuous anonymity might reduce the deadly copycat effect.

Ron Borsch's research underscores the importance of the first responder in life-or-death crises.

Interaction with responding/investigating police officers is virtually inevitable, and is best planned for beforehand. It will certainly happen after a use-of-force incident, and may occur with the simple routine of being pulled over by a police officer, or witnessing a crime and being interviewed by an investigating officer. In many jurisdictions, the private citizen carrying a gun is required to notify the officer of that when any official contact is made. Check handgunlaw.us to see whether that is the case in any given state you might be in while carrying.

HARVEY HEDDEN

The person I invited to address this topic is Harvey Hedden. He and I first met at the great old Second Chance Shoot in Michigan, and we worked together for nineteen years at

ASLET and more than thirteen at ILEETA, where we were founding members in both cases. As Executive Director of ILEETA, Harvey continues to be a leader in cutting-edge police training. An advocate of Second Amendment rights, Harvey is well positioned to advise on armed citizen/police interaction. He and I both believe that the law-abiding armed citizen and the police officer are natural allies in the "war against crime."

Court aftermath, of course, is a huge concern. The late, great WWII combat vet Lt. Col. Jeff Cooper (USMC, Ret.) was one of the 20th century's most significant authorities on gunfighting. He said Problem One was winning the gunfight, and Problem Two was surviving the courtroom aftermath.

JIM FLEMING, ESQ.

I asked my friend and colleague Jim Fleming, Esq. to address this issue. Jim is a Minnesota defense lawyer who, over the decades, has righteously earned fame for his defense of innocent people wrongly accused. He is also an ex-cop and firearms/concealed carry instructor. Jim and I have taught multiple CLE (Continuing Legal Education for practicing attorneys) courses on management of the lethal force case, around the country. Go to Amazon.com and order Jim's book "The Bison King," the story of how he exonerated a wrongfully accused man imprisoned for criminal homicide. And his book "Aftermath," which focuses on how to manage a righteous use of deadly force in self-defense. And his latest, "The Second Amendment and the American Gun: Evolution and Development of a Right Under Siege." Jim's advice on this was born in courtroom experience, and is something you can take to the bank.

Post-incident support is a critical element, in a world where anyone can bring suit against anyone for anything. The defense in State of Florida v. George Zimmerman, arising from a very controversial shooting on February 26, 2012, and culminating in a full acquittal on July 13, 2013, left the defendant with a seven-figure legal bill. It is not at all uncommon for the cost of defending criminal prosecution or lawsuit to go into six figures. Few people have the resources to handle that. Today, we have a burgeoning cottage industry dedicated to post-self-defense support.

MARTY HAYES, JD

I asked Marty Hayes, JD, founder of one such organization, the Armed Citizens Legal Defense Network (armedcitizensnetwork.org) to write the chapter on that. Why ask one of the players? Because Hayes is the man who established that industry with ACLDN, the first such organization. I have worked with Marty in training for more than a quarter century and have always found him scrupulously honest. In the spirit of total disclosure, I've been on the advisory board of ACLDN since its inception. I've seen it work.

Finally…

I want to profoundly thank the professionals who made this book what it is. I know you will benefit from reading their work, as I have benefitted from knowing and learning from them.

Respectfully,
Massad Ayoob
October 2016

Chapter 1:
INSIDE THE DEFENDER'S HEAD

BY JOHN HEARNE

T he self-defense community is infamous for focusing on "hardware issues" and debating ad nauseum the alleged superiority of certain calibers or the best shooting stance. When we do discuss "software issues," one of the popular topics, filled with misinformation, is how capable people are of performing well under life-and-death stress. Some folks flippantly dismiss these performance concerns and suggest that more "testicular fortitude" is all that is needed. Others take the position that one is destined to devolve into a quivering mass of Jello with flippers for fingers and that high levels of performance are simply impossible due to "body alarm reaction," "tach-psyche effect," "survival stress response," "Hick's Law" or some other psycho-babble excuse. As with many topics, the truth lies not at the extremes but in the murky middle with some caveats such as "it depends" and "it's based on the individual" and "you have to train properly."

The argument that high levels of performance under stress are impossible can quickly be disregarded with the most modest appreciation of history. Most of us have recognized that some people are able to perform remarkable feats of skill and rational thought while facing death squarely in the face. Whether we reference Jim Cirillo's gunfights, the hit rates of LAPD's Metro units, or Captain Sullenberger's ability to expertly land a crippled jet on the Hudson, it is obvious that at least some individuals can perform exceptionally when needed.

Unfortunately, there are numerous examples of people performing poorly under stress. With the proliferation of video cameras in police cars, it is not difficult to find tragic examples of officers being utterly incapable of delivering the most fundamental of skills when faced with a real threat. For instance, annual statistics from the FBI tell us that practically every year, the majority of police officers are feloniously killed without ever removing their service weapon from the holster.

These observations raise an interesting question – if high levels of performance are possible, how do we increase our likelihood of performing well? Before offering specific advice, we need to recognize that some people are more gifted in this area than others. The research literature seems to suggest that 10-20% of the

RESEARCH LITERATURE SEEMS TO SUGGEST THAT 10-20% OF THE POPULATION ARE "NATURAL SURVIVORS." FOR THE REST OF US, RELEVANT, REALISTIC, AND RECENT TRAINING BECOMES THE BEST OPTION.

population are "natural survivors" and more able to respond calmly and rationally during a crisis.

The good news is that proper performance under stress is not limited to this gifted group. For the rest of us, relevant, realistic, and recent training becomes the best option for reliable performance across a variety of domains – whether we are considering gunfighting or aviation emergencies. Jeff Cooper famously noted that the purpose of training was to make copers out of non-copers. There is an incredible amount of truth in that observation. In order to understand why these are our best solutions, it is necessary to examine what scientists have learned about the human animal.

OUR TWO BRAINS

While the analogy is crude, it is not unreasonable to view your head as housing two distinctly different brains. The first brain is older and its solutions, while imperfect, are time-tested and proven over hundreds of thousands of years of evolution. We'll label this brain the "emotional" brain. The emotional brain offers many of our most basic responses, most notably fight, flight, or freeze.

In this day and age, we tend to scoff at some of these responses such as freeze. At first glance, freezing while facing a life threatening situation does not make much sense – how could this possibly keep us alive? However, this response evolved in a world where we were hunted by larger predators that hunted by sight and located prey by movement. In a world before firearms, freezing when you saw the lion first might keep you alive long enough to share your genes.

With these responses, the emotional brain also brings with it a powerful ally in its simple responses – adrenaline. While many view adrenaline and its long list of associated symptoms as negatives, the release of adrenaline brings significant advantages. Adrenaline is basically nitrous for the body – it allows greater strength, a reduction in sensations of pain, and if one is executing a primitive option, it makes our fight or flight much more effective.

While the emotional brain is very good at its primitive responses, it does have some major shortcomings. The emotional brain does not possess the ability to analyze and synthesize complex solutions. The emotional brain is not a very effective tool user either, especially when the tool is more complex than a rock or stick.

Our second brain is best labeled the "rational brain." It is a far more recent evolutionary development and it has accomplished amazing feats. Our rational brain is the seat of our problem-solving abilities and speech. Our rational brain is what allows us to design skyscrapers and fly spacecraft. Civilization itself is founded on our ability to use our rational brain for communication and planning.

When I picture the emotional brain, I tend to think of a large grizzly bear. This bear is very strong, can move very quickly, and can destroy most anything it can touch with its claws. It is a strong, nasty brute that can dominate with its strength or run away very quickly if necessary. It is perfectly at home in nature and can solve "natural" problems very well. This brain can decide very quickly to run away but it cannot reload a pistol or properly respond to a stalling aircraft.

I picture the rational brain as an early human, moving through the harsh, resource scarce world of the ice ages. This human wears carefully-crafted clothes to protect him from the cold and carries with him highly developed weapons that allow him to kill dangerous creatures many times his size. Using his problem solving abilities and language abilities, he manages to work as part of a carefully coordinated team to make sure the tribe does not starve.

Understanding human performance in life-and-death stress revolves around the interplay of these two brains. Generally speaking, people who perform well under stress are those who are able to allow the rational brain to stay in charge of solving the problem at hand. Any time we are using tools (firearms and other force options are just specialized, life-saving tools) or facing complex situations (such as assessing the lawfulness of our choices), we only perform well if the rational brain remains in control.

Whether the rational brain or the emotion brain ends up in control is ultimately up to a subconscious process. This process is much like a crusty old baseball coach who is an expert at swapping the right player at the right time to maximize the odds of winning. This coach is very difficult to fool and knows with great certainty how good your skills are, the last time you practiced, how much sleep you've had, whether your heart is really in it, and many other considerations that enter into the calculus of which brain to use.

While not as sexy as sub-6 second *El Presidentes* or any other feat of great technical ability, much of performing well under stress revolves around training the subconscious to allow the rational mind to stay in control when things are at their worst. In order to understand this process, we must recognize that there are certain circumstances under which the sub-conscious is more likely to default to the emotional brain in order to mitigate them. These situations include: the potential for catastrophic consequences (death, injury, or ego damage); situations with limited time; our current anxiety level; situations we haven't seen before; and close proximity of the threat.

Essentially, the subconscious is answering the question – how bad? The more the answer is "really, really bad!!!" the more likely it is that the emotional brain will take over. In the self-defense world this perfect storm would look like an adversary suddenly producing and firing a firearm at extremely close range. In fact, these circumstances describe the manner in which most police officers feloniously die in the line of duty every year. The need to avoid these perfect storms of circumstances also shows us why situational awareness is so critical and can offer such an overwhelming advantage.

If the circumstances are

HOW WELL THE MENTAL MAP MATCHES THE UNFOLDING REALITY WILL BE THE DEAL-BREAKER BETWEEN CONTINUING TO TRUST THE RATIONAL MIND OR DEFAULTING TO THE EMOTIONAL MIND.

not considered so bad that the subconscious defaults to the emotional brain immediately, then the subconscious will ask this question – are we in control? Control doesn't necessary mean that we are driving the events unfolding around us but rather, do our perceived abilities match or exceed the difficulty of the circumstances being faced? Factors that make answering "yes" to this analysis include: having seen the problem before, having won in similar circumstances, having plans stored away for this sort of problem, and having a "mental map" that matches the unfolding circumstances.

Of these various factors listed above, the mental maps that we have or have not created will likely be most important. The term mental map is shorthand for an incredibly complicated process in which the mind creates a model of the surrounding environment and creates expectations about how that world works. When the subconscious is evaluating whether to trust a situation to the emotional or rational mind, how well the mental map matches the unfolding reality will be the deal-breaker between continuing to trust the rational mind or defaulting to the emotional mind.

For instance, if your mental map includes the belief that merely racking a pump shotgun will make bad guys flee, and then the bad guys don't run when your ballistic talisman is cycled, your subconscious will likely not trust anything else the rational mind has to offer during that situation. Alternatively, if your mental map includes the possibility that shooting someone several times in the chest might not stop a dedicated attacker, your subconscious will be more likely to trust the rational mind when it suggests that transitioning to a head shot might be the next best course of action.

This need for valid mental maps creates one of the subconscious' greatest considerations. While the mind recognizes the need for mental maps that match, it will be much worse when the mind has no frame of reference for what it is experiencing. Any time the mind is experiencing novel stimuli, there is a much greater likelihood of a transition to the emotional brain. Based on tens of thousands of years of evolution, if something suddenly appears for which the mind has no reference, the mind will assume that it is bad – really, really bad.

If these processes seem subjective, there's a reason – they are. There is very little objective assessment in these processes; they are driven by perceptions, and different individuals can reach very different conclusions based on the same set of observations.

For instance, suppose you are standing in a room with only one door and you are along the wall furthest away from that door. Suddenly, a polar bear appears between you and the door – you are suddenly trapped with an amazing natural predator that sees you as nothing but a slow moving sack of protein. There are three possible reactions to these circumstances. If your reaction is, "Oh my God! I'm going to die!" you're probably right. You'll most likely freeze in place and watch helplessly as you learn your place in the food chain.

A second option is this: upon seeing the polar bear materialize, you think, "Damn! He's going to look good as a rug in front of my fire place." If this is your reaction, and you have the tools and the necessary skills to use them, the polar bear is the one with the serious problem. The history of human conflict tells us that you will in all likelihood emerge as the victor.

Between these extremes is a middle ground, a middle ground that is obtainable through hard work and prior preparation. If the sudden appearance of the polar bear makes you think, "Damn! I have a problem but I can solve it," then the odds are you'll be able to use whatever firearm you're carrying (you are carrying a firearm aren't you?) and emerge as an adrenalized victor.

Ultimately, people who perform well under stress tend to have a lifelong commitment to teaching the subconscious to ignore the cries of the emotional brain and to trust their well-trained rational brain. They use a variety of mechanisms to develop this trust, including training, hunting, high-risk sports, competition, visualization, etc. Regardless of the particular mechanism(s) used, the results are undeniable.

BRAIN MECHANISMS AND WIRING

While the idea of having two brains running around inside your head may seem esoteric, modern neuroscience has vastly expanded our understanding of how the brain actually works at a mechanical level. If we can understand how certain portions of our brain work, then we can start to leverage these systems to our advantage.

Our brain works on a simple premise – if you do something a lot, it must be important. If a task or motor program is identified as important, the brain will begin to prioritize it and find ways to make it quicker and more efficient to execute. The more important a task is, the more the brain will prepare itself to be able to perform it. Eventually, the optimizations make the well-developed motor programs far less susceptible to the effects of stress.

The most basic example of this is the ease at which motor programs can be accessed based on frequency of use. Think of a stack of file folders on your desk. Every time you use one, you put it back on top of the pile. Eventually, the files you are using the most will end up at the top of the pile. These folders will be more accessible and the ones you can grab most easily when under time pressure. Motor programs work in much the same way. If you perform certain motor programs regularly, they become primed for execution and are more accessible to the brain than what you learned a year ago but haven't practiced since. This is why the concept of recency in our training is so important.

As another example, the brain seems to have two distinct memory systems. If you've ever memorized the capitals of the states for tomorrow's test, you've taken advantage of the brains explicit memory system. Explicit memories are intentionally placed into the mind and unless the placement is done very intensely, the contents of our explicit memory system can disappear quickly.

You also have an *implicit memory system*. The

THE CONTENTS OF OUR EXPLICIT MEMORY SYSTEM CAN DISAPPEAR QUICKLY.

implicit system is where we store how to perform physical tasks. For instance, if you've ever gone a long time without riding a bicycle and then rode one successfully, you can thank your implicit memory system. The implicit memory system is the home of so-called "muscle memory" which is really just a way of saying "well developed neural programs which can be executed without conscious thought." Tasks performed from muscle memory are actually physically and measurably different. For instance, the amount of muscle activity and the amount of limb stiffness are much lower in these types of tasks. These tasks are performed very efficiently and the more they are performed the more efficient they become. Ultimately, you end up using less brain resources to execute the task.

It is important to remember that these efficiencies come from actual physical changes to the structure of the brain. Through a process called *myelination*, a fatty, insulating substance is laid down on the particular neural pathways being used most frequently. The deposits of myelin actually increase the speed at which electrical impulses move through the brain. Unfortunately, nothing is forever and this process will reverse itself if a pathway isn't used regularly. The need to maintain myelination points towards the importance of a life-long dedication and practice of whatever lifesaving skills you need to be able to perform, it is literally "use it or lose it."

Whenever scientists study how well someone has learned something, they use three standards. The first and lowest level can be called "untrained" which means someone has not had formal training and/or demonstrated proficiency. The next level is "learned" which means that instruction has been offered and the student has demonstrated basic proficiency in the task. The highest level is "overlearned," which means that the task has been practiced beyond basic proficiency.

These standards are relevant because we know that overlearned skills have distinct attributes. These include greater accuracy, speed, and fluidity of movement; reduced muscle tension; longer term retention; greater ability to complete complex tasks based on the overlearned material; higher base level to which the skill will decay without practice; reduced rate of skill loss without practice; greater accessibility under stress; and reduced amount of mental resources to execute the task.

These advantages can be summarized in one word – *automaticity*. A commonly accepted definition is "the ability to do things without occupying the mind with the low-level details required, allowing it to become an automatic response pattern or habit." Increasing levels of automaticity in basic skills offer major benefits. First, it is highly likely that these skills will be accessible under life and death stress. Second, because these skills place little, if any, demand on the brain, the mind is able to execute these skills while actively problem solving. For the shooter, possessing skills with high levels of automaticity allows one to instantly present the firearm, seek cover, maneuver when needed, and even evaluate the lawfulness of a particular action, all in the heat of the moment.

APPLICATION AND ANALYSIS

There is one final concept we need to understand in order to understand performance under life and death stress – *task complexity*. When used in the purest sense, task complexity is a score that measures the difficulty of performing a specific job. The task complexity score increases as the number of decisions needed increases, the amount of perceptions needed increases, and the complexity of motor skills involved increases. Research tells us that tasks with greater complexity are best performed during lower arousal states (lower pulse, breathing, blood pressure, etc.) or, effectively, when we are functioning more in our rational mind. For purposes of this chapter, we can also think of task complexity as the difficulty of the scenario we are trying to win. For instance, shooting a home intruder when you're fully awake and barricaded in your safe room with a long gun is a much simpler scenario than a solo police officer responding to a chaotic, large scale terrorist event.

The failure to appreciate these concepts – recency, implicit memory, myelination, overlearning, automaticity, and task complexity – explains a lot of the misinformation that is heard when human performance is discussed. If we just consider the necessary motor skills, we must recognize that unless the needed skill was overlearned to begin with and then practiced regularly to maintain recency, it is unlikely that it will be seen during periods of life and death stress. By their very nature, skills possessed merely at the learned level are not very accessible under stress. If they haven't been practiced recently, the brain may have trouble finding those skills and may not trust them to solve the problem at hand.

If I were to express this concept visually it might look something like this:

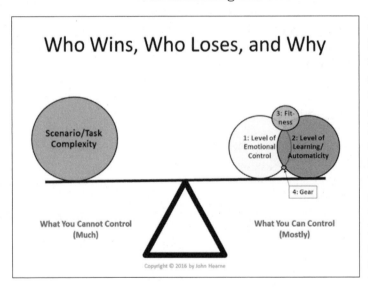

In order to win, I must have more emotional control and skill than the problem I am confronting. If my emotional control and skill are greater than the problem I'm confronting, then I will win. If the problem is greater than my emotional control and skill, then I'll lose. A dominating win comes from bringing dramatically more emotional control and/or skill to the fight than the scenario requires. Losing badly would be the result of facing a problem that dramatically exceeds one's abilities.

"Level of emotional control" encompasses many different aspects needed to win a fight, such as situational awareness, tactics, etc., but all of these require the ability to analyze the situation, and analysis is rooted in the rational mind which can only be used when the emotions are controlled. To use an older term, emotional control contains all of the aspects of the combat mindset.

"Level of skill" contains many facets based on role of the actor. It may include firearms skills, empty hand skills, verbal skills, etc. If we were discussing firearms skills, it would include marksmanship and gun handling.

> **NEITHER FITNESS NOR GEAR CAN EVER PROVIDE ENOUGH BENEFIT BY THEMSELVES TO OVERCOME A LACK OF SUFFICIENT EMOTIONAL CONTROL AND SKILL.**

There are other ways to tip the balance in my favor, including physical fitness (much more important for law enforcement and military), and the equipment I'm using. However, neither fitness nor gear can ever provide enough benefit by themselves to overcome a lack of sufficient emotional control and skill.

Before moving to specifics, it is important to note that the complexity of the scenario we are handling is not always entirely out of our control. Situational awareness and an acceptance of what we are seeing can sometimes help reduce the complexity of a potential problem. As noted trainer Tom Givens reminds us, we must know "who's around us and what they are doing," and we must not rationalize or downplay the danger signals we are seeing. It is much easier to avoid a bad situation entirely than to try to fight out of a worst-case scenario because you didn't see the danger signs, or if you did see them, failed to accept them and plan/act accordingly.

PROPER TRAINING AND PREPARATION

In light of this information, how to best prepare for self-defense situations most efficiently has priorities that are different than many seem to think. These priorities are:

1. Remove novelty.
2. Build valid mental maps.
3. Develop robust motor programs for relevant skills.
4. Keep mental maps and motor programs re-

freshed and recent.

Developing one's level of emotional control is a much more complicated task, with techniques not as well-established as those for building motor skills. Building emotional control can be addressed in many different ways and a multi-prong approach seems to be best, as opposed to relying on one single method. Of all the concerns we can address, making sure that the brain does not face a novel situation is probably the most important.

As mentioned earlier, the pattern-loving subconscious is naturally fearful of novel situations and is more likely to trust the emotional brain and its classic responses of fight, flight, freeze, or posture when confronting something it has not seen before. While many so-called experts will tell you that you need to train with photo-realistic targets to overcome the so-called "innate hesitation to kill," the reality is that the first time the subconscious sees the sights superimposed on someone's chest should not be in an actual confrontation. This isn't about a hesitation to kill but about removing the novelty from the experience.

The primary goal of self-defense training should be to expose the brain to all of the situations it is likely to encounter and need to address. This is why simply teaching someone to shoot is inadequate training for self-defense. Being able to shoot a fist size group on a B-27 in no way, shape, or form resembles the task complexity of being accosted in a parking lot in reduced light by someone who does not telegraph their intentions until the last possible moment and uses a major threat of force.

Given the brain's heavy use of vision to create its view of the world, and research from the military on its value, one of the most underused training tools is

SOMEONE WITH BASIC FIRE-ARMS SKILLS AND A RESPECTABLE MENTAL LIBRARY WILL BE FAR MORE PREPARED TO DEFEND THEMSELVES THAN SOMEONE WHO MERELY PRACTICES THEIR SHOOTING SKILLS IN A STERILE RANGE ENVIRONMENT.

probably the video simulator, especially the models that allow the use of the student's actual, live firearms. Since a student could complete a large number of scenarios in just a brief bit of time, they could build a respectable mental library of how threats unfold and how to properly respond to them. Someone with basic firearms skills and such a mental library will be far more prepared to defend themselves than someone who merely practices their shooting skills to an intermediate or advanced level in a sterile range environment. Such simulators would also help form valid mental maps, our second priority.

While having valid mental maps is an important factor in allowing the rational mind to stay in control, mental maps also set us up for success or failure during actual events. For these reasons, having accurate maps is crucial. The importance of valid mental maps can best be seen in situations where someone else's maps were inaccurate. A classic example of this would be a belief that only certain genders or races or ages engage in crime. If your mental map for an armed robber is limited to a young black male wearing a hoodie, you will only be prepared for such a threat and will be effectively blind to an armed robber who is an older white female.

Mental maps are also where we plan out our most desirable actions during a fight, such as seeking cover or post-fight actions. If we want to perform any of these actions, we must build a map that includes them. Besides video simulators, mental visualization, and force-on-force training are other tested methods that help create these crucial maps.

Our third priority is to develop robust motor programs for relevant skills. Robust and relevant are the key considerations. The motor programs we will bet our lives on must be "sturdy in construction." They should be as simple as possible and they must be heavily practiced so that they can endure the stress of a critical incident. Also, the skills we choose to develop must be relevant – that is, likely to be used in a problem we are likely to face. For instance, while being able to deliver accurate rifle shots at 1,000 yard is an impressive feat, unless one is a military sniper the skill isn't relevant to dealing with violent street crime.

Since we are discussing relevant skills, I would be remiss if I didn't address a common fallacy in this arena. When training and firearms discussed, concerns about fine and gross motor skills are often raised. Many authors have maintained that fine motor skills, those involving smaller muscles and significant hand-eye coordination, cannot be performed during periods of extreme stress. While this is a valid concern for some situations, current research tells us that the use of fine motor skills is possible if the skills are practiced properly.

In fact, the blanket position that fine motor skills are not possible fails the most casual examination. For instance, the mere act of removing a pistol from a retention holster involves the use of fine motor skills. Those who argue that the slide must be pulled backwards to chamber a round during the reload ignore the fact that the shooter managed to push the magazine release button, an object that is almost always smaller than the slide catch lever or release. Finally, we cannot hit our target unless we can execute the finest of the fine motor skills – trigger control. If fine motor skills were impossible under stress, no police officer would be able to draw their weapon during a fight, reload it, or hit with a single round, ever.

Fine motor skills are a training concern because they do degrade more quickly when your arousal level is elevated, unless the skills are overlearned. Fine motor skills are also vulnerable to degradation from lack of practice as they are more vulnerable to recency effects. This means that we must spend more training time on fine motor skills in order to make sure they are overlearned and we must practice them more often to ensure they can be executed when needed. Finally, our level of emotional control will dictate how aroused we become and how much our fine motor skills degrade, if at all.

When it comes to developing skills, the goal is to make sure the most important skills are overlearned until we develop automaticity. By their very definition, skills executed with automaticity are as robust as the brain can create. The most efficient way to reach this level is to receive quality instruction from a solid teacher and then practice the skills regularly on your own time. As part of this process, periodic review by a skilled coach, to ensure skills are being practiced correctly, can be an important component. This is will never be a quick process as we are making actual physical changes to our brains – myelination and automaticity simply take time and work.

The final priority is to keep our mental maps and motor skills refreshed and recent. It is a sad truth that our skills and mental maps start to degrade the instant we stop practicing. As noted, regular practice is key to building automaticity. But even once automaticity is developed, we must practice on a regular basis to make sure those gains are not lost.

Similarly, our mental maps will degrade if they are not refreshed and updated. Besides making sure we have recently visualized and solved likely scenarios, we must also be aware that criminal methods can change over time and, consequently, our mental maps must change to reflect these new realities.

FINAL THOUGHTS

The best available research now tells us that people can perform well under life-and-death stress. However, such performance is almost always the result of continuous practice and development. This practice and development takes place across a many different domains. While raw shooting skill can be important, it is not the most important factor. For instance, we must cultivate within ourselves the ability to work within the rational mind and not give in to the panic associated with the emotional mind. We do this by placing ourselves in stressful situations, learning to accept the pressure, and then learning to perform amidst the stress. We must make sure that we have already faced the most likely scenarios in training before we confront them in the real world, in order to remove novelty and allow the rational mind to execute its plans. Performing well under life-and-death circumstances is possible, but it is never accidental.

ABOUT THE AUTHOR

John Hearne has been a federal law enforcement officer since 1992, serving primarily in uniform patrol. He currently serves as an instructor (firearms, tactics, active shooter, and use of force), an armorer, and a field training officer for his agency. John's firearms instructor certifications include:

– **Federal Law Enforcement Training Center (FLETC)**
 (Pistol, Revolver, Shotgun, Rifle, Select-Fire)
– **Federal Bureau of Investigation (FBI) Police Firearms**
 Instructor
– **National Rifle Association (NRA) – Tactical Shooting**
– **Rangemaster Advanced Instructor Certification**

Hearne has been a Rangemaster instructor since 2001 and has helped teach armed citizens, law enforcement officers, and military personnel across the country. He is also a noted researcher and speaker and has been speaking at a variety of national and international venues since 2005.

Chapter 2:

PSYCHOLOGICAL AFTERMATH OF A CITIZEN'S USE OF LETHAL FORCE

BY **ANTHONY SEMONE,** Ph.D

B ecause of the work of Artwohl, Christensen, Lewinski, Ayoob and many others, much is now known about the psychological effects experienced by a person in association with self-defensive use of deadly force. At the onset of the confrontation, for example, it is common for the person to experience tunnel vision, auditory exclusion, alterations in perceived time, and the loss of fine motor control, among others. In the time frame following the encounter, it is unsurprising to observe symptoms associated with the altered state of consciousness produced by the encounter with death, including memory impairment, dissociative symptoms, and disruption to basic biological functions such as eating, sleeping, and sexual behavior. At points further along the temporal dimension from the shooting, flashbacks, social withdrawal and isolation, avoidance, and hypervigilance may well occur. (This listing of symptoms is not exhaustive.) While these data are largely gathered from subjects in the law enforcement community, they have been extrapolated here to the private citizen who has employed deadly force.

The rate of a person's recovery from the symptoms of complex stressful events will vary as a function of their pre-existing resilience with respect to the stressing stimulus complex and the efficacy of post-stimulus exposure to corrective interventions. Resilience is understood as "the capacity to recover quickly from difficulties; toughness," and it can be brought about in any given individual by graded exposure to the stressing stimulus complex. That exposure can be via mental imagery, mindfulness techniques, and/or scenario based training. Interventions employed for post-exposure recovery typically involve initially Critical Incident Stress Debriefing. Extended debriefing and graded exposure to stimulus complexes that continue to provoke negative experiences can be employed to ameliorate persistent symptomatology. Social support, however, is the major source for developing both resilience and symptom reduction secondary to the intimate understanding of the complex psychological response to a deadly force event.

PRIVATE CITIZEN - LAW ENFORCEMENT

Generally speaking, private citizens do not share with law enforcement officers those factors central to developing resilience. For the most part, private citizens are not members of an insular group whose esprit de corps permeates its daily existence. Private citizens do not typically undergo the extensive psychologically-based selection process that looks for resilience, nor do they benefit from resilience-producing experiences of academy training. In fact, it is reasonable to hypothesize that a significant percentage of private citizens undergo minimal training, if any at all. Also, law enforcement officers, as part of their governmental appointment as "keepers of the peace," have available to them the additional protections afforded by a network of professionals including psychologists, clergy, medical assistance programs, defense attorneys, and more. Indeed, any given use of deadly force by an officer has the potential of availing him of qualified immunity and summary judgment against potential legal consequences.

THERE IS AN EMBEDDED SOCIAL, CULTURAL, AND POLITICAL PREJUDICE AGAINST PRIVATE CITIZEN USE OF LETHAL MEANS OF SELF-DEFENSE.

However, private citizens who use lethal means to counter an imminent attack that reasonably threatens him or her with grave bodily harm or death may well do so at their own peril. That seems on the face of it inarguably true. Absent training, absent a cohesive supportive community, absent embedded professionals who are proximately available to him or her, the private citizen is left mostly alone to deal with the aftermath of that use of deadly force, and with a greater likelihood of the occurrence of complex psychological consequences. More critical, however, in this author's view, is this: private citizens do NOT have formal, visible governmental authority and sanction to engage in protecting and serving the public, even with deadly force. So there is an embedded social, cultural, and political prejudice against private citizen use of lethal means of self-defense. Private citizens who secure the means and take the responsibility for their own safety and that of their loved ones are seen as vigilantes or lone wolves. They are seen as inveighing against the collective and they frighten others because of their individualist ideology.

Hence, it is precisely in the presence of this deeply

embedded societal bias that the use of lethal force will undergo scathing scrutiny from that citizen's social, cultural, and political systems. And that scrutiny may well bring with it the full weight of governmental and media effort, especially when the use of force involves the death of a racial minority. As recent history has amply documented, neither private citizen (nor law enforcement officer for that matter) will escape that consequence (though arguably the LE will be more protected). This author would propose that, in the vulnerable citizen, the durability of the "poetic justice" inherent in the Mark of Cain will be the most enduring of symptom complexes with which the citizen will have to contend.

HYPOTHETICAL USE-OF-FORCE SCENARIO

You have just been required to use deadly force to ensure your continued life. In doing so, you met all requisite legal conditions, just as your father and your prolific reading of self-defense literature taught you. Upon recognizing that the attacker was down and out, you replaced your weapon in your truck while dialing 911 to report a self-defense shooting. You have your hands in the air as the first arriving officer orders you to turn around and get on the ground. As you are doing that you have a knee in your back, propelling you forcefully to the pavement. You then become aware of another sharp pain in your neck as what seems to be another knee immobilizes you. You experience a very rapid heart rate, irregular in character and you fear a heart attack. You are transported by EMS to your local hospital where you are diagnosed with an anxiety attack and released to the custody of law enforcement officers. (You will subsequently be diagnosed with cervical vertebral fractures and under go surgical repair. You will also undergo medical treatment for rotator cuff injury.) "Ah, excuse me Officer Friendly, I'm not the bad guy here."

The stress will continue with the interaction among you, law enforcement, and the prosecutorial side of the legal system: from initial arrest and incarceration, to probable cause hearing(s); preliminary hearing (s); response to continued jailing; securing bond (where possible given the charge); continuing threats against your family because you defended yourself successfully against a member of the community; threats against you while in jail; securing your own defense counsel; securing the funds (you may well go bankrupt) necessary to support a defense team, to include at least one investigator, one crime scene reconstructionist, one use-of-force expert, one prior firearms trainer as a fact witness (assuming you had any training), and of course one defense attorney where defending you will not be his or her first rodeo as an attorney who specializes in self-defense cases.

Now, let us assume that you get through the many pretrial motions, unfavorable rulings given by an anti-gun judge, and that you luck out and you meet your burden of production and are allowed to enter the defense of self-defense. However, your use of force expert is sharply curtailed in what he is allowed to introduce as expert testimony, the judge having ruled in a Frye hearing that such testimony requires the use of licensed psychologists or psychiatrists. Since your expert is not one of those professionals, he is precluded from testifying about those issues for just that reason, notwithstanding his credentials as an expert in the use of deadly force. Of course said judge was able to drag out some broadly construable case law as justification for his decision. In any case, that's what you're left with, but I digress.

And if it seems the gods are against you, consider further that you live in a jurisdiction that has gone progressively statist for the last three elections, electing politicians opposed to private citizen carry of lethal weapons. Those elected officials also represent the exact constituency reflected in the social, cultural, and political group of the individual whose life you admit to having taken. And it is precisely at jury selection that multiple additional stressors come into play deriving from the fact that the jury is not made up of your peers, but rather those of the decedent. And it is just here that the societal impact of your defensive use of deadly force will begin to have its say on the outcome of your legal case. Media outlets in the community will pounce immediately upon the shooting as the grist for their anti-gun mill and echo the dismay of the paper's similarly-biased readership.

Now, consider this: when, for example, you first contacted your wife following your being detained by LE and taken to jail, with the one phone call you were allowed by the jailer, your wife, amidst sobs, reported to you that your 11-year-old daughter came home from school also in tears as she reported one of her classmates having announced for all to hear that, "Your Daddy is a BAAADDDDD MAAANNN. He killed a poor, innocent boy who my Mommy told me had just turned his life around. I don't ever want to play again with you."

You and your family begin to feel shunned and distanced by your neighbors. Your children are ignored by their peers and no longer have their usual play-friends to "hang with." As a consequence of this social system response to your defensive shooting, your family becomes increasingly disenfranchised from its social system. Your and your family's responses to the reaction of the milieu in which you live will amplify further the shame and humiliation. Why?

The media will report this: You have just taken the life of a poor, disenfranchised boy that, according to all reports was unarmed – "after all, it was just a 'toy gun'." The newscaster will report in somber tones on the nightly news report, that the teenage boy was from an impoverished neighborhood; that he never had the "privilege" you have enjoyed your entire life; and, besides that, quoting a family member: "how was he gonna get the money to pay for the new clothes for the coming school year? Stealing from you, while not the correct thing to do, didn't deserve the death penalty."

This encounter will not, however, have been your first experience with "The Mark of Cain." And it will not be your last. The psychologist (whom your defense attorney retained pro bono), in his continuing debriefing process with you, advised you, as the old song goes: "(It's) only just begun." Indeed so, it has only just begun, because in these times the defender must now anticipate the second judicial attack, the civil suit.

IT DOES NOT GET ANY MORE REAL THAN THIS

What follows is taken in part from public records and in part from this author's direct interview with the person (hereinafter "D") who used deadly force in a confrontation with a neighbor in his community. After five hours of deliberation, the jury by unanimous decision found him Not Guilty of all charges. He had been charged with 1st degree Murder, 3rd degree Murder and Manslaughter. Be mindful that the shooting took place in 2012, but it was not until 2013 that the case even came to trial. Since the jurisdiction in which it took place did not provide for bail since the primary charge was 1st degree murder, D remained in prison for virtually one year before the trial even began. Because he was deemed by the classifying officer to be a vulnerable prisoner, for his protection he was placed in solitary confinement for that entire time.

In late Spring of 2012, in a small suburban community, a confrontation took place between D and his next-door neighbor. It was not the first such encounter between the two, the latter reportedly angry over property-line boundary violations committed by D's dogs that were defecating on his property. There were as well arguments apparently having to do with a dilapidated, termite-infested shed in D's backyard. Over time, there apparently had been escalations in the acrimony between the two neighbors, including an occasion on which D believed that his neighbor had poisoned his dogs. D also saw him as responsible for tipping over log piles as well as killing a rabbit that was being fed by D's girlfriend. (At the end of the trial, the DA admitted that the decedent may well have been a bully, but that didn't mean he deserved to be killed.)

D's primary response to those incidents was to call his local township police and file a report. On interview, he reports to this author that he did in fact do that but that the police response either never took place or was ineffectual. He added that one officer advised him to send a registered letter to the attacker telling him to stay off his property. It is important to recognize that the attacker, a former Marine, was a person who was well liked by a number of people in that neighborhood. As well, the attacker had a sign posted in is yard that read: "Intruders will be shot. Survivors will be shot again."

In any case on the day of the shooting, a confrontation took place between the two men as D was leaving his property in his truck. As he was backing out from his driveway, he saw his neighbor approaching at a brisk pace and reportedly hollering, "I'm going to go over and get those dogs." D testified, "I thought he was going to kill my dogs (and) hurt B (his girlfriend). (So) I stopped my truck and got out. I put it in park, took off my seat belt and got out. He was right there; he said I'm going to fix you. I grabbed the pistol off the seat. The way he said "I'm going to fix you." It was like a growl. He was raging, he was seething. .... I thought he was going to kill me. (I) could see (him) pulling something out of his pocket.... (I) thought it was a gun. I fired.... I stopped shooting when he was no longer a threat. (I) then called 911 to get help for (him)."

MANAGING THE AFTERMATH

The interview between D and this author (a portion of which is reproduced below) took place four years after the shooting incident and three years from the verdict. In D's own words (save for omitting names and locations and for enhancing grammatical structure), here are some of his comments about the long-term psychological effects of the deadly force encounter. Note specifically those comments he gives about the critical need he felt for being able to tell his whole story; for being able to feel understood, and understood by peers, by people who were connected to the self-defense community. As well, note his disdain for the legal system, despite the verdict. His report of his psychological experiences post-shooting are as compelling a narration of the effects of the Mark of Cain as this author has ever read or heard:

Most impactful (experience) from verdict to this date psychologically I would have to say (is) the public's reaction and how people look and act towards me now.

It's something (the shooting) that is brought up once a week from other people.

It's always having to deal with the elephant in the room. Meeting new people... do they know? Do they not know? Sometimes people will ask about it; sometimes people will have gallows humor or make a joke about it.

Two weeks ago I was out with two people talking and one guy said he was having trouble with his neighbor. The other guy said: Well don't ask (him) about that. He meant it as a joke but I didn't take it that way. He was referring to me.

You have to let it roll off your back. Some people don't realize how life altering this situation was. They see me walking around and looking okay and assume I'm okay, but I'm not. You have to learn to deal with it or you won't be able to associate with anybody. It's the new normal. *(Emphasis added)*

My internal experience (is) a combination of sadness and a bit of anger. I'm sad that this is what I'm known for now. That's the big aspect of it. Everything I've accomplished up to now, all the accolades, they mean nothing now.

For my obituary I'm going to have to come up with the cure for cancer (to erase the stigma of the shooting).

And a little bit of anger that people aren't more sensitive to the situation. A person died; (that's) not to be joked about; the seriousness of the entire situation; there were no winners; making a joke is not very sensitive; I don't see people making those comments to a woman who had been sexually assaulted.

(I felt) trepidation at your (referring to this author) contact but I hope that it can help me turn a bad situation into a positive. I could very easily have said after the acquittal I'm not going to speak about this again. This would not have been a benefit to anybody. But I still have my demons, but it helps to get it out. (I) still have some trepidation to bring

it out because it brings up upsetting thoughts and feelings. But that's what the new normal is.

(It) irks me when I see phony PTSD; if you really had it you wouldn't be talking about it the way you are.

Lawyers are the winner. System is the winner. They (prosecution) lost (but) they still made their money.

Both the decedent and I were the smallest part of the whole thing. (The) prosecution (is) making a big deal about being out for justice. Baloney! There are two people's lives and he and I were just two small parts to further individual agendas (and) careers. (This trial) was supposed to be about truth and justice. (It's) Not.

Prosecution didn't really have anything to convict me on. They had four shell casings. I admitted this. What's the purpose? This wasn't like OJ. One week to get it done. The judge said to jurors, expect a week, jurors getting antsy so we went long in the evenings. We shortened our defense case; but it was over.

Disappointed in the pace (of the trial). (I) always thought that high paid people in these positions should act accordingly. I didn't have my day in court. Winning is the goal. We're here not to hear you story. We're here to get you home. Defense attorney didn't want to carry it on.

I had my mother call Massad; see what he thinks about the case. Massad's comment was "What's he even being charged for." I said finally somebody understands.

When I was in (the) class: I'm now in the company of other people who understand!! Ordinary folk do not understand. There are people who do know what I'm talking about. Part of the reason I did (the presentation at the class) is just that; when I was reading and learning nobody ever talked about the aftermath; it's now coming to the fore. More prevalent. More questionable prosecutions.

I had hoped for the opportunity to sit down and talk to the Prosecution but that doesn't happen anymore. It's not like (TV).

So the more opportunity to give voice to what

happened to a knowledgeable audience, the better. Still (it) sticks in my craw that I couldn't say my piece. What was reported in the newspaper was a lie. Couldn't explain. I did not get my whole story out.

(We used a) forensic psychologist to see what I was all about psychologically. (She was) a help to (my attorney) to understand. (Prosecution) was trying to paint me as a gun nut. (Psychological) testing made an impression on jury. That was a big help.

Trial covers the range of emotions from anger to sad to funny. Prosecutor looked ridiculous hammering on her (defense psychologist) credentials (but) she put him in his place.

Irks me even today the cursory investigation. They got blinders on immediately. Forensics team (was) told you are going to a murder scene. Rush to judgment as to murder. This is now four years since the shooting. You called on the day. Good karma.

(The prosecutor) was up for reelection – charge what you want. (There was all the) media attention for him (to help) in his reelection. Maybe only his 3rd or 4th case he tried himself. He thought (he had) a slam-dunk. Tried to block my self-defense defense. But I knew I had to be the first one to 911.

I'M THAT GUY. (Emphasis added) Just something you have to deal with. I meet a girl. When do you bring that up what I did? Do you wait till they are emotionally invested? I never read about that anywhere.

How do I explain the four-year gap? Another residual is that I need to get my record expunged. Especially because (on employment applications) it's now (have you) ever (been) "charged with a crime." Now I have to go get a lawyer to get my permit back.

Still follows me to this day. In January of this year, (I was) in a bar and a guy killed another guy, (who was) six feet behind me. Actor shoved an older guy and broke his neck. Blood all over. Put me back in another place. I showed arriving officer my driver's license and the officer talked with me about 15 seconds. I asked the officer for any info about the guy and got ignored.

I'm not anti-cop. (although my) local department is under DOJ scrutiny. (I have had) three surgeries from excessive arresting force; ruptured two disks in (my) neck; rotator cuff injury and surgery.

(The shooting) will produce major changes in your life!

CAVEAT EMPTOR

Even a cursory review of the Defendant's statements provides eloquent testimony to the pervasive and enduring psychological effects secondary to his justifiable use of deadly force. These statements he made are occurring four years post shooting event. As he talks, it has all the vocal quality of what clinically is known as "talking in real time," that is, as if in the time and space of the occurrence of the event.

When this author asked him how he got through it all, his immediate response was family and (real) friends. He was clear in pointing out that his use of deadly force separated his friends from his acquaintances, and within the latter group, even those whom he had known for many years had abandoned him. He lost all his financial resources and has to depend upon family to survive again. The injuries he sustained secondary to his arrest left him unable to work, forcing him into continued dependence upon his family as he awaits a favorable decision on his disability payment status. He is now in the process of moving to another state where he will be closer to his family of origin and where he believes he will be able to be regarded as a person in his own right, and not as "That Guy."

As noted earlier, private citizens encounter the complex stress associated with their use of deadly force as the "lone survivor." There are no fellow officers who arrive, lights on, sirens loud to provide a secure perimeter. There is no officer to whom he is especially close to provide a secondary weapon to replace the weapon he used in the engagement. Transport to secure environment does not happen. There is no police chaplain to notify the family of the shooting and to provide them with reassurance as to their loved one's safety. There is no immediate response from a police psychologist/police surgeon to conduct a defusing with the relevant officers and who will provide formal incident debriefing for the officer following the IACP OIS protocol.

The bottom line, however, is that private citizens who chose to go armed in the service of the protection of our life and the lives of those we hold close to our heart, well, we do that at our own psychological peril.

ABOUT THE AUTHOR

Dr. Anthony Semone has amassed considerable education, experience, and training within a broad range of psychological disciplines. In doing so, he has afforded himself the ability to work within the fields of Forensic Psychology, Clinical Neuropsychology, Clinical Psychology, and Police Psychology.

Dr. Semone holds certifications from the NRA as an instructor in Home Firearms Safety, Personal Protection and Pistol, as well as in Law Enforcement/Security Firearms; from the Smith &Wesson Academy as a Reduced Light Training Instructor, Advanced Instructor in Police Use of Force and Risk Management, and as a Master Use of Force and Control Instructor; from the Lethal Force Institute as a Stressfire Instructor in Combat Pistol and Shotgun; and from the PA State Police as Lethal Weapons Instructor. He is also certified by the Lethal Force Institute as a Police Instructor in the Ayoob/Lindell Method of Weapon Retention and in the Kubotan/ Persuader. He has taken advanced firearms training from such internationally recognized instructors as Ray Chapman, Marty Hayes, Chuck Taylor, Clive Shepherd, Bob Taubert, Bert DuVernay, Tom Aveni and Clint Smith.

Dr Semone has been qualified in both state and federal courts and has provided in those contexts expert testimony on Use of Force, Body Alarm Reactions and their Impact on Eyewitness Identification, Post-Shooting Trauma and PTSD. He has assisted the Massachusetts State Police and the Baltimore County (MD) Police Firearms Training Units in designing instructional programs so as to incorporate known psychological principles to enhance the efficacy of those programs. He is presently involved in gathering data on the relationship between heart rate variability and decision-making ability in officer use of force.

Chapter 3:
MEMORY AND DECISION MAKING UNDER STRESS

BY **ALEXIS ARTWOHL,** Ph.D

WIN, WIN, WIN

Rules number one, two, and three of self-defense: Win, Win, Win. Why three? People using force to defend themselves will face three survival challenges: 1) physical, 2) legal, and 3) psychological. Physical is number one, because the next two won't matter if the defender doesn't physically survive. However, for many people who survive a threat, the most stressful part of the event will now unfold: the aftermath. The defender has committed an assault or homicide, which is a felony crime. The only question will be, was it justified self-defense?

You can be assured that being investigated for a felony crime will not be fun, and incarceration could be the outcome. The threat to your life and/or the stress of the investigation also have the potential to be psychologically devastating. Understanding how the mind operates is important not just for preparing to survive an attack, it will be critical to guiding you through the legal/emotional challenges ahead.

MEMORY BASICS

"Your brain does not process information,
retrieve knowledge or store memories."
~ Robert Epstein, the empty brain

Most people go around thinking they have a pretty good memory. Nothing could be further from the truth. Memory researcher Schacter (2001), in his book *The Seven Sins Of Memory*, points out the many ways in which our memory fails us in our everyday lives. Epstein (2016) points out how the computer analogy for the brain, where people "store" and "retrieve" memories, is not at all accurate.

People think their memory is better than it is in part because they are rarely challenged on its accuracy. Major memory gaps, inaccurate details, and false memories are common in everyday life, and can become worse during stressful situations (Sapolsky, 2004). This is usually merely annoying, such as forgetting what we did with our car keys. However, if you get tangled up in the criminal justice system you may find that the devil is now in details.

The criminal justice system you encounter may be unaware of the normal, and sometimes severe, biological limitations of memory. Although behavioral scientists can make some empirical observations about the failures and successes of memory, Epstein (2016) points out they are in fact very limited in their understanding of how memory actually works, and that it is a puzzle that will not be solved for many years to come

NARRATIVE VS. HISTORICAL TRUTH

Given that memory for detail is known to be poor even during everyday life, what happens when people are caught up in a highly stressful event? The gist of the event may be more memorable because the emotional intensity makes it stand out in a person's memory. People tend to think a lot about dramatic events and this repetitive thinking can also strengthen the memory compared to more mundane things that we ignore as soon as they are done. However, this does not mean the vivid, highly-rehearsed memory is necessarily an accurate representation of reality.

The research literature on eyewitness testimony has repeatedly shown that eyewitnesses are often wrong, especially when it comes to details (Morgan, et.al., 2004, Sharps, et. al., 2009; Wells and Quilivan, 2009). This can include eyewitnesses who are absolutely certain that their memories are accurate when in fact they are not. A person's beliefs about what happened can be called their "narrative truth": a completely truthful accounting of what they think happened. However, this truthful account can also be a not entirely accurate reflection of what actually happened.

What really happened can be called the "historical truth." This discrepancy between narrative and historical truth is common and normal, but it can create havoc in the criminal justice. DNA evidence has exonerated several hundred people who had been convicted of crimes they did not commit. 70% of those convictions relied heavily on eyewitness testimony that turned out to be faulty. (Wells and Quilivan, 2009). If you are the subject of an investigation and your narrative truth does not line up perfectly with historical truth, you could be branded as a liar and this will not help your legal survival.

SELECTIVE ATTENTION

Selective attention is one factor explaining why people often have poor memory for details of events. The human brain is extremely powerful and does amazing things. However, one thing it's not good at is being able to pay attention to everything all the time (Shomstein and Yantis, 2004). In fact, your brain can typically pay conscious attention to only one important thing at a time, known as selective attention.

Every millisecond of your life, your brain is allocating your attention to a very limited data set based on what it thinks is most important at the moment. This is often done without conscious thought. Chabris and Simon (2010) summarize their extensive research on selective attention in the book *The*

Invisible Gorilla. They point out that, not only are you paying attention to less than you think you are, you are unaware of just how limited your attention really is. People can be looking right at something and not see it because their attention is focused on a different detail of the environment. This is called inattentional blindness and happens to people all the time (Mack and Rock, 1998).

All perception happens in the brain. The eyes, ears, and other sensory organs are merely sending signals to the brain. It's up to the brain to decide what those signals mean. If the brain ignores the signals, then no conscious perception is happening and the result will be no concrete memory. People also experience inattentional deafness, are unaware of injuries, do not accurately track time, misperceive stimuli, and a host of other perceptual issues that result in perception of an event that is not congruent with reality.

PERCEPTION AND BIAS

Once the brain has paid attention to something, it then needs to decide what it thinks it means, i.e., perception. The brain takes the raw data it is receiving and, based on a lifetime of learning, interprets this data as images, concepts, events, etc. The brain is full of expectations about how the world operates. These expectations are known by various terms including schemas, heuristics, stereotypes, and biases (Kahneman, 2011; Schacter, 2001).

Bias is a politically loaded word, but the brain must be biased in order to make sense of the world and allow decision making, especially in rapidly unfolding situations. Some biases are in fact accurate and useful. A concrete example is that the brains of people raised in a culture that uses forks, knives, and spoons, are biased to automatically view any fork as a tool to spear food, regardless of color, material, size, number of times, etc. Based on this bias, the brain would not try to use a fork to scoop up soup. Bias allows the brain to automatically use utensils without conscious thought and without having to laboriously relearn the best way to use them with every food-related situation. Without bias, much of which is below conscious awareness, the world would be perceived as chaotic and confusing, where few things had meaning and decision making would be slow and difficult; similar to how a traveler would feel if suddenly plunked down into totally foreign culture and environment. Bias also plays a part in optical illusions. An Internet search can quickly bring up many amazing illusions that capitalize on bias to fool the brain into perceiving things incorrectly.

Like many things, bias cuts both ways. It allows us to function efficiently in the environment we are familiar with, but it can result in perceptions that are not entirely accurate, especially when the context of a situation might lead the brain toward a certain conclusion. One example is self-defense situations where a defiant and uncooperative suspect refuses to follow officers' commands, then compounds the situation by reaching into a pocket or waistband, pulling out a small object and pointing it at the officers. This foolish behavior of the suspect, often taking place under low-light conditions, has now biased the officers to perceive the suspect as potentially dangerous. In the context of this event, the normally innocent behavior of retrieving an object from a pocket can now be interpreted by a worried brain as reaching for a weapon.

BIAS CAN RESULT IN PERCEPTIONS THAT ARE NOT ENTIRELY ACCURATE, ESPECIALLY WHEN THE CONTEXT OF A SITUATION MIGHT LEAD THE BRAIN TOWARD A CERTAIN CONCLUSION.

The brain has also learned through a lifetime of experience that there will always be an action-reaction gap, where the person who makes the first move has an advantage over the person who has to respond to it. This particular bias will motivate the brain to take no chances if lives are on the line. As the suspect – who has now created bias in the minds of the officers to perceive him as a threat – points the small object at the officers, he has increased the odds that the officers will shoot him in self-defense. Even if the object is a cell phone, officers may in fact perceive a gun due to all the situational cues that have biased their brains in that direction. Similar consequences can happen with non-police shootings, military combat, and other volatile situations.

Sometimes people demand that expectations and misperceptions must play zero legitimate part in any self-defense situation; but, in fact, that is simply not possible, especially during rapidly unfolding situations. The more time the brain has to process information, the better it will be able to consciously and carefully sort through incoming information to double check the accuracy of perceptions, but the luxury of time is not always available in self-defense situations.

Note that schemas that bias us to perceive and react to the world in certain ways are different than premeditated bigotry, which leads to deliberate mistreatment of individuals. The former is inevitable, the latter is not acceptable.

DECISION MAKING

Decision making is complicated and happens at a conscious and subconscious level. One simplified classification of decision making is the difference between rational vs. intuitive decision making (Epstein, 1994; Kahneman, 2011; Klein, 1998; Pinizotto, et.al., 2004; Sharps, 2010). Different scientists use different names but agree on the general characteristics of each. People are rarely using only one type of decision making at any given moment; it's a matter of which one is predominating.

Scientists characterize rational decision making as generally being oriented toward conscious, thoughtful problem solving using analysis, logic, and deliberate reasoning. The human brain can harness the power of this powerful thought process to achieve amazing things, such as space flight and understanding physics. It encourages us to "look before we leap" and not jump to hasty conclusions. It is easier to engage in this type decision making when we are calm and have time to think about how we want to handle the situation. As powerful as it is, it does have a potentially fatal flaw in a sudden emergency: it takes time.

Therefore, mother nature provides us with an alternative way of making decisions: intuitive decision making. This has the general characteristics of being more subconscious, more driven by emotion and habit, more automatic, and more action oriented. It also happens effortlessly and far more rapidly than rational decision making. An example would be a driver automatically slamming on the brakes when they perceive something darting in front of their car. The advantage in a sudden survival situation is obvious, assuming you are properly trained. People will often say things like, "It happened so fast I didn't have time to think about it." This can be problem when the criminal justice system is now very interested in what you were thinking during a self-defense situation in which you suddenly needed to take action. If you reply, "I didn't have time to think," that may not go over well, even though it is totally normal.

STUDIES RELEVANT TO SELF DEFENSE SITUATIONS

Several studies have been done on thinking and perception in officer-involved shootings. If police officers are subject to the influence of the human performance factors discussed above, the same will be true of everyone else.

Artwohl (2002) gave a self-report survey to 157 officers involved in shootings and asked them to reflect upon whether or not they experienced a variety of perceptual and memory phenomenon. She found the following results:

• Diminished Sound (did not hear loud sounds such as gunshots, etc.) 84%

• Tunnel Vision (inattentional blindness to most details except immediate focus) 79%

• Automatic Pilot (gave little or no conscious thought to what they were doing) 74%

• Heightened Visual Clarity (could see minute details within their narrow focus) 71%

• Slow Motion Time (sensation of time slowing down) 62%

• Memory Loss/Event (includes dramatic details they simply weren't paying attention to) 52%

• Memory Loss/Own Actions (this can include complex, purposeful behavior) 46%

• Dissociation (felt disconnected from themselves and/or the event) 39%

• Intrusive Thoughts (thoughts not immediately relevant to the tactical situation) 26%

• Memory Distortion (false memories about things that never happened) 21%

• Intensified Sounds (sounds seemed much louder than normal) 16%

• Fast Motion Time (sensation of time speeding up) 17%

• Temporary Paralysis (feeling like they were temporarily frozen into inaction) 07%

Klinger (2004) did similar research:
• Diminished Sound 82%
• Tunnel Vision 51%
• Heightened Visual Clarity 56%
• Slow Motion Time Perception 56%
• Fast Motion Time Perception 23%
• Intensified Sounds 20%

Other researchers, including Artwohl (2003), Honig and Sultan (2004), Lewinski (2008) and Ross, et. al., (2012), documented similar perceptual/memory results with police officers in actual shootings or scenario training.

Trainers sometimes ask, "How can we train our officers so they don't experience these factors?" The answer is, "That's not possible." Extensive training might be able to somewhat reduce some perceptual issues in some situations with some people, but perfect perception and memory are not consistent with the biological limitations of the brain.

PERFECT PERCEPTION AND MEMORY ARE NOT CONSISTENT WITH THE BIOLOGICAL LIMITATIONS OF THE BRAIN.

DECISION-MAKING TRAINING

The time to start preparing to defend your life is before a threat happens. Self-defense situations are usually sudden and unexpected, are rapidly unfolding, and are over quickly. Given that you will likely revert to automatic, intuitive decisions in a sudden emergency, your brain will rely primarily on past learning and biases.

The solution? Training, training, training. The more realistic the training, the better (Davis, 2015; Murray, 2004; Ross, et al, 2012). Target shooting is useful to improve your firearms skills, but moving beyond that to decision training is desirable. Ideally, the training would require you to make quick decisions when presented with realistic scenarios that require you to make choices, such as take cover, retreat, issue warnings, use your weapon, etc. Having a good trainer/coach is always a plus. If your access to this type formal training is limited, you can still do mental rehearsal training in which you envision yourself in situations you might encounter and how you might defend yourself and/or others. In the absence of preparation, a sudden survival situation may result in freezing instead of acting, or doing something counterproductive. Training should build confidence as well as skills, in-depth knowledge about concealed carry equipment and other issues, (Ayoob, 2008), and good decision making under stress.

This does not mean envisioning always using your weapon. Whenever possible, you want time to be on your side. Think and rehearse how you can give yourself time to call 911 and retreat to safety. For instance, you can rehearse always locking your car door the second you get into it, and driving safely away if someone suspicious approaches your car. You can train yourself to do always a perimeter check around your house to make sure everything is locked up once you get home. Situational awareness will give you time to spot and avoid threats. However, anyone can be suddenly faced with a deadly situation where "When seconds count, the cops are only minutes away" and immediate action is your best chance for survival.

You will face major challenges once the threat is over and you now have to deal with first responders and the legal system. You want to educate yourself about what to expect and mentally rehearse how you will face those challenges as well.

CONTROLLING EMOTIONAL INTENSITY

One of the survival skills you want to practice is regulating your emotional intensity level. When a person faces a life-threatening event, it is normal for their body to be flooded with stress hormones that are activating all body and brain systems to instantly fight or flee. (Artwohl and Christensen, 1997; Grossman and Christensen, 2004). In the absence of training and mental preparation, the person may freeze instead simply because they are unsure what to do.

This heightened state of physical and emotional intensity, properly focused, is good for survival, as intuitive decision making kicks in and we become action oriented. If you are attacked and are fighting for your life, kicking into high levels of emotional intensity will help you fight instead of being a passive victim. However, once the immediate threat is over you want to start calming yourself down so you can become more focused on rational problem solving. This could include tasks such as scanning for other threats, rendering first aid, calling 911, and dealing with the first responders, etc. One technique is slow, regular, deliberate breathing, which helps your nervous system reduce intensity levels. Self-talk is another common technique. Everyone has something that works best for them and you want to practice this skill as part of your self-defense repertoire.

> "FEAR IS AN AUTOMATIC PHYSICAL REACTION TO A PERCEIVED THREAT THAT WILL RESULT IN PREDICTABLE PHYSICAL, EMOTIONAL, PERCEPTUAL, AND COGNITIVE CHANGES BECAUSE OF HIGH PHYSICAL AROUSAL STATES. IT'S IMPORTANT THAT YOU UNDERSTAND THESE AUTOMATIC REACTIONS, NOT ONLY FOR YOUR PHYSICAL SURVIVAL, BUT FOR YOUR LEGAL AND PSYCHOLOGICAL SURVIVAL AS WELL."
>
> ~ ARTWOHL AND CHRISTENSEN, DEADLY FORCE ENCOUNTERS

SITUATIONAL AWARENESS

Ask any expert what is your single best self-defense strategy and they tell you: situational awareness (Davis, 2015). Situational awareness should be practiced all the time. Selective attention limits your brain's ability to pay attention to more than one important thing at time, so you want to be always scanning your environment and learn to notice things and people that don't seem right. If you are with another person you can divide up tasks, such as assigning one person to stash the groceries in the car while the other person focuses on scanning the environment. Predators take advantage of selective attention by focusing their attention on their prey, and waiting for the prey's attention to focus on something else. Then they spring the attack and ambush their prey.

THE INVESTIGATION PHASE

Once you have successfully defended yourself and/or another person, you will now face one of the most stressful parts of the event: the aftermath (Davis, 2015, Fleming, 2015). Your two challenges now will be legal and psychological survival.

Your mental processes will be key to helping you successfully navigate the legal challenges. As soon as you are no longer under immediate threat, you want to start calming yourself down and consciously review your post-shooting survival plan which you have hopefully already trained and prepared for. You will be playing three roles in a dramatic situation: victim, witness, and suspect. Being the victim of a crime will be stressful in and of itself. You will also be an eyewitness and investigators will want to question you to get information about what just happened. Additionally, you will be a suspect in an assault or homicide case. Everything that you say and do will be observed and noted by the criminal justice system.

As the threat subsides you need to engage your rational brain to start problem solving the aftermath. Your first and immediate behavior should be to

> YOU WILL BE PLAYING THREE ROLES IN A DRAMATIC SITUATION: VICTIM, WITNESS, AND SUSPECT.

call 911 and prepare yourself to cooperate with the first responders in their efforts to secure the scene. Shortly after calling 911, your next call should be to your legal representative who will hopefully also respond ASAP to the scene to help you deal appropriately with the aftermath.

You will need to start making decisions about how and when you will interact with the investigators. The investigators are not your friends or enemies. They have a job to do and will want to question you. Your job is make good decisions about if, when, and how you will respond to their questions. Educating yourself ahead of time about your legal rights and responsibilities, and consulting with your legal representative can help you in the decision making process. Investigators, being human, also experience the same kind of perceptual and decision-making errors as the people they are investigating (Rossmo, 2009). The same applies to everyone else in the criminal justice system. For this reason, you and your attorney need to pay attention to the investigative process in case errors cause it to go haywire.

TIMING OF INTERVIEWS

Your first opportunity to interact with the legal system comes in the immediate aftermath as first responders arrive. They will want to get enough information to secure the scene and figure out the basics of what just happened. Hopefully you have mentally prepared and trained for this phase of your self-defense situation, you have been successful in calming yourself down, and you can make good decisions about assisting the first responders.

How much detail, if any, you provide to investigators will be up to you. The intensity of the immediate aftermath may not be the best time for your brain to sort out all the details. If you decide to answer questions at the scene or shortly thereafter, your best bet may be to provide investigators with only a brief "public safety statement" in which you are providing the basic facts so they can secure the scene, figure out who your assailants are, collect any physical evidence, identify other eyewitnesses, and make sure all injuries are taken care of.

No matter how well you have calmed yourself down, this will still be an anxious time. This anxiety may cause you to ramble, and make emotional and/or irrelevant statements, so you want try and curb this tendency so you can be coherent and factual. Having your legal representative on the scene can assist you with staying on task.

If you choose to provide a detailed statement beyond a brief public safety statement, you may want to wait until you have calmed down and have had some recovery time (IACP Officer Involved Shooting Guidelines). This may include one or two sleep cycles. Research has shown that our brains are very active when we are asleep (Stickgold and Ellenbogen, 2008). One of the many tasks the brain is performing during sleep is to sort out, make sense of, and consolidate memory (Walker, 2006). Memory researcher Geiselman (2010) found that cooperative eyewitnesses to an event provided better statements when they reported, "I felt rested at the time of the interview," than if they reported not feeling rested. Being interviewed is an anxiety-provoking experience, even for police officers who were questioned about training scenario they had just participated in (Lewinski, 2008). Anxiety and fatigue can inhibit the ability to recall information, so getting some sleep, being rested, and having had a chance to calm down may well enhance your ability to be a better eyewitness.

DO NOT BE PUSHED BY THE INVESTIGATOR'S QUESTIONS INTO SPECULATING, FILLING IN THE GAPS, OR OTHERWISE GUESSING ABOUT WHAT MIGHT HAVE HAPPENED.

If you choose to make a statement, be prepared for the fact that it's likely your perception of the event will not be a perfect match for what actually happened (Artwohl, 2002; Artwohl, 2003; Schacter, 2001; Lewinski, 2008; Ross, 2013; Ross, et. al., 2012). You might even experience some significant memory gaps and false memories. You want to be absolutely truthful and not be pushed by the investigator's questions into speculating, filling in the gaps, or otherwise guessing about what might have happened.

If you choose to provide more than one statement, it's not likely that each statement will contain exactly the same information every time (Epstein, 2016). This is normal given that memory is not precise "recording" of what happened, but is a creative and reconstructive process that can be influenced by multiple factors, including the behavior of the persons asking the questions (Fisher and Geiselman, 1992). It's important that you and your legal representative understand the basic science about selective attention, perception, and memory, so that you can respond appropriately during statements, and defend yourself if others try to use these normal memory processes to discredit you as a witness.

PSYCHOLOGICAL SURVIVAL

Being involved in a life-threatening event of any type is highly stressful. A self-defense situation has the added stress of the defender now being viewed as a suspect in a crime and being forced to deal with the criminal justice system. It will take an emotional toll on you and your family. It's normal for a traumatic event to be distressing and disruptive for a period of time, especially if the event becomes prolonged. The good news is that human beings are naturally resilient and most will bounce back after traumatic events (Stix, 2011). They may never be the same, but that does not mean they will be worse off, and in fact may even feel they benefitted in the long run.

You and your family members can likely benefit from a debriefing from a licensed mental health professional who has expertise in traumatic incidents (Best, et.al., 2011). The purpose is to get an education about what to expect, how to recognize if psychological recovery is not going well, and a known counselor to go to for further help if recovery becomes stalled. You don't need to talk about the details of the event with the counselor unless you want to. Make sure you clearly understand whether or not the counselor is licensed and has legally privileged confidentiality, and what the limits of confidentiality are. The path to recovery is different for everyone and should be a conscious and deliberate task that you facilitate for yourself. Support from friends and family is a crucial part of this process.

Only about ten percent of people will develop chronic post-traumatic stress disorder from an event. It's unclear why some people are more vulnerable than others. As with most physical and mental health issues, it's likely a complex combination of each person's genetic predisposition and how that interacts with the sum total of that person's lifetime experiences. If recovery becomes stalled and post-traumatic stress disorder sets in, it's crucial to get professional help from a trauma specialist.

REFERENCES

Artwohl, A. (2002). Perceptual and Memory Distortions in Officer Involved Shootings. *FBI Law Enforcement Bulletin*, October 2002.

Artwohl, A. (2003). No Recall of Weapons Discharge. *Law Enforcement Executive Forum*, Volume 3, No.2, May 2003.

Artwohl, A. & Christensen, L. (1997). *Deadly Force Encounters: What Cops Need to Know to Mentally and Physically Prepare for and Survive a Gunfight.* Boulder, CO: Paladin Press.

Ayoob, M. (2008). The *Gun Digest Book of Concealed Carry*. Iola, WI: Krause Publications.

Best, S.; Artwohl, A., Kirschman, E. (2011). Critical Incident Reactions and Early Interventions. In *Handbook of Police Psychology*, Jack Kiteaff, Ed. Prentice-Hall.

Chabris, C. and Simons, D. (2010). *The Invisible Gorilla*. NY: Crown Publishers.

Davis, K.R. (2015). *Citizen's Guide to Armed Defense*. Iola WI: Krause Publications.

Epstein, R. (2016). https://aeon.co/essays/your-brain-does-not-processinformation-and-it-is-not-a-computer. May 18, 2016.

Epstein, S. (1994). Integration of the Cognitive and Psychodynamic Unconscious. *American Psychologist*, 49(8):709-721.

Fisher, R.P. & Geiselman, R.E. (1992). *Memory-Enhancing Techniques for Investigative Interview-*

ing. Springfield, IL: Charles C. Thomas.

Fleming, J. (2015). *Aftermath: Lessons in Self-Defense*. Monticello, MN: Riversedge Publications.

Geiselman, R. E. (2010). Research Note: Rest and Eyewitness Recall. *American Journal of Forensic Psychiatry*. April, 2010.

Grossman, D. & Christensen, L. (2004). *On Combat*. Brasseys, Inc.

Honig, A.L. & Sultan, S.E. (December, 2004). Reactions and Resilience Under Fire: What an Officer Can Expect. *The Police Chief*, Vol. LXXI, No. 12, 54-60.

Kahneman, D. (2011). *Thinking, Fast and Slow*. NY: Farrar, Straus, and Giroux

Klein, G. (1998). *Sources of Power: How People Make Decisions*. Cambridge, MA: MIT Press.

Klinger, D. (2004). *Into the Kill Zone*. San Francisco: Jossey Bass.

International Association of Chiefs of Police: Police Psychological Services Section. *Officer-Involved Shooting Guidelines*. www.theiacp.org.

Lewinski, W. (2008). The Attention Study: A Study on the Presence of Selective Attention in Firearms Officers. *Law Enforcement Executive Forum*. 8(6):107-138.

Mack, A. & Rock, I. (1998). *Inattentional Blindness*. MIT Press, Cambridge, MA.

Morgan, C., Haslett, G, Doran, A., Garrett, S., Hoyt, G., Thomas, P., Baranoski, M., Southwick, S. (2004). Accuracy of Eyewitness Memory for Persons Encountered During Exposure to Highly Intense Stress. *International Journal of Law and Psychiatry*, May-June, 2004, Issue 3, Vol. 27, 265-279.

Murray, K. (2004). *Training at the Speed of Life*.

Pinizotto, A.J., Davis, E.F., Miller, C.E. (2004). Intuitive Policing: Emotional/Rational Decision Making in Law Enforcement. *FBI Law Enforcement Bulletin*, February, 2004, Vol, 73, No. 2.

Ross, D.L. (2013). Assessing Lethal Force Liability Decisions and Human Factors Research. *Law Enforcement Executive Forum*, 2013, Vol. 13, No. 2.

Ross, D.L., Murphy, R.L., Hazlett, M.H. (2012). Analyzing Perceptions and Misperceptions of Police Officers in Lethal Force Virtual Simulator Scenarios. *Law Enforcement Executive Forum*, Volume 12, No. 3.

Rossmo, K. (2009). *Criminal Investigative Failures*. NY: Taylor and Francis Group.

Sapolsky, R.M. (2004). Stressed Out Memories. *Scientific American Mind*, 14(5)28-34.

Schacter, D. (2001). *The Seven Sins of Memory*. Houghton Mifflin: New York.

Sharps, M. J. (2010). *Processing Under Pressure: Stress, Memory and Decision Making in Law Enforcement*. Flushing, NY: Looseleaf Law Publications.

Sharps, M.J., Janigian, J., Hess, A.B., & Hayward, B. (2009). Eyewitness Memory in Context. Toward a Taxonomy of Eyewitness Error. *Journal of Police and Criminal Psychology*, Vol. 34:36-44.

Shomstein, S. & Yantis, S. (2004). Control of Attention Shifts between Vision and Audition in Human Cortex. *The Journal of Neuroscience*, November 24, 2004, 24(47):10702-10706

Stickgold, R. and Ellenbogen, J.M. (2008). Quiet! Sleeping Brain at Work. *Scientific American Mind*, August/September, 2008, Vol. 19, No. 4.

Stix, G. (2011). The Neuroscience of True Grit. *Scientific American*, March, 2011.

Wells, G.L. & Quilivan, D. S. (2009). Suggestive Eyewitness Identification Procedures and the Supreme Court's Reliability Test in Light of Eyewitness Science: 30 Years Later. *Law and Human Behavior*, Vol. 33: 1-24.

Walker, M.P. (2006). Sleep to Remember. *American Scientist*, Vol. 94, July-August, pp. 326-333.

 *Dr. Alexis Artwohl is an internationally recognized behavioral science consultant to law enforcement as a trainer, researcher, and author. She has done extensive training in the USA and Canada as well training in Mexico, the United Kingdom, and Jordan. Dr. Artwohl is a member of the advisory board of the International Law Enforcement Educators and Trainers Association.*

Chapter 4:

VIOLENT ACTORS/ VIOLENT ACTS: A CONCEPTUAL AND PRACTICAL OVERVIEW

BY **WILLIAM APRILL**, Ph.D

The basic premise of the self-defense/tactical training industry is a contradiction in terms: focused preparation for an eventuality that one fervently hopes will never materialize.

This risk encounter – an unplanned, physically violent encounter between what Dr. Sherman House of Revolver Science calls a "civilian defender" and a type of criminal offender we'll refer to as a violent criminal actor (VCA) – exists in somewhat of a conceptual black hole for far too many defensive practitioners because attention is overly focused on the individual performance of those on the "good guy" side of the risk encounter. In hopes of expanding our consideration and better preparing to defend ourselves and those we protect, we will undertake to counter that trend and focus quite deeply on the topic of those who would see us broken, violated, and murdered at their whim and through their will.

At the most basic level, we must understand violence to understand those who traffic in it. Violence has been defined by the World Health Organization as "the intentional use of physical force or power, threatened or actual, against oneself, another person, or against a group or community, which either results in or has a high likelihood of resulting in injury, death, psychological harm, maldevelopment or deprivation." Among the committee of commas the issue of intentionality arises, highlighting that one can cause injury without specific intent but that violence is the application of force as an affirmative desire, an exercise of will. The student and practitioner of self-protection will focus less intently on the data for self-directed and collective violence and more on interpersonal violence (IPV), both in family/intimate partner and community contexts.

Our attention is certainly merited, as worldwide estimates of violence truly boggle the mind:

• Somewhere around one million deaths occur annually from IPV, not including acts of war, state action, and terrorism.
• The incidence of non-fatal IPV is difficult to calculate, impacting an estimated 15-75% of populations studied.
• The economic cost of IPV defies imagination, with over $200B in direct cost added to over $500B in cost to victims in the U.S. alone.

In the U.S., though, rates of violent crime are at or near historic lows after rising dramatically from 1960 to the commonly accepted peak in the early 1990s. Theories to explain the decline from that era to the present run the gamut from the aging of the U.S. population as a whole, the dramatic shift to more aggressive policing and incarceration policies across the nation, attendant expansion of the prison populations, to increased rates of abortion in at-risk demographics and the reduction in childhood exposure to lead. Murder, especially, has declined in frequency to levels not seen since the 1950s, leading by proxy to widespread argument that "we're safer than we've ever been."

Of less interest to researchers but of great import to civilian defenders, though, are some features of violent crime data that complicate the picture somewhat. The first is the issue of aggravated assault, which is to say those assaults demonstrating intent to produce grave injury manifest in use of weapons, choice of victim(s) of vulnerable status, the degree of injury caused, and indifference to human life. Aggravated assault rates, though generally perceived to be declining with the general crime rate, are more volatile in recent years and offer insight into the complications of using crime statistics to assess risk of violence.

A VCA IS MORE TYPICALLY INTERESTED IN ASSAULT, ROBBERY WITH INJURY, RAPE, AND MURDER THAN IN THE THEFT OF CAR STEREOS OR VALUABLES.

First, many aggravated assaults fall into the unofficial category of "rehabilitated murders" in that the victim received injuries that would have resulted in death in even the recent past but survived through advances in EMS services, ultra-rapid transport, and pre-hospital trauma life-support, arguably reducing the murder rate. Moreover, the impact on trauma care of having the nation on a war footing for over a dozen years now cannot be underestimated, as personnel from EMTs to trauma surgeons have mainstreamed advances in technical practice that only the horrors of war can provide. As a serving officer in a large Eastern metropolitan area described it: "if somebody's hit in the head 10 times with a bat and lives after 12 hours of surgery, you can't blame him living on the bad guy!" Additionally, there is widespread reporting of criminal acts that would have justified an aggravated assault charge in the past (a kick to the head of a downed opponent with a shod foot, for example) now being accepted as routine by police agencies and judged "simple assault" on a charge sheet. In short, the murder rate may be subject to suppression by advances in saving lives and the aggravated assault rate equally so by the shifting community standards of violence evidenced in any number of "wilding" or "rat-packing" videos available online.

WHO POSES RISK?

The civilian defender must devote considerable attention to the violent criminal actor (VCA) in order to properly understand "street crime" and the risks entailed. VCAs are differentiated from the mainstream of offenders by their emphasis not on property crime but on a criminal repertoire that includes violence against others as a matter of daily course. A VCA is more typically interested in assault, robbery with injury, rape, and murder than in the theft of car stereos or valuables in plain sight.

The demographics of arrest data can lead to some general awareness of who might pose a risk of violence, though this approach has clear limitations. A statistically "average" VCA might well be described as:

> **THINKING THAT WE KNOW WHAT "A BAD GUY" LOOKS LIKE AND IGNORING OTHER FACTORS CAN BE FATAL ERRORS.**

- Male.
- Young, with +/- 60% between 18-35.
- Decidedly "normal looking" (as highlighted by the FBI's consistent finding that murderers of law-enforcement officers hover slightly under U.S. average height and weight for adult males).

The life histories of VCAs, though, begin to show substantial divergence from expected norms. Again, a typical VCA arrestee might display a broad menu of maldevelopment, environmental risk factors, and dysfunction:

- Predominantly raised in a lower socioeconomic status households.

- Fewer completed years of educational attainment.
- Prior history of arrest (>75%).
- Prior history of incarceration (>30%).
- Re-offense despite being under criminal justice supervision (up to 30%).
- Significant and early history of association with peers who themselves have criminal history.
- Prior offenses as a juvenile, with early onset.
- Early personal exposure to violence, especially weapon violence.
- Significant criminal justice involvement among family members.
- History of substance abuse within the family and in the offender.
- History of mental illness within the family and in the offender.

In short, those arrested at some point during their career arc as a VCA demonstrate early and sustained alienation from virtually all normative social structures, early resistance to authority, histories of physical victimization and the predilection to act out violently against others. Risk-aware defensive practitioners, though, must pay special heed to the pitfall of assuming that the above described characteristics are subsumed only under particular racial or ethnic backgrounds. Thinking that we know what "a bad guy" looks like and ignoring other factors can be fatal errors.

HOW DOES THE VCA ARISE?

Attempts to understand and prepare for interactions with the VCA must necessarily involve not only descriptive findings, as above, but also some attempt at reviewing causal explanations for the presenting problem itself. In this endeavor, though, there are seemingly as many theories to explain criminal violence as there are questions about it, and very little consensus to guide us, resulting in an often frustrating and fruitless effort. In brief, then, let's review some of the more promising models of understanding causes of criminal aggression:

1. SOCIAL/SOCIETAL INFLUENCES

Though they may get little sympathy in the more socio-politically conservative quarters of the self-defense community, it would be foolish to dismiss the prejudicial impact of the social systems surrounding the young person who develops into a VCA.

Neighborhood features such as extreme poverty, high crime rates, prevalent substance use and abuse, low levels of social cohesion, the scarcity of intact nuclear families, and high levels of transience all contribute to stressful and unsupportive settings for development. Families themselves may contribute to maldevelopment when they feature little in the way of corrective discipline, monitoring of behavior, display of affection, and too much physical abuse and neglect.

The presence of deviant peers and family members (those with existing patterns of criminal behavior) also provide malign influence on developing youths who observe and model the use of force to achieve one's desired ends. In addition, the larger culture of poverty may lead to too few positive examples of success through "playing by the rules," lending credibility to those who earn a living through criminal activity. Developing youth also often receive deviant instruction, explicit support for and training in the commission of crime, from peers and family members. As one incarcerated violent offender explained: "If he's gonna wind up doin' it, best he hear the right way about it from me."

The effects of these and other risk factors compounded can produce an almost inescapable breeder reactor of violence and crime, a criminal supra-culture rather than subculture. A horrifying but common manifestation of this phenomenon was related by an officer in a major metropolitan area on the West coast, who disclosed that the use of gunshot

> **IN THIS SORT OF SOCIAL CONTEXT, THE MORE REALISTIC QUESTION MAY BE HOW ANYONE AVOIDS BECOMING A VIOLENT OFFENDER.**

location technology in his area results in the finding that less than 20% of gunshots result in a call to the 911 system, and that in one incident at least five guns were used to fire at least 110 shots and not a single call to 911 was made. In this sort of social context, the more realistic question may be how anyone *avoids* becoming a violent offender.

2. MEDIA INFLUENCES

Complaints that American culture seems to be on a path of decline toward coarseness and brutality are seemingly as old as the Republic itself. Increasingly, though, researchers have striven to explore the effects of violent behavior in popular media on children, with particular attention paid to the possibility of violent content in television, music, music videos, films, video games, and streaming media resulting directly in increased violence in the behavior of child consumers. There is no dispute that a "double saturation" of media violence is occurring: the amount of media in children's lives and the amount of violence in media. In little over a half-century, televisions have gone from rare to ubiquitous, with over 99% of U.S. households having one or more. Increasingly, children have televisions in their own bedrooms, allowing for unchaperoned viewing. Moreover, computer and mobile Internet access devices such as smartphones are challenging the saturation rate of television sets and allowing children to view far more violent and salacious material without adult intervention. At the same time the rate of violent acts in available media is increasing, with the result that children may be exposed to hundreds of instances of violence in media per hour, and up to an estimated 250,000 acts observed, including tens of thousands of murders, by age 18.

Though data so far have demonstrated that the effects of "violence contagion" from media to behavior are transitory in nature and affect generally only the youngest of children, it would be short-sighted to presume that there will never be evidence of causation, especially as the age of initiation drops, the degree of violence (in video games especially) rises, and total "screen time" on television and computers edges toward 50 hours per week in youth.

3. EVOLUTIONARY/GENETIC INFLUENCES

Human aggression has long been a field of interest for psychologists, biologists, and anthropologists, with the resulting development of collaborative inquiry into how traits (including a propensity for violence against others) propagate through generations and manifest in the present as criminal behavior. Fundamentally, the discussion of present behavior is a snapshot of traits passed along by genetic winners, those successful transmitting their genes to offspring. From that prospect, violence poses a quandary: participation in IPV raises the risk of death, the ultimate failure of inclusive fitness, but at the same time must convey some adaptive benefit that would justify its persistence.

While it's not difficult to imagine scenarios in a challenging and resource-poor past where the use of violence might have conveyed significant material and evolutionary benefit (murder of a successful hunter and the theft of his game providing sustenance to one's own offspring without the risks of hunting being assumed by oneself, for example), how would this selection for trait exist in the modern world? One might look to the persistent phenomenon of "death-row brides" to see a hypothetical modern example. Convicted violent criminals of the most heinous character (from Ted Bundy to Charles Manson) have been pursued and married by women well-aware of their status and apparent unsuitability as mates.

The very characteristics that might generally disqualify an incarcerated murderer from consideration may be not an impediment to attracting potential mates but rather an actual benefit if some women feel a force of attraction whose primordial roots overwhelm conventional mate-choice practices. In one reported case, an inmate facing execution for the murder of a law-enforcement officer was able to conceive children with three different women (including a corrections staffer) during his trial. It may be reasonable to see in this sort of event an evolutionary benefit both for the killer, whose genes continue on, and for his mates, who may benefit from the prestige of having such a demonstrably dangerous mate and genitor of their children. Moreover, it is possible that this practice may lead to concentration and over-representation of maladaptive traits in already at-risk populations.

4. CHEMICAL DYSREGULATION IN THE BRAIN

Researchers in the medical and biological sciences have attempted to sound out the roots of troubled human behavior in the organ of the brain itself for centuries, and the brain's many neurotransmitters have been a subject of intense interest. Grossly speaking, systems or "circuits" in the brain can be associated with specific feeling, thinking, and action states, and the cells making up those systems are activated and deactivated by electrical impulses involving neurotransmitters, or "chemical messengers."

Popular press translations of research notwithstanding, there is no easy answer to the questions around causation of violence, though some progress toward consensus of association has developed. Studies implicating norepinephrine, testosterone, monoamine oxidase, and others have been conducted, but a center of gravity appears to be forming around dysfunction in the dopamine and serotonin systems.

Serotonin is generally thought of as an inhibitory neurotransmitter ("brakes") deeply involved in regulation of emotion and behavior, while dopamine is seen as having an activating function ("gas") on initiating motivated behavior and the processing of rewards. In specific regions of the brain, low serotonergic activity is strongly associated with aggressive behavior in humans and animals and, complementarily, higher dopaminergic activity in the same areas is associated with increased aggression as well.

Given the increasing sophistication of detecting neurotransmitter abnormalities and their increasing predictive power (including, possibly, the risk of future murder recidivism), the importance of understanding the role of such chemical messengers cannot be underestimated. It is important to remain aware that, even if certain variations in chemistry are found in specific regions of the brain, the picture of any violent offender is not complete until the effects of life stressors and other environmental influences are understood. That caveat notwithstanding, the promise of increased understanding in this area may be almost unlimited.

5. ORGANIC BRAIN SYNDROMES

These disorders are generally thought of as changes in mental function, feeling, and behavior, caused by a disease of the organ of the brain, its very tissues, as opposed to the action of any mental illness. A general consensus is emerging that physical damage to specific areas of the brain, particularly the amygdala and a part of the pre-frontal cortex known as the ventromedial prefrontal cortex, is strongly associated with aggressive and criminal behavior. Studies have repeatedly shown that subjects with injuries to those areas demonstrate increased incidence of violence and criminality over the lifespan when compared to normal control populations. Given the importance of the implicated areas of the brain in emotional regulation, impulsive behavior, and perception of threats, the contribution of organic syndromes to violence seems significant. Further, history of head injury, including traumatic brain injury (TBI), is widespread among both incarcerated violent offenders and in children who grow up in the compromised environments described above.

HISTORY OF HEAD INJURY, INCLUDING TRAUMATIC BRAIN INJURY (TBI), IS WIDESPREAD AMONG BOTH INCARCERATED VIOLENT OFFENDERS AND IN CHILDREN WHO GROW UP IN COMPROMISED ENVIRONMENTS.

Another form of damage to the brain common in environments one might refer to as VCA-generative is lead toxicity. The links between early exposure to lead and violent criminal behavior are robust and growing, with sobering parallels between incidence of lead exposure and rates of aggravated assault. The connection appears so sound that a prominent lead researcher has stated that up to 50% of the decrease in crime rates since the 1990s may result from reductions in environmental lead.

The severity of risk of organic brain syndromes to its subjects and from its subjects may best be summarized in the finding by Centers for Disease Control and Prevention that at least 11% of deaths, injuries, and hospitalizations of TBI patients are due to assault, indicating how frequently they are engaged in violent encounters.

6. MENTAL ILLNESS

Public and expert opinions are as diametrically opposed on few subjects as they are on the relationship between mental illness (MI) and violent crime. There is little support in the research community for the notion that mental illness (disorders of thinking, feeling, mood, and behavior that are not better explained by causes such as those detailed above) is a significant driver of violent crime rates. Among lay observers, however, the belief that MI causes violence and that anyone committing a violent offense is suffering from MI is widespread and deeply rooted. On one matter, the connection between mental illness and incarceration, there is no debate, though. Over one million diagnosed and diagnosable people are serving terms in America's prisons and jails, often for they types of offenses that treatment and supportive services could obviate. Other sad facts are that those with MI are disproportionately victims of violent crime due to their vulnerabilities, that successful prosecutions of their victimizers are rare, and that they harm themselves at rates up to 20 times that of the general population.

The best available data paint a portrait very different that that common in public perception: simply having a mental health diagnosis causes no increase

VIOLENCE THAT CAN BE HONESTLY ATTRIBUTED TO THE MENTALLY ILL IS A TINY FRACTION OF THE OVERALL CRIME RATE.

in the likelihood of committing a violent crime over the lifespan. People with chronic and severe mental illness (such as schizophrenia and bi-polar disorder) demonstrate higher incidence of violence, but in addition to those qualifiers the difference is explained by a history of violence before the onset of illness, lack of treatment, violence against caregivers, and most significantly, substance abuse. Moreover, even in subjects with serious mental illness, less than 10% of their crimes are shown to be directly related to their symptoms, with the vast majority related to lifestyle and conditions such as pre-existing violent disposition, poverty, hunger, deprivation, and again substance abuse.

The persistent belief in American culture that to enact violence one must be mentally ill is reinforced by spectacular cases such as the shooting of Rep. Gabrielle Giffords and the school attack in Sandy Hook, CT. Those sorts of cases are in fact extreme outliers, not least in the degree to which they show the outcome of severe mental illness on a long timeline with little to no treatment and positive support. The public aftermath of such events leads generally to a mis-directed effort to change the mental health/legal system interface "to prevent such tragedies going forward." This sort of campaign typically focuses on placing people on disqualification or prohibition lists such as those created under the "NY SAFE Act" in place in New York State since 2013. Such registries require the breach of patient confidentiality by treating professionals who are required to notify the state of any belief that a risk of harm to self or others exists. These lists are subject to any number of bureaucratic abuses and misuses, of course, not the least of which is that citizens with thought, mood, and impulse control disorders may be barred from exercise of firearm rights despite little evidence that they pose an elevated risk to the public.

An uncomfortable reality to many is that up to 25% of Americans may be diagnosed with MI in any given year. This finding must be counterbalanced with the fact that the vast majority respond well to treatment and the passage of time and do not go on to chronic and severe disorders. Violence that can be honestly attributed to the mentally ill is a tiny fraction of the overall crime rate; the result of a combination of diminishing likelihoods: the percentage of those with MI diagnoses, reduced to those with chronic and severe diagnoses as well, reduced to those with co-existing substance abuse disorders as well, reduced to those as well with the pre-existing histories of violent aggression that are the best predictor of future violent crime.

IF SO MUCH IS WRONG, WHAT'S RIGHT?

As to the bulk of violent crime, then, the risk-aware civilian defender must look away from glib assumptions about risk to focus on the most relevant vectors: those few for whom violence is not a symptom or a rarity, but a certainty. In clinical terms the behavior caused by most MI is distressing to the subject, or ego-dystonic, with violence as no exception. The violence perpetrated by the VCA on the other hand is ego-syntonic, causing no distress or discomfort and even experienced as rewarding and reinforcing.

This vast distinction leads to consideration of the VCA as best described not by a frank mental illness but rather Antisocial Personality Disorder (APD). APD is like other personality disorders in that it is a long-standing pattern of maladaptive interaction with the world that affects feeling, thinking (notably perception and attribution), and behavior, causing significant impairment and distress. Also, APD and other personality disorders share the characteristics of early onset, persistence over time, and pervasive impact across all domains of life (work, relationships, school, family, etc.).

The hallmark symptoms of APD are disregard for and violation of the rights of others, callous disregard and lack of empathy, and the inability to experience remorse or take others' perspective. In practice, APD subjects will act impulsively and aggressively, lie, cheat, steal, manipulate, and mistreat others without compunction, resulting in failure in responsibilities and relationships, frequent conflict with others, criminal justice system involvement, and violence. Up to 3% of the American population may meet the criteria to be diagnosed with APD, across a spectrum from least to most severe in expression.

This variation in intensity of behavioral symptoms has caused tremendous conflict among researchers and clinicians as conceptualizations of the disorder have changed markedly over time. The very name seems to defy development of consensus, morphing from Psychopathy to Sociopathy to Sociopathic Personality, to the current Antisocial Personality. One of the nodes of contention in the mental health community is around psychopathic traits, and involves debate over whether they are merely characteristics of APD, modifiers that would indicate increased severity of APD, or constitute a distinct diagnosis independent of APD. It should be noted that no current classification system holds psychopathy as a separate diagno-

> ## "ALL PSYCHOPATHS ARE SURELY ANTISOCIAL, BUT NOT ALL ANTISOCIALS ARE PSYCHOPATHS."

sis, though advocacy in that direction is unceasing, and we shall consider the psychopath as, at the very least, the most severely ill of VCAs and APD subjects from this point forward.

In the words of one researcher, "all psychopaths are surely antisocial, but not all antisocials are psychopaths." The civilian defender must acknowledge the reality of the psychopathic VCA in order to appreciate and prepare for the pinnacle of risk s/he presents. On a practical level, this sort of VCA is remarkable for extreme brutality, suddenness of action, and the use of instrumental violence. Instrumental violence is cold, calculated, predatory, goal-oriented, and detached from high levels of emotional arousal that one might assume motivate extreme violence. It is this abstract quality of violence, along with complete lack of remorse and empathy, that render the VCA so alien to the understanding of the general population and so critical to the mindset of the civilian defender. One can expect no capacity for sympathy, pity, or emotional consideration from a VCA, but rather under-arousal, perverse gratification in deviance, and the efficient, effective use of indiscriminate force to achieve the desired end. In short, the VCA represents a "top-of-the-food-chain" human predator not bound by any conventional morality or parameters of behavior, and one for which the civilian defender must prepare robust and effective response sets, as there will be time for little else in the risk encounter.

CAN IT GET WORSE?

In a word, yes. The complex systems that interact to produce the malignant VCA are difficult for NORPs (colloquially, "Normal, Ordinary, Rational People") to imagine, much less appreciate, understand, and learn from, but the effort is invaluable. A critical data set was gathered by a study of incarcerated violent offenders in a Southwestern state prison system.

When asked to identify their motivations for rape and aggravated assault, the following were endorsed:

- Relief, from anger, frustration or rage 82%.
- The exercise of power and control 75%.
- The thrill or excitement 62%.
- The "high" of the experience 58%.

When asked to describe the emotional states expected to be achieved by having committed rape or aggravated assault, the following feelings were endorsed:
- Powerful 73%.
- Happy and excited 65%.
- Able to achieve anything 65%.
- A sense of accomplishment 58%.

Horror aside, the simple implications of behavioral economics would seem to apply. In the developmental environments described above, rife with deprivation, dysfunction, and violence, is it reasonable to expect that anything else in the truncated life of the VCA other than violent subjugation of others allows him to feel and think those things? Actions that produce such strong and positive internal experience will likely be repeated.

Further exploration of the genesis of the problem is illuminating as well. An invaluable resource is the work of the award-winning sociologist and violence researcher, Lonnie Athens, Ph.D., the author of The Creation of Dangerous Violent Criminals (1992) and many other works. Dr. Athens uses data gathered from incarcerated VCAs themselves to describe the process of making a child into what we most fear, the process that shaped their own lives, revealing this process:

1. Brutalization – the immersion and saturation of the subject into a world governed by the power of violence; including violent subjugation of the subject's will by those stronger in the home and social environment on pain of physical assault; personal horrification, in which the subject sees significant others brutalized and experiences helplessness; violent coaching, in which older, trusted others explicitly advocate and enforce the use of violence as a personal responsibility, expectation, and right.

2. Belligerency – the realization that only the use of violence can counter brutalization and the deci-

sion to face the fear inherent in deciding to harm another. In order to justify violence and create psychic distance from one's brutalizers, the subject decides to use violence only when its necessity can be attributed to someone else; in this phase, the subject is intentionally violent for the first time, though projecting responsibility onto the opponent.

3. Violent performance – the establishment of capacity to regularly attempt to seriously injure or kill others. This stage requires increased confidence in the ability to cause injury and is compounded by rage at the subject's brutalizers, the desire to protect significant others, and desperation fueled by the knowledge that defeat will result in increased brutalization by the opponent; transition to the final stage is only achieved by the personal identification and public acceptance of the subject as capable of violence and successful in its application

4. Virulence – repeated successful and/or remarkably reckless violent acts have created a persona which has social currency, lending an aura of fear and notoriety to the subject; s/he is gratified and exalted by this new-found approbation, but at the same time must now commit to further violence to uphold the reputation and expand prestige. At this final stage, no perceived slight or offense may be overlooked and the subject commits to a perpetual state of readiness in which the attempt to gravely harm or kill anyone providing any degree of provocation is justified, despite any risk or inhibitory pressure.

Dr. Athens notes that completing all four stages of the process will result in the creation of a dangerous, violent criminal whether or not other prejudicial factors such as a genetic pre-disposition toward sociopathy, or even poverty, are present during development. We may be confident, though, that the high incidence of such accelerants will reduce neither the number of VCAs created nor the severity of the risk they present to the civilian defender.

WHERE DO WE GO FROM HERE?

It would seem to go without question that risk-aware civilian defenders would have long ago made the commitment to do whatever is necessary to prepare for the likelihood of violent encounter with the VCA, and yet experience belies this notion. It is not enough to carry firearms or other safety/rescue equipment without a fully-informed mental map of the expected terrain. There is clear evidence that VCAs are both born and made to act with ruthless and indiscriminate violence, and that the twisted developmental process forced upon them has rendered them incapable of seeing themselves and the world accurately. Their experiences have shaped them, perversely, to feel morally affronted by, at risk from, and under physical attack by the actions and very existence of seemingly normal, peaceable, law-abiding citizens. In contrast to this manifest existential threat, the average person struggles, in the words of the late trainer Paul Gomez, "to get aggressive enough fast enough," and is left brutalized, broken, bereft, bereaved, or dead.

....

IT IS NOT ENOUGH TO CARRY FIREARMS OR OTHER SAFETY/ RESCUE EQUIPMENT WITHOUT A FULLY-INFORMED MENTAL MAP OF THE EXPECTED TERRAIN.

....

In order to manage risk and attempt to prevent these negative outcomes, the civilian defender must undertake some hard work, starting with:

1. Development of immediate and robust physical skill-sets.

2. Commitment to violence against the VCA; in face of an attempt to kill, restraint is not a virtue,

3. Institution of personal habits that convey rectitude, seriousness and capacity to defend oneself and

significant others; helping the VCA de-select and move on.

4. Recognition of the fact that our consent and understanding are not required for violent criminal actors to immerse us in their world of hate and pain, of rage and blood.

ARBITRARY GLOSSARY

Behavioral economics – the use of principles from both economics and psychology to explore human decision-making; human irrationality, cost, benefits, and human-scale matters of choice are emphasized.

Bipolar disorder – a serious mental illness characterized by unusual and debilitating changes in mood, from excessively high to excessively low.

Belligerency – aggressive or warlike status marking engagement in conflict.

Dysregulation – abnormality in the function of a body system.

Inclusive fitness – the relative success of an organism and its kin at surviving and passing along its genes to offspring.

Maldevelopment – faulty or abnormal growth or maturation.

Prejudicial – harmful or detrimental.

Psychopathic traits – there are many, but we're most concerned with callousness, lack of guilt or remorse, absence of empathy or compassion, and cruelty.

Rectitude – moral uprightness; in this context, good judgment, and most importantly, righteousness.

Schizophrenia – a chronic and serious mental illness that affects thought, emotion, and behavior; difficulty distinguishing internal artifacts from reality is the hallmark symptom.

Virulence – the most harmful and injurious phase of a microorganism's lifespan; the period of greatest risk to others.

William Aprill is a licensed mental health professional with more than 19 years experience across the continuum of clinical care. He presently maintains a private practice and consultancy specializing in post-traumatic interventions and other disciplines.

William is a former deputy sheriff (Orleans Parish, LA, Criminal Sheriff's Office) and Special Deputy U.S. Marshal (Eastern District of Louisiana). He is a decorated competitive shooter and has taught civilian, law enforcement, and military personnel in various fighting skills since 1990. He maintains an active schedule both as student and teacher, having been instructor rated by several top-tier trainers and studying under many of the most influential members of the combative arts community.

Through his company April Risk Consulting, William

has been invited to present his material on violent criminals and their decision-making, defensive incident aftermath, mindset development, defensive preparedness, and other material to civilian, law enforcement, and military audiences across the country, including:

- **International Association of Law Enforcement Firearms Instructors**
  (IALEFI)Annual Conference
- **Georgia Association of Law Enforcement Firearms Instructors**
  (GALEFI) Annual Conference
- **Louisiana Homicide Investigator's Association**
- **Illinois Homicide Investigator's Association**
- **Rangemaster Tactical Conference**
- **The 1-Inch to 100 Yards Warrior Conference**
- **Tactical Response Alumni Weekend**
- **Lethal Force Institute**
- **Defense Training International**
- **Orleans Parish (LA) District Attorney's Office**
- **New Orleans Police Department, Crisis Transportation Service**
- **Jefferson Parish (LA) Juvenile and Adult Courts**
- **Orleans Parish (LA) Drug Court**
- **Louisiana Association of Drug Court Professionals**

William is a co-founder and Training Director of Paul-E-Palooza, the memorial conference and fundraiser for the family of the late trainer Paul Gomez, and has presented across the country in collaboration with Craig Douglas/Shivworks, Lethal Force Institute, Rangemaster, Active Response Training, Sharp Defense, Point-Driven Training, Tactical Response, Safety Solutions Academy, Modern Defensive Training Systems, Immediate Action Combatives, Defense Training International, Armed Dynamics, and others.

He has been referenced in publications including RECOIL magazine, The Tactical Wire and The Journal of the Armed Citizen's Legal Defense Network, and is the subject of two Personal Defense Network DVDs of his original training material on defensive decision-making and mindset development.

Chapter 5:

THE CRIMINAL ASSAULT PARADIGM

BY CRAIG S. DOUGLAS

The typical progression of the average person down the road of self-defense and preparedness is to purchase a handgun and then seek some type of formal instruction in its use. That same person may find that they enjoy the benefits of training and shooting, and soon this new interest evolves into something of a hobby. This in turn leads to years of investment and training in "defensive" shooting skills that leaves one with the impression that they have done their due diligence, and have taken the necessary measures to learn how to protect themselves and their loved ones with a firearm, should the need ever arise. The new aficionado is firmly entrenched in shooting culture.

But what happens if that student of defensive pistol craft is ever fortunate enough to test their skills in a training venue where they have real opposition and intent from a living, breathing, thinking human being? Often, they find that much of what they learned in live fire simply isn't coming out as cleanly, or even at all, when they try to apply their skills in a training format that replicates the likely conditions present in a typical criminal assault. This is very similar to the martial artist that trains for ten or twenty years in some form of empty hand combat and is soundly trounced in a street fight. Why and how does this happen?

The contextual considerations that frame any activity literally define how it should be trained. All pistol training has sight alignment and trigger press concepts within it, but the conditions under which one has to apply them to win a small bore bulls-eye match are very different than the conditions of a USPSA match. So it is with using a handgun to effectively thwart a criminal assault within a typical criminal assault paradigm. This phrase will essentially be used as shorthand for how most criminal assaults occur, the likely conditions that are present during them, and how this affects handgun training.

Most people who teach concealed carry skills for state licensure have never been subjected to the brutal reality of a real criminal assault and, to use the words of Col. Dave Grossman, are much like "virgins discussing sex" when it comes to understanding what is actually involved in ending a violent criminal assault with a firearm. Paradoxically, most of the people who have experienced real violence may very well not be inclined to teach firearms skills, or even able to pass on any meaningful lessons from their experience.

UNEQUAL INITIATIVE

Two core themes usually present within the criminal assault paradigm that are often notably absent from defensive firearms training are those of *un-equal initiative* and *un-proportional armament*. Even in training that is conducted in an oppositional structure, most of the time both parties are completely aware of a starting point. There's a buzzer or whistle, or a coach saying "Go!" Thus, most oppositional training begins by consent. This is an equal initiative event, where both parties are aware they will engage in some kind of motor skill with a firearm and are prepared to do so.

A criminal is not interested in engaging in this type of contest of skill and arms. His end state is very simple: get paid. Most career criminals are surprisingly sophisticated and adept at laying the groundwork for successful criminal enterprise, so it's doubtful that a real-world event that required using a firearm defensively would exhibit equal initiative. What's more common is that a criminal selects a place that is conducive to a crime against a person and carefully assesses people who pass through his hunting grounds for certain characteristics, including inattention, distraction, and task overloading.

For example, consider coming out of the supermarket and trying to get in your car as it begins to drizzle lightly. You speed up to get out of the rain just as your cell phone goes off. It's your spouse and you answer. Then you drop a bag of your purchases while fumbling with your key fob as you're trying to cut the conversation short with your spouse who is insistent upon having this conversation right now. A stranger rapidly starts helping to pick up the scattered groceries as you say to your spouse over and over again "I have to GO!" This smiling stranger hands over the sack of groceries and then offers his hand. Of course one would probably shake it since after all this person chose to get wet to help someone else out, right?

Now a gun comes out and gets stuck under your chin while someone else who you didn't see rifles throuigh your pockets. Both predators quickly run off and hop in a car driven by a third and it's off to another baited field.

This scenario is much more plausible for a typical robbery and illustrates an unequal initiative event.

In the unequal initiative event, either the good guy sees what this is turning into and initiates on the criminal, or the criminal initiates on him. Rarely does the other realize that they are getting ready to be ambushed. This speaks to two things regarding motor skills particularly drawing a firearm – time and quality.

In most firearms training, the benchmark for time is in a vacuum without anything other than a target and timer. Endless presentations and manipulations are repeated to shave even a tenth of a second from a present standard. When attention is split from the task at hand, by even something as mundane as speaking, there is a significant addition in time. Usually when the verbal task load is present, the difference between that and when one is just waiting for a timer to go off is well upwards of a second. So now that 1.25-second draw from concealment that one has worked to achieve over months of dedicated work diminishes to something over two seconds.

Considering the verbal issue specifically, there's a transition point that exists between verbal and motor skills – a speed bump is a great way of thinking about it. This diminishes the quality of motor skills significantly and is one of the reasons that, when realistic criminal assault conditions are replicated in training, it's not uncommon to see very well practiced shooters who can't clear cover garments or get their guns in play. The quality of motor skills has diminished because the conditions present in real life have never been present in training. This is also an area where there are quite a few negligent discharges. Small adaptations to the presentation – like clearing the cover garment high and well away from the holster as you establish grip – are important. This may very well add a tenth of a second to a concealed draw, but it will insure that you don't have a jacket fall back into the presentation and get a hammer hooked on it. Surety trumps speed in a real-world event.

UN-PROPORTIONAL ARMAMENT

There's a high likelihood that, if one fails to seize

initiative, they may very well have their firearm concealed when the bad guy has his in hand, which leads to the idea of un-proportional armament. Revisiting the supermarket parking lot scenario, if you are held at gunpoint with a second person rifling your pockets, should you attempt to draw a gun or just comply?

There's not an easy answer to this problem and the reality is that fighting and compliance have both worked and failed. If one does try to fight there are a couple of other skills required to make it a fight with a firearm. A good student of verbal agility may very well be able to talk themselves into a position where their hands are closer to the gun before making a disarm attempt. Once that is achieved, fundamental competency in close range empty hand skills is paramount in creating the window to access a handgun. "Talking" one's way to a gun works for the good guy as well as it works for the predator. Having a good sense of wrestling or any vertical clinch art that allows one to control limbs and take a dominant position (for a draw or to wrestle your way on top should both of you topple to the ground) is a required skill for successful contact range presentation.

The nature of unequal initiative and un-proportional armament creates a significant deficit that can be completely un-winnable or at best give one 50/50 odds of winning. The objective then should be to place the adversary in the initiative/armament deficit. Quite often, when this is achieved the situation can be resolved without a shot being fired. It's doubtful that the vast majority of opportunistic predators are going to push a fight this hard. To reiterate the previous point, the criminal has no ego investment in who wins or loses. This is mostly economics, and there is probably someone a couple of blocks away who is unprepared and will make a far easier victim. The cost/benefit analysis runs both ways with victim and bad guy.

There are three other common elements in the criminal assault paradigm that are consistent from event to event; close range, more than one assailant, and the presence of a weapon.

CLOSE RANGE

Range or distance is something that any good student of defensive handgun skills should always be processing in real time. Range and time are inextricably linked, in that more of one affords more of the other. Certainly no one wants to be in an entangled gunfight or, perhaps arguably worse, the "no-man's land" of a two-way exchange just outside of arms reach. Yet quite often criminal assaults initiate at this distance. Why does this occur and how do criminals close in to this distance so often?

Closed environments with complex geometry and blind spots should be avoided, as these are pre-disposed to facilitating criminal assault. This is quite often a choice a person must make, and can be less convenient in daily life. If such an environment cannot be avoided, then what one must do is open up and consciously heighten their field of awareness.

> **RANGE AND TIME ARE INEXTRICABLY LINKED, IN THAT MORE OF ONE AFFORDS MORE OF THE OTHER.**

Much has been written on this idea without very much tangible advice given on how to achieve this state of being aware. After all, the word itself is not a verb...how does one "aware"?

Think about awareness as a field of vision that's in a constant state of flux between maximum expansion and maximum contraction. What we seek is the wider "field of view" in the environment that is more supportive of crime. We can actually physically feel when our field of vision contracts, and a good analogy is that it feels like looking through a drinking straw. The expanded, broader field of vision or awareness hopefully allows earlier detection of a potential problem, resulting in the opportunity for range and time.

With the newly expanded field of awareness, what specifically are we looking for? What does a bad guy look like? Quite often people rely on what may be inaccurate stereotypes that involve age, gender, or perhaps even race. The best advice is to essentially treat all strangers alike and focus on specific behavior that may indicate hostile intentions. Studying pre-assault cues, or body language that correlates to pending physical violence, is an area of study that merits attention from everyone who carries a gun. A good way to do this is to get on any video host site, like You-tube or Live Leak, and pull up some videos that display violence. Police dash cam footage and surveillance film provide ample examples of what to look for, and the point to concentrate on is the time right before things go physical. Watch the video and pay close attention. Watch a lot of them and see if you can pick out common body language that everyone exhibits right before things go to blows or guns. It's this area of study that may very well allow you to make the distinction between a benign stranger and a criminal actor, and act appropriately and decisively.

EVERY CRIMINAL ASSAULT THAT IS NOT AN AMBUSH WILL BEGIN WITH AN ENCROACHMENT PROBLEM.

Once early detection of a potential predator is made, essentially what we are left with is how to manage this encroachment. This is, more often than not, where people open the door for criminals to get close enough to overwhelm them. Most people have a conversationally normed distance, implanted in them by socialization, of barely outside of arm's reach. This is where dialogue is initiated and held by strangers every day without a thing going awry. This is too close to manage if someone initiates physical hostilities and is well within the marksmanship capabilities of the untrained gunman.

If a person can address an encroachment problem effectively early enough, that in and of itself may be all that's required to thwart a bad guy's plan. Now this should not be taken to mean that one should aggressively posture at every stranger that encroaches. The vast majority of strangers that encroach towards you in your lifetime will probably have no ill intentions. That said, every criminal assault that is not an ambush will begin with an encroachment problem.

There will probably be some type of dialogue from the encroaching party directed at emotional manipulation. An effective one is for the bad guy to make his approach with a couple of crumpled dollar bills in hand and open up with something like, "Hey buddy/lady you dropped some money back there." This is surprisingly effective for a number of reasons. Most normal, well-adjusted people want to believe their fellow man is good. This plays into the idea of the good Samaritan, and the average person will respond to what is perceived to be a kind act. It may very well provoke an immediate reaction of checking for one's wallet or even looking down into a purse. A darker reason this works to the criminal's advantage is that a citizen may very well be aware that he or she didn't lose any money, but takes the opportunity to avail themselves of a little extra cash. Career criminals are adept at these ruses, and the best way to manage these problems is to have a verbal "playlist" that avoids protracted dialogue, halts encroachment, and doesn't create unnecessary hostility with a benign stranger. Verbal agility and strategies are as important as marksmanship and gun handling, and are part of becoming a good problem solver. Good verbal strategies support halting encroachment and maintaining/increasing range so one has more time to react if necessary.

MORE THAN ONE ASSAILANT

More than one assailant is common in criminal assault. Swarms of assailants are increasingly more common than they were a few years ago, and it is a good practice to avoid pockets of able-bodied young men who appear capable of delivering harm. The classic criminal assault with a second assailant, though, is usually a pincer movement conducted from the blind spot. To put this in perspective let's re-address the encroachment problem. More than likely there's a verbal component from the predator and the objective is to get the citizen engaged in dialogue. While engaged in dialogue, the likely approach is from behind by the second adversary. This is a difficult problem to manage and requires a significant adaptation to how one normally reacts to forward encroachment. Even if one is aware of the potential that a second party may be coming from behind, the cost of looking may very well be the window that the initial adversary uses to throw a punch or draw a gun. So how do we maintain awareness and vigilance to a known potential problem and scan the area behind us for the most likely avenue of approach for a second adversary without making the job of the initial encroacher easier?

The key element here is movement, and the natural reaction to wanting distance and space – which is moving backwards – must change and adapt. Backwards movement is expected by any bad guy and it's quite easy to "steer" the uninitiated pretty much anywhere, once this basic reaction is understood.

One recommendation is to "arc" around the adversary and not move backwards. A good way of visualizing this is if one were to place themselves on the face of a clock with the predator standing at twelve o'clock and the citizen standing at 6 o'clock, the objective would be to try to cut a perfect arc up to either the 9 o'clock or the 3 o'clock position. This is not a natural or instinctive thing to do. In fact, it's quite counterintuitive, as are many of the best practices in self-defense. It's also not intuitive to look at the tiny metal post at the end of the reciprocating slide in an exchange of fire, but it is most assuredly the best practice to guarantee that the bullet goes where desired.

Arcing up to the three o'clock and nine o'clock positions provides two significant advantages in managing unseen space to the rear. First, by following the arc, we can literally maintain our primary field of vision with the known problem in front of us while simultaneously pulling what was behind us into our peripheral vision. This is significant because now we don't lose the primary problem by "checking our six."

The second advantage of this movement tactic is that, if indeed there is a second adversary, then what the good guy has done is remove him/her self from a 180 degree pincer problem and significantly narrowed the field of threat. Much has been written about dealing with multiple assailants, and one of the few successful tactics is lining them up as much as possible. The arcing movement does this not perfectly, but it does remove us from the unmanageable 180-degree problem and begin this process of "stacking" multiple assailants.

One more real benefit of the arcing movement goes well towards de-selecting us from a criminal selection process. The arcing movement is so out of pattern from average that, often, the reports back from those who have actually used this tactic are that the encroaching party gives the good guy an odd look and walks off mumbling. So, movement is a key element in managing a second adversary, which is common within the criminal assault paradigm.

PRESENCE OF A WEAPON

The final element of the criminal assault paradigm is the presence of weapons. More often than not there is a weapon utilized to enforce compliance. Handguns, despite being distance/projectile weapons, are still utilized at near contact range during robberies, home invasions, and car-jackings. This is due to the phenomenon I have termed compliance creep. Compliance creep is where someone holding a firearm gains compliance to their verbal demands, and after doing so tends to creep closer to the person at whom they are pointing the gun. This is common to anyone that forces compliance of another by brandishing a firearm and is an unconscious manifestation of emboldened "alpha" dominance. One can watch any number of police dash camera videos and see where a subject will give up and be completely passive while police shout at them continually to not move. Usually this ends with a proned subject literally being "stuck" with the muzzle of several different handguns during the handcuffing process.

Understanding this may very well allow a defender to draw a handgun closer to them for a gun grab attempt, or even just to shift a muzzle away from a loved one and towards themselves. Projecting raw fear and blubbering helplessness is the best way to try and trigger this alpha dominance response. Before trying this, you want your hands as close to a gun as possible so the tactic of using a "fence" or hand barrier/antenna is desirable.

The word "fence" was originally coined by U.K. combatives instructor Geoff Thompson to describe the hands being up, active, and in between a person and someone else who is hostile. A good fence can be used proactively and reactively. Proactively, a fence can be used to set up a gun grab or even a strike. The trick is making the fence look like something that's not "tactical," and good fence work should be sublime and at most make someone appear to be animated or described as "talking with their hands." Reactively, a fence is vital and it should be specifically constructed in such a way that the hands are high and compressed, thus keeping one's hands relatively close to one's head so they can quickly cover in the event of a sudden blow thrown towards one's head. If we think of a criminal assault as an unequal initiative event, then the immediate goal, should we get caught in the deficit, is to stay conscious and upright. Consciousness and mobility are what we must have in order to escape or to access a handgun.

To review the criminal assault paradigm, or what conditions may likely be present when one has to draw a handgun to use during a robbery, car-jacking or home invasion:

• There may be one move made, and the good guy needs to make it. Criminal assaults are unequal initiative events where either the good guy or bad guy ambushes the other. In the case of the bad guy initiating, it is usually done under circumstances invoking a cognitive task load purposefully for diminishing resistance.

• If one loses initiative, then the affair will be one of un-proportional armament. Compliance may very well be the key to surviving, but is still no guarantee. If one is going to make a move on a person bearing a weapon, then it must be drawn close enough to do so and this is usually done through ruse and artifice to invoke compliance creep from the bad guy.

• The best case is that a gun never comes out and people de-select themselves from a potential criminal assault before it initiates.

• Enhanced awareness and the expanded field of vision is key to seeing a problem early enough to have the range and time to act or react.

• A keen understanding of body language and actively seeking pre-assault cues may very well allow one to discriminate a person's intentions and act appropriately.

• Once a potential problem is successfully identified, then managing the encroachment with effective verbal strategies that don't invite people into unwanted conversations is the key element in not closing into the average conversational range, which is usually barely outside of arms reach. At the same time, this strategy should not be hyper-aggressive with unnecessary posturing, which may create a problem with someone who is indeed benign. Think of this is a pre-rehearsed playlist.

• Moving in an unpredictable arc around an encroaching adversary is an effective strategy for maintaining visual contact with a known problem and scanning your blind spot for a second adversary without creating a window of opportunity for the first. If there is a second person in play, then it's a significantly more manageable problem when the field of threat is reduced to less than 180 degrees.

• Finally, keep the hands high and compressed in a good fence. This keeps your hands available for striking or weapons grabs, or allows you to cover your head from an incoming blow.

Evaluate your training and ask some difficult questions. Has a large percentage of your firearms training been conducted under conditions that replicate realistic criminal assault? Are you able to apply your hard-earned range skills under those conditions? Do you need competence in other skills that allow you the chance to access your firearm? Despite preparing for a confrontation by training with and carrying a firearm, do you engage in behavior that makes you more likely to be selected for an event where you may have to use it?

The conditions present within the criminal assault paradigm require a truly interdisciplinary approach to effective problem solving. The skills and tactics outlined are not learned on ranges or in live fire. They are learned in an interactive way with a training partner, and mastery of them is just as important as learning how to press a trigger cleanly without disturbing the sights. In fact, the skills of recognition, awareness, avoidance and de-selection are probably the most important skills in the tactician's repertoire.

ABOUT THE AUTHOR

Craig Douglas, a/k/a "South-Narc," is a retired 21-year police officer and former commander of his agency's SWAT Team. Craig was a full time police officer from 1990 to 2011 and held line assignments in corrections, patrol, narcotics and investigations, and was also a narcotics group supervisor. He was the primary defensive tactics instructor at the Southern Regional Public Safety Institute from 1992 to 1999, and has personally trained over 5,000 police officers at the Academy level. Craig has extensive operational experience in an undercover capacity that is reflected heavily in the Extreme Close Quarter Concepts coursework. Craig has a 30-year background in Filipino, Indonesian, Brazilian and Japanese martial arts and is a veteran of the U.S. Army. He has been conducting training in the private sector in the U.S. and abroad for the past 13 years. The U.S. Army, U.S. Navy, USMC, DEA, and DHS have brought him in to present entangled shooting concepts in confined spaces, particularly vehicles.

Chapter 6:
THE ARMED LIFESTYLE

BY **MASSAD AYOOB**

The first thing to understand about the armed lifestyle is that it has multiple subsets. Assuming law-abiding people, we have those who own guns but never even load them except when hunting or on the range. Then there are those who keep loaded guns readily accessible for security purposes at home or at their place of work, but don't actually carry them on their person. Next up is the category of those who carry a gun only when they have a heightened reason to expect trouble. And, finally, there are those of us who choose to have a loaded firearm on our person pretty much 24/7. All of the above have, when armed, the same power...and all of the above have, all the time, the same responsibilities.

POWER AND RESPONSIBILITY

There is a saying in America that we all live by, like it or not, and it says something rather sad about our country that it had to come from a comic book. The source is Spiderman's doomed Uncle Ben, and the saying is, "With great power comes great responsibility."

It says something else sad that so many people don't realize Spiderman's uncle only got half of it. The equation should be, "Power and responsibility are commensurate." They must be in dead equal balance, because things get ugly when that particular scale tips in either direction.

Power without responsibility tends to become tyranny.

But responsibility, without the power to fulfill it, is the very definition of futility.

How does that apply to the armed lifestyle?

RESPONSIBILITIES

We may use the firearm as sporting equipment – as a tool to harvest game, or a remote control paper punch in a target shooting game that measures our concentration, self-control, and fine motor skill – but the law still sees it as a lethal weapon. Statistics show that a child is more likely to drown on our property than to die as a victim of a firearms accident, but nonetheless, we bear a responsibility to keep it out of that little kid's hands. And out of any other unauthorized hands: those of an intruder, for example, or our crazy brother-in-law who comes for an unexpected visit.

Gun safes and quick-release security gun boxes make sense here. If a firearm must be left in an unattended motor vehicle, a lock box bolted to the transmission hump makes sense, or at least, locking the pistol in the glove box and then locking the vehicle. In some countries, a stolen firearm is considered presumptive evidence of criminal negligence on the part of the legitimate original owner, and the burden of proof is now upon that theft victim to show that the thief had to go to extraordinary effort to defeat the security measures the owner had in place.

We have a responsibility to those around us to handle our firearms safely. Possession of arms is a right, not a privilege, but the law nonetheless punishes negligence when it causes harm to others.

And that's just for the firearms we keep at home. When we carry one in public, we do so with the recognition of the possibility, however remote, that we might have to fire it in public. This carries with it the implicit responsibility to become sufficiently skillful that we are unlikely to miss the intended target and strike an innocent bystander.

THE DEFENDANT WHO HAS SOUGHT OUT TRAINING IN HOW AND WHEN TO USE THE FIREARM IS FAR EASIER TO DEFEND.

This doesn't mean that the legitimate pistol-packer has to be a state champion shooter. I recall one of my defendants who was totally new to guns when she fired three shots in desperate self-defense, and scored three hits, stopping her assailant permanently. We won her acquittal when she was charged with manslaughter. But I also remember the entitled Yuppie who bought a revolver he never fired, and one panicky dawn fired at a shadowy figure on his lawn. He said he thought it was an armed looter, and that he just fired "a warning shot" without aiming. His bullet struck and crippled for life a workman he himself had called to perform home repair. The man who pulled that trigger paid dearly for it, as well he should have.

Attorney Lisa Steele, probably the top appellate lawyer in the country who specializes in self-defense cases that went wrong at the trial level, has noted that the defendant who has sought out training in how and when to use the firearm is far easier to defend. This is because the yardstick of judgment in use-of-force cases both criminal and civil is the ancient common law doctrine of the reasonable man.

The judge will instruct the jury, "You must ask yourself what a reasonable and prudent person would have done, in the same situation, and knowing what the defendant knew." This is a three-pronged test. (1) What would a logical, cautious person have done (2) in the exact same situation as reasonably perceived by the defendant, and (3) knowing what the defendant knew.

That last prong of the test opens the door for the defense to show the jury the defendant's training. The object is for the defense team to convince the jury of two things: that the shooter did what he or she was trained to do, and that what they were trained to do was in fact the appropriate thing to do. Toward this end, defense counsel calls each of the defendant's instructors to testify as to just what they taught the defendant. During their direct testimony, they will explain and document why they in turn learned to teach what they taught the defendant. This may be supported by separate expert witness testimony, confirming that the defendant's actions were within "the mainstream of common custom and practice" or "best practices" that professionals would have taught him to apply in dealing with that type of crisis.

(l to r) Ayoob, Attorney Don West, and West's client George Zimmerman.

The untrained defendant does not bring that very substantial supportive testimony to the table, or the witness stand, when twelve good people who likely have no background of their own in this topic weigh the defendant's culpability.

THE FIRST RESPONDER CONCEPT

When crisis strikes and you are there, like it or not a responsibility has fallen upon you to deal with it. It would be of great help if you had the proper tools for the task. The firearm is the best tool for neutralizing homicidal armed men. Yes, it is that simple.

Citizens who choose to lawfully arm themselves are simply following a cultural flow that we have seen expanding in America since the third quarter of the twentieth century, a flow back to much older values of self-reliance. In the year 1950, one would have been unlikely to find a residence that contained fire extinguishers, unless a firefighter lived in the given home. Yet, today, it is a rare home that doesn't have a fire extinguisher in the kitchen at the very least, and probably also in workshop or garage.

In the year 1950 if one had asked the family physician to teach them closed chest cardiac massage, as CPR was known then, the doctor probably would have said, "Go to medical school, then! That's something *we* do!" For generations now, anyone who doesn't know cardio-pulmonary resuscitation – and the Heimlich maneuver, and hemorrhage control and other raw basics of first aid – is considered rather derelict in their social responsibilities.

What was the difference? A practical, collective recognition of the laws of time and space. There are fewer than 1,135,000 firefighters and roughly a quarter of a million emergency medical technicians and paramedics in the United States at this writing. Each of them probably works only 40 full-time hours in every 168-hour week. A few weeks of that allotted time will be consumed each year in vacation, sick time, and in-service training time. The result is that we can't put a firefighter or a paramedic on every doorstep to protect every one of the 320 million people who currently populate the United States.

When flame blooms on the stove, the householder who can simply snatch up the extinguisher and put it out has probably limited the damage to some smoke and some scorching. But if all they can do is summon the Fire Department, the clock starts ticking. In the time it takes for them to get to the phone and tell the 9-1-1 operator…and the operator dispatches the message to the emergency personnel… and those people mount up and traverse the distance and get to the fire scene…

Well, do the math. By then, the entire home may be involved. The structure may burn to the ground, and flame and smoke may have killed everyone inside. A first responder with a fire extinguisher could have prevented that.

The citizen is present when someone nearby suffers a heart attack and goes into cardiac arrest. The same laws of time and motion apply. If it takes ten minutes for the ambulance and the EMS team to arrive, the patient is very likely to be irretrievably brain dead by then. A first responder with CPR skills could have saved that lost life.

Why did it take so long for so much of society to realize that the same principles that apply to fire service and emergency medical service also apply to police service? The nation's estimated 800,000 cops, like their EMS and Fire Service counterparts, are thin on the ground. The San Bernardino massacre of the innocent by jihadis saw a very swift response by local law enforcement: they were there in about four minutes. But, by that time, 14 people were dead and 22 wounded.

The shooting had taken place in a "gun free zone." There was no one present on the ground when the danger flared who was equipped to stop it. Since law-

> **WHETHER IT'S A STORE DEFENSE GUN, A HOME DEFENSE GUN, OR A CONCEALED CARRY GUN, IT'S A PIECE OF EMERGENCY, LIFE-SAVING RESCUE EQUIPMENT DIRECTLY ANALOGOUS TO THE FIRE EXTINGUISHER OR THE AUTOMATIC ELECTRONIC DEFIBRILLATOR.**

breakers by definition break laws, "Gun Free Zone" signs do absolutely nothing to stop them. Indeed, it may make the given premises a more desirable killing ground for homicidal fanatics and madmen. Going back to the 1990s, mass shooter Buford Furrow admitted after his capture that he chose a Jewish day care center as his place to open fire because he feared that other venues he scoped out might have armed security who could shoot back. "Gun Free Zones" have thus become hunting preserves for psychopathic murderers.

The only people who obey those rules are, again by definition, the law-abiding. Thus, the "Gun Free Zone" becomes only free of good people with guns who have the wherewithal to stop the carnage. See the chapter in this book by subject matter expert Ron Borsch.

Whether it's a store defense gun, a home defense gun, or a concealed carry gun, it's a piece of emergency, life-saving rescue equipment directly analogous to the fire extinguisher or the automatic electronic defibrillator, there to help the user save innocent lives, not to end them.

LIVING ARMED

To get an idea what it will feel like carrying a gun in public for the first time, think back to when you were a child and got your first wallet or purse. For a week or more, you probably felt like a large wallet or purse with a small child attached. "If I lose this, boy am I gonna be in trouble! What if someone takes it from me? Hey, this ain't comfortable or convenient!"

But, after that week or so, you acclimated. Eventually, it became a part of you. A "new norm." The final adaptation was when you realized that when you were out and about without it, you were acutely aware of its absence. You knew that something was missing that you just might need if things didn't go as planned and hoped.

Carrying the gun is very much like that.

Unlike wallet or purse, there will be places where you can't carry it. This will depend not only on current state law, but sometimes on city ordinances as well. In jurisdiction A, a "No Guns" sign may have the power of law, and carrying the weapon there can result in arrest and a heavy conviction. In jurisdiction B, the law may say that if your gun is spotted and you are asked to leave, you have only to peacefully

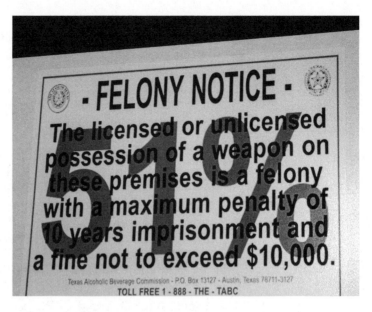

depart and the matter ends there…but if you don't leave, you are subject to arrest for Trespass After Warning.

Texas Attorney Charles Cotton

Carrying in different levels, if you will, of "Gun Free Zones" may carry different penalties, even in the same city and state. For example, Charles Cotton, a Texas attorney famous for his knowledge of gun laws there, points out that ignoring a 'no guns' sign in the Lone Star state is a relatively minor class C misdemeanor, but refusing to leave such premises when asked jumps up to a Class A misdemeanor, which can bring up to a year in jail and a four- or five-year loss of license to carry.

Some say, "It's only a misdemeanor." Those who work in the criminal justice system realize that "only" a misdemeanor is "only" up to a year in jail, and a gun-related crime on your record.

People who carry regularly use the term "NPE" which stands for "non-permissive environment." This is the situation where it is particularly important for the firearm to go undetected, or the carrier may suffer unpleasant consequences. As noted above, those consequences may involve serious legal penalties. Or, it may simply be that where you work, the company policy is "no guns."

Let's look at that particular situation a bit more closely. There are some who will say, "Concealed means concealed. If no one sees it, there's nothing to worry about." And there are those who'll say, "My right to live supersedes my boss's right to forbid guns in his workplace. I can always get another job, but I can't get another life."

All those sentiments are understandable…as far as they go. But there are other considerations, too. One is the simple matter of property owners' rights versus the right to keep and bear arms. Consider, though, that when one is fired for illegally carrying a gun, that will probably be mentioned by the now former employer whenever contacted for a reference by a prospective future employer. "He only obeys the rules he likes" is not the sort of glowing recommendation that is likely to secure a new position.

TRAVELING ARMED

It is imperative that the lawfully armed citizen know the laws of the given jurisdiction. Let's say that you are a resident of New Hampshire, the "Live Free or Die" state. If while carrying a gun you cross the southern border into Massachusetts, which does not have carry permit reciprocity with any other state at this writing, you will be committing a felony the moment you cross the state line. However, if you have obtained the difficult-but-not-impossible-to-acquire Massachusetts non-resident carry permit, you will be fine.

And if you instead drive west into neighboring Vermont, you will also be fine because for longer than anyone reading this has been alive, the Green Mountain state has allowed any law-abiding citizen regardless of their state of residence to carry without a permit, and merely forbidden anyone to do so if they have been convicted of a felony or adjudicated mentally incompetent. Indeed, for many decades Vermont was the ONLY state that allowed permitless carry, which some prefer to call Constitutional carry, though it has now been joined in that by several other states.

But if you continue your journey through Vermont and cross that state's border with New York, things change. New York offers neither any reciprocity with any state, nor any option for a non-resident to be permitted to carry a gun. First offense illegal concealed carry is a serious felony there, with mandatory prison time.

It's a classic example of what lawyers call *malum prohibitum*, which means in essence "it's bad because we passed a law against it." This stands in contrast to *malum in se*, which translates to evil in and of itself: "we passed a law against it because it's bad." Much gun law follows this pattern. As famed defense attorney and firearms instructor Jim Fleming likes to say, "We don't have to like reality. We do have to face it."

> "WE DON'T HAVE TO LIKE REALITY. WE DO HAVE TO FACE IT." ~ JIM FLEMING

At this writing, the best resource by far on the topic of gun laws is the website handgunlaw.us. It is unwise to trust anything in print on the topic, because the reciprocity agreements between state

Attorneys General change regularly, often without widespread public announcement. For example, the state of Nevada for many years recognized the home-state carry permits of Florida residents. However, when Florida for administrative reasons extended the longevity of their carry permits, Nevada authorities decided that was a longer period than they liked and ended their reciprocity with Florida. This was not widely announced, and visitors from the Sunshine State who routinely visited Las Vegas every year and carried their guns where legal there did not realize that doing as they had always done had now criminalized them. When Nevada subsequently chose to recognize Florida again, that wasn't widely publicized either.

Handgunlaw.us maintains constant contact with all the states' AG's offices (and with gun owners' civil rights groups in the various states) and thus stays current with things. It is strongly recommended that the armed citizen do a here-and-now check at handgunlaw.us before crossing state lines. For a smartphone app in the same vein, consider Legal Heat.

EFFICIENT, DISCREET CARRY

The concealed handgun can't be used to protect yourself and others if it is not readily accessible. If it is not discreetly concealed, well…it is no longer concealed.

Open carry is a hot-button issue in both the gun culture and the eye of the public. In some weather this can add comfort to the carrier, since cover garments can be unduly hot. There is also an intimidation effect on potential criminals, and there is documentable evidence of that.

However, that which intimidates bad guys will inevitably intimidate good guys, too. We live in a society where, for generations, media and politicians have relentlessly demonized guns and

DO WE HAVE A RIGHT TO ALARM INNOCENT PEOPLE?

people who own them. Because people unidentifiable as law enforcement carrying guns in public are an aberration of the norm, it follows that some by-standers will perceive "aberrant person with power to kill me and others." Do we have a right to cause that alarm to others? We do not know if one of those passers-by, or fellow diners in the restaurant where we are open carrying, may in the past have been victimized by a criminal armed with a gun. We should be able to understand how we strangers with visible guns in their presence may alarm them. It puts us in the position of a smoker in the presence of someone who has a severe allergy to tobacco smoke. Yes, we have a right to smoke, but not a right to trigger someone's allergy. Yes, we have a right to bear arms, but do we have a right to alarm innocent people needlessly when we know, or should know, that might happen?

There are other concerns with open carry. One is that the exposed handgun becomes an inviting target for thieves, bullies, and show-offs. More than one good person innocently carrying a holstered gun has been disarmed by someone who had no right to touch them, sometimes with tragic results.

Finally, any experienced cop can tell you that sometimes bad people make false complaints to the police about good people. If that person has spotted your small, gray semiautomatic pistol in your exposed holster, he can maliciously and falsely call police and tell the officers that you threatened him and pointed your gun at him, an act of felony aggravated assault which can bring many years of incarceration. Because he will be able to correctly describe your gun due to your openly carrying it, his false accusation gains credibility. That could all have been avoided by simply carrying concealed.

This is why most in the gun culture recommend discreet, concealed carry. The concealed carrier has the element of surprise against the bad guys, and is much less likely to suffer an attempted "gun-grab."

And the concealed carrier will not offend, alienate, and antagonize innocent people.

APPROACHES TO HANDGUN CONCEALMENT

My old friend and fellow trainer Clint Smith coined the phrase, "A personal defense gun shouldn't be comfortable, it should be comforting." Whenever I've seen Clint in his natural habitat, he was carrying one or another .45 or .44 caliber handgun. As a former combat Marine and street cop, he wants to know that if the feces unexpectedly hit the fan, he has a gun with the power, accuracy, and cartridge capacity to deal with the problem. I don't blame him.

An opposite school of thought holds that when there is no particular threat, it's more than enough to carry a very small gun. A tiny single action .22 caliber novelty revolver, for example, or better, the Lilliputian Ruger LCP (Lightweight Compact Pistol) in .380 caliber. If tucked in the waistband or slipped in a pocket (always use a holster for either application, please!), the LCP will need precious little adaptation to always be on the shooter's person, and always within reach if one should unexpectedly but desperately need it. The current generation of subcompact 9mm pistols with single-stack magazines, or that old stand-by the small-frame, snub-nose revolver in .38 Special or even .357 Magnum, are also very easy to conceal with the right carry systems, even in suit-and-tie environments in which the firearm cannot be exposed.

Each individual who chooses to be lawfully armed needs to find his or her own optimum ground. Factors will include body shape and size, dress code in given times and places, and habituation. Those of us who, like Clint Smith, lean toward "serious fighting handguns" follow a practice called "dressing around the gun." A suit-coat one size large will drape enough to well conceal a full-size service pistol in an inside the waistband (IWB) holster, and the pants of the same suit will need to be an inch or two larger in the waistband to allow for comfortable carry of the discreetly concealed IWB scabbard.

Experts generally recommend carrying spare ammunition, at least one full reload. Noted gun expert John Farnam determined back in the 1970s that the average person could fire a gun with a long trigger pull and reset, such as a double action revolver, at a rate of four shots per second measuring from first shot to last, and a semiautomatic pistol with short trigger pull and reset at approximately five rounds per second. (World champions can shoot at roughly twice that speed.) A gun without spare ammunition is a temporary gun. Moreover, most malfunctions in handguns are related to the ammo (revolver or auto) or the magazine (auto), and can only be rectified by dumping what's in the gun and reloading. It's emergency safety-rescue equipment; remember, being able to keep it up and running is of paramount importance.

In the gun world, a lot of people seem to think, "anyone who carries more hardware than I do must be a paranoid 'mall ninja,' and anyone who carries less than I do is a pathetic sheeple." Don't fall into that trap. Assess your own needs realistically and equip yourself accordingly. Another person's perceived needs may differ from your own.

10 COMMANDMENTS OF CONCEALED CARRY

In 2010, when I was writing for Harris Publications' "Pocket Pistols" annual, publisher Shirley Steffen asked me to write an article titled Ten Commandments of Concealed Carry. I did, and it kind of went viral. I offer it to you here:

COMMANDMENT I: If you choose to carry, always carry as much as possible.

Hollywood actors get to see the script beforehand, and nothing is fired at them but blanks. You don't have either luxury. Criminals attack people in times and places where they think the victims will not be prepared for them. It's what they do. The only way to be prepared to ward off such predators is to always be prepared: i.e., to be routinely armed and constantly ready to respond to deadly threats against you and those who count on you for protection. It's not about convenience; it's about life and death.

COMMANDMENT II: Don't carry a gun if you aren't prepared to use it.

The gun is not a magic talisman that wards off evil. It is a special-purpose emergency rescue tool: no more, no less. History shows us that—for police and for armed citizens alike—the mere drawing of the gun ends the great majority of criminal threats, with the offender either surrendering or running away. However, you must always remember that criminals constitute an armed subculture themselves, living in an underworld awash with stolen, illegal weapons. They don't fear the gun; they fear the resolutely armed man or woman pointing that gun at them.

And, being predators, they are expert judges of what is prey and what is a creature more dangerous to them than what they thought a moment ago was prey. Thus, the great irony: the person who is prepared to kill if they must to stop a murderous transgression by a human predator is the person who is least likely to have to do so.

> # THE PERSON WHO IS PREPARED TO KILL IF THEY MUST ... IS THE PERSON WHO IS LEAST LIKELY TO HAVE TO DO SO.

COMMANDMENT III: Don't let the gun make you reckless.

Lightweight pseudo-psychologists will tell you that "the trigger will pull the finger," and your possession of your gun will make you want to kill someone. Rubbish. The gun is no more an evil talisman that turns kindly Dr. Jekyll into evil Mr. Hyde than it is a good talisman that drives off evil. Those of us who have spent decades immersed in the twin cultures of American law enforcement and responsibly armed citizenry know that the truth is exactly the opposite. A good person doesn't see their weapon as a supercharger or excuse for aggression, but as brakes that control that natural human emotion. The law itself holds the armed individual to "a higher standard of care," requiring that they do all that is possible to avoid using deadly force until it becomes clearly necessary. Prepare and act accordingly.

COMMANDMENT IV: Carry legally.

If you live someplace where there is no provision to carry a gun to protect yourself and your loved ones, don't let pusillanimous politicians turn you into a convicted felon. Move! It's a quality of life issue. Rhetorical theory that sounds like "I interpret the law this way, because I believe the law should be this way"—which ignores laws that aren't that way—can sacrifice your freedom, your status as a gun-owning free American and your ability to provide for your family. If you live where a CCW permit is available, get the damn permit. If you don't, move to someplace that does. Yes, it is that simple. And if you are traveling, check sources such as handgunlaw.us to make sure that you are legal to carry in the given jurisdiction. Don't let the legal system make you a felon for living up to your responsibilities to protect yourself and those who count on you. If you carry, make sure you carry legally.

COMMANDMENT V: Know what you're doing.

Gunfights are won by those who shoot fastest and straightest, and are usually measured in seconds. Legal aftermaths last for years, and emotional aftermaths, for lifetimes. Get educated in depth in the management of all three stages of encounter beforehand.

COMMANDMENT VI: Concealed means concealed.

If your local license requires concealed carry, keep the gun truly concealed. The revealing of a concealed handgun is seen in many quarters as a threat, which can result in charges of criminal threatening, brandishing and more. A malevolent person who wants to falsely accuse you of threatening them with a gun will have their wrongful accusation bolstered if the police find you with a gun where they said it was. Yes, that happens. Some jurisdictions allow "open carry." I support the right to open carry, in the proper time and place, but I have found over the decades that there are relatively few ideal times or places where the practice won't unnecessarily and predictably frighten someone the carrier had no reason to scare.

COMMANDMENT VII: Maximize your firearms familiarity.

If you ever need that gun, it will happen so quickly and terribly that you'll have to be swift and sure. If you don't, you'll still be handling a deadly weapon in the presence of people you love. Making gun manipulation second nature—safety as well as draw-fire-hit—is thus doubly important.

COMMANDMENT VIII: Understand the fine points.

Don't just read the headlines or editorials, read the fine print. Actually study the laws of your jurisdiction. What's legal in one place won't be legal in another. Cities may have prohibitions that states don't. Remember the principle, "ignorance of the law is no excuse."

COMMANDMENT IX: Carry an adequate firearm.

A motor scooter is a motor vehicle, but it's a poor excuse for a family car. A .22 or a .25 is a firearm, but it's a poor excuse for defense. Carry a gun loaded with ammunition that has a track record of quickly stopping lethal assaults. Hint: If your chosen caliber is not used by police or military personnel, it's probably not powerful enough for its intended purpose.

COMMANDMENT X: Use common sense.

Common sense—encompassing ethics and logic and law alike—must be your constant guide and companion when you decide to carry a gun. Not idealism, not rhetoric. When you carry a gun, you literally carry the power of life and death. It is a power that belongs only in the hands of responsible people who care about consequences, and who are respectful of life and limb and human safety—that of others as well as their own.

FINAL THOUGHTS

The gun carries responsibility with it, in return for the power to protect oneself and others from deadly dangers that cannot be neutralized with lesser force. People fear that which they cannot control; the firearm gives them a mechanism of control that realistically allows them to cope with certain dangers which have created reasonable fear. The well-adjusted person competent with first aid doesn't hope for someone to suffer injury or heart-attack so they can show off their skills, and the well-adjusted armed citizen doesn't hope for an opportunity to shoot a criminal. Each is simply a responsible member of society who is prepared for life-threatening emergencies and, being so prepared, is now more free to go on and enjoy a happy and productive life.

Chapter 7:

FINDING RELEVANT TRAINING

BY TOM GIVENS

Here's a typical conversation. Him, "I'm entitled to my own opinion." Me, "No, you're not."

In this age of Facebook, Google and You Tube, it seems everyone is an "expert," whether they have any background in the topic at hand or not. I think we can agree that the use of firearms for self defense is a technical field. To be entitled to an opinion in a technical field, one should have specialized training, education and experience in that field. Without those, an opinion is absolutely worthless.

I have been involved in defensive firearms training for 40 years, and a full time trainer for the past 20 years. I am a graduate of the FBI police firearms instructor school, the NRA Law Enforcement Firearms Instructor and Law Enforcement Tactical Shooting Instructor schools, and several other instructor programs. I have trained under everyone from the old guard like Jeff Cooper, Chuck Taylor, Clint Smith, Massad Ayoob and Ken Hackathorn, to newer guys like Southnarc, Jeff Gonzales, and many more. I have written five published textbooks on firearms training and well over a hundred gun magazine articles. I have been accepted as an expert witness on firearms and firearms training in half a dozen federal district courts and another half dozen state courts. I won several state and regional championships in IPSC, before it became USPSA, and I have won 2 state championships and a couple of regional championships in IDPA competition, where I hold a Master rating in three divisions. I spent eight years in the Army National Guard, with teaching duties, achieving the rank of E-7. In the civilian world I have worked in uniform in a patrol car and in plain clothes as an investigator. I have seen violence first hand, and I have investigated a metric butt-load of it. I do have a right to my opinion.

I elaborately made this point because there is so much nonsense available in print and on the internet from self-appointed experts who don't have these credentials. A student of mine recently remarked that getting one's self-defense advice from the Internet was much like getting your marital advice from Hustler magazine. Good point.

The problem is that when you are setting up your own training program you are preparing for an event where your life or the life of a loved one may be literally at stake; plus, after the event, your life, freedom and livelihood are still at risk if your training was inappropriate. There are so many training companies and individual trainers out there now that the new concealed carry student can be frustrated and bewildered. I will try to offer you some solid advice on how to select trainers and courses to set yourself up for victory in a self-defense confrontation and to limit your legal liabilities afterward.

All trainers are what I call "prisoners of our own experiences." This means that our training, education and experience form a prism, through which we see the training world. This colors our perception of what skills are important to you, and how they should be taught. Since various instructors' backgrounds can be radically different, so can be their views on teaching.

In firearms training, the word "context" is critically important, as it is in almost every sub-category of armed self defense. If we are selecting a holster, we look at context. Do I need a hunting holster, a secure police duty rig, or a discretely concealable carry rig? If selecting a pistol, do I need a target gun, a hunting gun, or a concealed carry handgun? Context is king. Thus, when discussing firearms training the very first thing we need to do is to define our mission.

For the purposes of this discussion, our mission will not be military operations nor uniformed police patrol duties. Our task will be to ensure our ability to protect ourselves and our loved ones from death or grievous bodily harm at the hands of an unlawful, predatory criminal attacker. With our end goal well defined, we can look at different training paradigms and see how they fit our needs.

BACKGROUND OF THE FIREARMS TRAINER

Most firearms trainers in this country will come from one of three backgrounds: military service, police work, or competitive shooting. Some have experience in two of these fields, and a smaller number have experience in all three. This, of course, forms the basis of their curriculum and training methodology. If they came from the police or military world they usually had entry-level training, such as a police academy or military basic training. They went on to more advanced training, with periodic in-service training. If they worked for an enlightened agency or unit, they were sent to outside schools for more training. If not, the best went to outside schools on their own dime and their own time. Coupled with field experience, this forms the core of their training philosophy. Let's look at the three major trainer groups separately.

Let's start with the military paradigm. There are a lot of trainers coming out of the military right now, especially former Special Operations soldiers with a lot of field experience. Unfortunately, a lot of that experience is totally unrelated to domestic, U.S. self defense, both as to circumstance and to operating under U.S. criminal and civil law. I would caution the civilian concealed carrier to take pains to select a military background trainer who has successfully made the transition to training American citizens operating in U.S. cities. Here are some of the key points that make much military-based training inadequate or even improper for the citizen with a carry permit.

I WOULD CAUTION THE CIVILIAN CONCEALED CARRIER TO TAKE PAINS TO SELECT A MILITARY BACKGROUND TRAINER WHO HAS SUCCESSFULLY MADE THE TRANSITION TO TRAINING AMERICAN CITIZENS OPERATING IN U.S. CITIES.

First, the soldier is almost always armed with a long gun, with the handgun relegated to the back-up-gun role. This very rarely applies to the private citizen, especially away from his home. In your case, the concealed handgun on your person is the only gun you will get to use in self defense. You can't go get anything better once the action starts. If you could go, why would you come back?

Next, the military operator works in teams, not alone. He has friends with long guns with him, each with specific duties and areas of responsibility. Not so for the lone defender.

Once contact is made, the soldier can radio for additional support, ranging from more troops to an air strike. You cannot.

There are two factors, however, that really separate the military world from that of an armed citizen. First, the soldier understands and accepts the concept of "acceptable casualties." In planning any military operation, from platoon level to corps level, you have to figure in casualties from enemy action, equipment failures, and bad luck. You have to start out with enough men to lose some and still accomplish the mission. In our world, the acceptable level of friendly casualties is ZERO. If your plan involves losing one of your children while the rest of the family escapes, I can tell you now, Mom is not going to go for it.

> **IF YOUR PLAN INVOLVES LOSING ONE OF YOUR CHILDREN WHILE THE REST OF THE FAMILY ESCAPES, I CAN TELL YOU NOW, MOM IS NOT GOING TO GO FOR IT.**

The other issue is that the soldier understands and accepts the concept of "collateral damage." This includes the injury or death of uninvolved non-combatants. This is inevitable in warfare, and unavoidable. In our world the acceptable percentage of non-involved bystanders killed or injured is ZERO.

Finally, especially in Special Operations, use of firearms is almost always OFFENSIVE in nature, not DEFENSIVE. One ex-.mil trainer for whom I have utmost respect has not really been successful at making the transition to civilian training. I recently saw an ad from his school saying in bold letters, "We will make you the aggressor!" The problem is, in U.S. criminal and civil law, "the aggressor" is a synonym for "the defendant." Remember that your training resume will follow you into court in any criminal or civil action that may arise from your defensive use of deadly force.

The next group would be trainers from a purely law enforcement background. They typically have a lot of experience in managing chaos, and usually have a lot of experience investigating violent crimes. Thus, they tend to have a pretty good idea what interpersonal violence involves. This does, not, however, ensure that they have made a good transition to teaching private citizens. Here are some key points to consider.

First, the police officer has a sworn duty to seek out, confront, and arrest very bad people for doing very bad things, and to press forward in the face of armed resistance. This is the opposite of what the citizen should be doing, namely avoidance, deterrence, de-escalation and evasion. Using the firearm is a last ditch, desperate measure, as a last resort for the armed citizen.

Other differences include the fact that the officer will usually have a full size service pistol and lots of spare ammo, body armor, armed and trained partner(s), a long gun in the car, and direct real-time radio contact with armed friends. The armed citizen often has none of these advantages. In fact, even if you could call for help on your cell phone (you won't be able to until the action is over), the average response time to priority one calls in major American cities is eleven minutes! In eleven minutes, responding officers will have absolutely no impact on the outcome of the fight, they will simply take a report about it.

Also, most police officer-involved shootings in the U.S. involve uniformed patrol officers, who operate in a world vastly different from that of a legitimate private citizen. The circumstances are radically different, which requires radically different training. Contrary to what you see in movies and TV shows, SWAT officers in this country fairly rarely shoot suspects. Their job is to contain the suspect safely and get him out and into custody. SWAT really stands for "Sit, Wait, And Talk." Detectives also rarely shoot anyone. They mostly shuffle paper and talk to people in a controlled environment. The vast majority of police shootings involve uniformed patrolmen doing a fairly short list of duties.

Most shootings involving uniformed police officers will take place during the conduct of one of three activities: traffic stops, bar enforcement and domestic violence calls. Patrolmen will stop a car for rolling through a stop sign, believing they will be writing a "routine" ticket. They may be unaware that the driver has a kilo of cocaine in the trunk, a stolen pistol on the seat next to him, and a few warrants for his arrest on file. As the officer walks up, he is suddenly confronted with an armed assault. As a private citizen you should not, under any circumstances, be making traffic stops. That eliminates a huge danger area for you.

Cops also have to go into seedy dive bars on a regular basis to enforce a laundry list of statutes. They have to look for violations of liquor laws, gambling laws, drug laws, prostitution, parolees, etc. Seedy dive bars are often full of career criminals who are violating their probation or parole, are illegally armed, are holding drugs and so on. The predictable outcome is that cops are often involved in a fight for their lives in these dark, cramped, crowded spaces.

I have done a fair bit of research in this matter, and it appears that over 99% of bar fights occur in bars. Stay the hell out of bars and you will probably never be involved in a bar fight. This eliminates the second major source of police shootings.

The third group involves calls regarding domestic violence complaints. Officers go inside the houses, apartments and trailers of people who are already drunk and enraged. What a shock—they are then involved in a lot of shootings. I do some training periodically for a small rural Sheriff's Office that only has a dozen deputies. In the last few years they have been involved in three shootings, and all three began as domestic disturbances. You should not be going into other people's homes and sorting out their marital problems while they are drunk and fighting. That eliminates the third major danger area.

Next issue. Police trainers tend to have a distorted view of engagement distances, because of their duty to arrest. Whether the arrest is for impaired driving or First Degree Murder, at some point in the process the officer has to physically put his hands on the offender. This is the suspect's last chance to assault the officer and escape, and the moment of physical contact is the most dangerous for the officer. We have tried for decades to find a way to put handcuffs on a suspect by telekinesis, but it just doesn't work. This is why such a large percentage of police line of duty deaths occur at a distance of 0-5 feet from the assailant. That's not where the incident began, but it is where it ended.

Then there are trainers with only a competitive shooting background. They may be able to teach you a lot about fast, accurate shooting, and you would be well served to seek out a proven champion shooter in IDPA, USPSA or Steel Challenge shooting to polish up your shooting skills. Be careful, however, about nuances that may not serve you well in real life self-defense. For instance, we see ready positions in competitive shooting that muzzle everything downrange, all of the time. In many shooting sports,

> **POLICE TRAINERS TEND TO HAVE A DISTORTED VIEW OF ENGAGEMENT DISTANCES, BECAUSE OF THEIR DUTY TO ARREST.**

there are penalties for shooting non-threat targets, but not for muzzling them. On the street, muzzling innocents can get you charged with various felonies, from Reckless Endangerment to Aggravated Assault, depending on the jurisdiction. Even if you are acquitted, you lost. Attorneys, bondsmen, and so forth are not free. We see gunhandling that would facilitate getting disarmed in the real world, but not on a shooting range. We also see highly specialized guns and holsters that could not be used on the street. If you choose to shoot in competition, that's great. I've been involved in small bore rifle competition in school, PPC competition early in my law enforcement career, and as noted, both IPSC and IDPA matches. You must be careful, however, to mentally separate match shooting and preparation for actual armed conflict.

Finally, the major problem with competitive shooting is a preoccupation with inconsequential increments of time. Lost time measured in scant hundredths of a second mean nothing in a fight, but accumulate and become significant in a match with 10-12 stages. For self defense, we want the most robust techniques, meaning they work reliably over a broad range of circumstances and under suboptimal conditions. They may not be the very fastest techniques under optimal match shooting conditions, where you have a clean gun, clean ammo, clean magazines, and are uninjured.

> **LOST TIME MEASURED IN SCANT HUNDREDTHS OF A SECOND MEAN NOTHING IN A FIGHT.**

So, in summary, we need trainers who understand the realities of criminal predation against private citizens and understand the criminal and civil legal framework under which we must function.

Now let's look at the circumstances we need to consider, again to put the training in proper context.

USING RELEVANT THREAT DATA

When people begin to set up a defensive training program, there are certain sources they tend to look to. Sometimes these are not the best sources of information, however. One commonly used source is the

FBI's Uniform Crime Reporting section (UCR) Law Enforcement Officers Killed and Assaulted Summary (LEOKA). Unfortunately, each year in the United States typically somewhere between 50 and 75 police officers are murdered in the line of duty. Thousands more are seriously injured, but modern trauma care holds the fatalities down to this figure. The LEOKA report features a brief summary of the incident in which each officer was murdered the previous year. Usually, the summary of each incident gives the officer's name and age, type of agency (municipal, county, state, federal, etc.), assignment (patrol, SWAT, detective, etc), and a summary of the incident. For example, Officer Smith, a city patrol officer, was checking a suspicious car at 3:00am behind the local mall when he was shot to death by the driver.

A lot of people look at these summaries and try to base a civilian training program built on the distances, number of shots, etc. involved in these cases. Of course, the majority of these will be totally off base. Why would a citizen be checking a suspicious car behind the mall at 3:00 a.m.? As stated earlier, police patrol officer shootings do not generally reflect what a citizen will be dealing with.

Some trainers talk to the local department's Firearms Training Unit (FTU). Again, very little relevance to private citizens. Others look at competition shooting records. Still, little relevance.

There are some much better sources of information for us. The Bureau of Justice Statistics (BJS) is a section in the U.S. Justice Department whose sole function is to generate an annual report on crime in the U.S. This gives us a better picture of the threats a private citizen may face.

Here are some numbers from the BJS, which you may find alarming. In 2006, according to the BJS, there were 5,685,620 violent criminal incidents in the country. That's right, 5.7 million. That's Murder, Aggravated Assault, Robbery, Rape and Assault. Those are the only crimes included. With the exception of Assault, these are the very

IN 2011, THE AGGREGATE NUMBER WAS UP TO 5.8 MILLION (VIOLENT CRIMINAL INCIDENTS). THAT'S ONE VIOLENT CRIMINAL INCIDENT PER EVERY THIRTY ADULTS.

crimes that we carry guns to defend against. In 2011, the aggregate number was up to 5.8 million. That's one violent criminal incident per every thirty adults. (The odds of you needing that gun are a bit higher than one in a million, aren't they?)

According to the BJS, in 2013, 1.1 million Americans suffered at least one violent victimization. And no, it's not all gang on gang. In 2013 there were 737,940 violent criminal incidents in which the victim and offender were unknown to each other, in other words, stranger violence.

Most states have a parallel organization to the FBI. In Tennessee, for instance, it's the TBI. Every police agency in Tennessee is required by law to report every crime reported to them to the TBI. The TBI then puts out an amazingly detailed report each year. You can see when most robberies and aggravated assaults occur, and in what locations. The TBI report breaks down robbery locations, for instance, showing the number in banks, convenience stores, residences, and even vacant lots. This is the sort of data we need when setting up a training program.

For information relevant to armed private citizens, we can also look to law enforcement agencies whose personnel wear plain civilian clothing and concealed handguns. One such agency is the FBI. Their policy requires the handgun to be concealed if they are away from their own office and in civilian clothing. In fact, every year roughly half of their shootings result from someone mistakenly trying to rob or car-jack a Special Agent, unaware of his law enforcement status.

During the period from 1989-1994, for instance, the FBI averaged about 20-30 shooting incidents per year. This is after the change-over to semiauto pistols, and again involves plain clothes agents. During that period, 92% of their shootings occurred at a distance of 6-10 feet, and the average number of shots fired by agents was 3.2 rounds.

The Drug Enforcement Administration (DEA) also has personnel in casual civilian clothes, and due to the nature of their work they tend to be involved in more shooting incidents than the FBI. In 2007 alone, they were involved in 44 shooting incidents.

The average engagement distance was 14.6 feet and the average number of rounds fired was five. I might point out that the typical American sedan is 16 feet long, so their average engagement distance was about one car length.

From 1996 to 2014, I owned an indoor range and training center in Memphis, Tennessee. Memphis is one of the most violent metropolitan areas in the entire country, with a violent crime rate per capita about three times that of Los Angeles. Over that 18-year period, we trained about 45,000 students for a state issued carry permit, and about 45% of those went on to further training. Over that period, we had 65 students that I know of involved in defensive gunplay. These are students that reported back to the school or were reported to me through law enforcement channels. Of these, we had 62 victories, 0 losses and 3 forfeits. Of the 62 students who were armed on the Big Day, all 62 won. However, we had three students that were unarmed when their moment of truth came, and they all died. All three were murdered in separate street robberies, and ALL THREE WERE UNARMED AT THE TIME. As this is being written, a month ago the last defendant in the murder of the last unarmed student went to trial and was convicted. According to testimony from eye witnesses, the student had handed over his wallet and cell phone and was standing there with his hands in the air when he was shot in the face and killed. "Give them what they want and they'll go away" may not be the best strategy. What if what they want is your life? If you wait to see if they're really going to kill you, and they do, it's too late to stop them from killing you.

Let's look at the 62 students who were successful. Slightly over 90% of the incidents took place at a distance of 3-7 yards. One of the things we stress in training is not to let unknown people, with questionable intent, get too close before verbally challenging them, moving to a better position, making eye contact, or some combination to keep them a bit

> **IF YOU WAIT TO SEE IF THEY'RE REALLY GOING TO KILL YOU, AND THEY DO, IT'S TOO LATE TO STOP THEM FROM KILLING YOU.**

further out. Distance favors the skilled adversary, which should be you. Of these incidents, 90% occurred away from home, at convenience stores, shopping malls, ATM kiosks and other public spaces. The average number of shots fired was 3.8, although some incidents involved only one shot while others involved 8-12 rounds.

Distances also varied greatly. Two incidents occurred at contact distance, 0-2 yards. In one of those cases there was intentional physical contact, in the other the physical contact was purely accidental. At the other end of the spectrum, we had shootings at 15, 17 and 22 yards. The majority, however, occurred between 3 and 7 yards (92.1%).

So, in looking at the FBI, DEA and Rangemaster student shooting numbers, we see some clear commonalities. The involved Good Guys were in plain civilian clothing with concealed handguns. The predominant distances were 6-10 feet (FBI), 14.6 feet

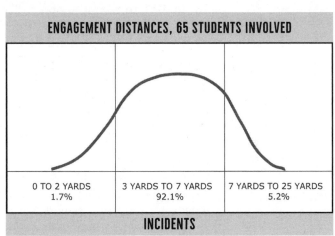

ENGAGEMENT DISTANCES, 65 STUDENTS INVOLVED

| 0 TO 2 YARDS 1.7% | 3 YARDS TO 7 YARDS 92.1% | 7 YARDS TO 25 YARDS 5.2% |

INCIDENTS

(DEA) and 9-21 feet (Rangemaster students). Remember, one reason our average distance is farther out is because we have no duty to arrest. Agents were moving in on suspects in a lot of these shootings, while our guys are trying to keep their distance. Most occur in public places (where there are potential victims, thus there are Bad Guys).

If you will recall, most uniformed police shootings involved traffic stops, bar enforcement, and domestic violence. In looking over the student-involved shootings, we tend to see four themes that recur. The most common reasons students are forced to defend themselves seem to fall into one of these categories, which we call "The Four R's." They are Robbery, Rape, Road Rage and Respect. Under the present

Incident Based Reporting System now widespread in American law enforcement, if you are shot and survive, none of those four foundational reasons for your shooting will be reported. You will just be listed as an Aggravated Assault.

THE TRUTH ABOUT "AGGRAVATED ASSAULT"

I'd like to use my remaining space to educate you a bit about Aggravated Assault. In the past, offenders such as armed robbers, car-jackers and rapists who shot a citizen were usually charged with Murder if the victim died, and Attempted Murder if the victim survived. This practice has largely been abandoned in the U.S. in recent years, for several reasons. Now, if the victim survives, the offender is usually charged with Aggravated Assault. In fact, the FBI Uniform Crime Report no longer even has an entry for Attempted Murder. It's either Murder or an Aggravated Assault.

People often ask me a question prefaced with, "I know the odds of my needing my gun are one in a million, but....". Sorry, Sparky, those odds are way off! Aggravated Assault simply means you survived an attack in which a suspect tried to kill you, but he was just inept. The FBI definition of Aggravated Assault is "an unlawful attack involving a weapon or other means likely to cause death or great bodily injury." In other words, someone tried to kill you but you survived.

People look at the murder rate and find there are only about 15,000 murders each year in the U.S. Their conclusion from that is that the odds of needing a gun are very low. In a typical year in the U.S., there are about one million Aggravated Assaults. Again, that's a million ATTEMPTS to unlawfully kill a victim. In 2006, for instance, there were 1,209,730 Aggravated Assaults.

The reason the total number of murders in this country is fairly low is not a lack of trying, it's because of modern trauma care. Modern trauma care, especially in big cities, is a true miracle. The VAST majority of people who are shot, stabbed or bludgeoned by criminals don't die from their injuries, so they are not Murders, they represent Aggravated Assaults. In my city, for instance, in 2013 there were 154 homicides (including 20+ justifiable homicides). There were, however, 9,165 Aggravated Assaults! Roughly 3,500 of those Aggravated Assault victims were shot. The rest were attacked with weapons other than firearms. In a city of 645,000 people, that's one Aggravated Assault per every 70 residents, in a single year! So, your odds are not one in a million. They are one in seventy, just for that one crime.

THE REASON THE TOTAL NUMBER OF MURDERS IN THIS COUNTRY IS FAIRLY LOW IS NOT A LACK OF TRYING, IT'S BECAUSE OF MODERN TRAUMA CARE.

Let me put a human face on this for you. I know a young woman named Jackie. Jackie came home from the grocery store one night and as she got out of her car in her own driveway, she was accosted by an armed robber with a sawed off shotgun. He fired a shot at her that mostly missed. The pattern of shot impacts on the garage door behind her shows most of the pattern missed her, but she caught the edge of the pattern in her face and right shoulder. Her right eye was macerated and had to be removed. It is now a glass eye. Her left eye was damaged to the point that she is legally blind. She also permanently lost the use of her right arm (she was right handed). Jackie almost died, and was in the hospital many weeks, but she survived. Since she lived, the suspect was only charged with Aggravated Assault. Jackie, however, will spend the rest of her life one-armed and blind. Her son was six years old when she was shot. She will not see him grow up, get married, have a grandchild, or see anything else. She is permanently blind. Jackie was 28 when this occurred.

This is often what Aggravated Assault actually means. Victims routinely survive, due to trauma care, but may be blind, lose a limb, be paraplegic from spinal wounds, undergo several corrective surgeries, lose the ability to work to support their families, and other tragic consequences. But, since they didn't die, the crime is treated as a minor affair.

Murder, Aggravated Assault and Forcible Rapes make up a total of about 1.25 million serious violent crimes each year in the US. Do the math. That's most certainly not a one-in-a-million chance, and that's not even including 600,000 Robberies each year.

WHAT TO LOOK FOR

Unfortunately, much of what passes for defensive training these days is "edutainment," a word coined by famous trainer Pat Rogers. It's a combination of education and entertainment, and unfortunately, the entertainment side is often more heavily weighted.

If you want to go to man camp and spend five days crawling on the ground, shooting thousands of rounds through your AR or AK, that's fine. It's great fun. Chalk that up to your vacation budget, NOT your training budget. When you're at your office or at the mall, you won't have a chest rig and a rifle. You'll have a concealed handgun and a spare magazine (unless you want to be another "forfeit"). The

Surveillance video shows Givens student (female in foreground) winning actual gunfight with armed robber: Student quickly side-steps and brings gun up in two hands, on the way to eye level.

Student fires, two handed, at eye level, and hits well.

only gear you will get to defend yourself and your
loved ones with will be that gear which is on your
person when the incident occurs.

So, our training program should be geared toward
excellence in the following areas:

Develop an alert, aware state of mind, accepting
the fact that violence can occur anytime, anywhere.
Do not be surprised or astonished that someone is
unlawfully attacking you. Instead of "I can't believe
this is happening!," your mental response should be,
"My day at bat."

Acquire a reliable, functional handgun you can
shoot well, a good carry system (belt, holster and
ammunition carrier), and wear it on a routine, daily
basis. You do not get to pick which day you will need
your gun. Someone else makes that decision for you,
and you will typically be informed at the very last
minute!

Work on a safe, efficient, fast presentation of the
handgun from its concealed mode of carry. Practice

in the clothes you will wear daily. If you ever need that gun to save a life, you will need it quickly. You will have a very finite amount of time once the flag flies. The faster you can access your equipment, the more time you have to make life-altering decisions, and if necessary, get good hits.

Learn to keep your gun running. If it runs empty, reload it. If it malfunctions, fix it.

Do the bulk of your practice on getting solid hits in the 3- to 7-yard range, quickly and reliably. Do some practice at 15-20 yards, but not much. In short, concentrate on the skills we are most likely to need.

Contact info:
Tom Givens
Rangemaster.tom@gmail.com
www.rangemaster.com

ABOUT THE AUTHOR

After completing a 25-year career in law enforcement and specialized security work, Tom Givens opened his own pistol range in Memphis, TN in 1996. For 18 years, it was the primary source of handgun carry permit certification for the greater Memphis area. Soon joined by his wife Lynn, the training duo formed Rangemaster Firearms Training Services to share their expertise with a much broader audience. They now travel across the country and around the world to arm responsible citizens with the skills and knowledge they need to effectively protect themselves and their families.

Tom has now been working in firearms instruction for nearly 40 years. He has trained security officers; law enforcement officers at the local, state, and federal level; and foreign government agents.

Tom has made hundreds of arrests, including numerous armed felons, and he has successfully used a handgun to defend himself and others against armed criminals. Tom designed and oversaw all training courses at his range, and he now does the same for RFTS all over the coun try and abroad.

Chapter 8:
ARMED CITIZENS FIGHT BACK: LESSONS LEARNED

BY "SPENCER BLUE"

With the followings statistics, I have attempted to eliminate targeted crimes. These include assaults on law enforcement officers, domestic or other intra-family assaults, and crimes motivated by the victim's involvement in criminal activity (gang activity, narcotics sales, etc.). Once I eliminated these targeted crimes, a pattern emerged. The distances between suspect and victim at the time the attack began were shorter than targeted crimes. In incidents involving firearms, both victims and suspects fired fewer shots. The attacks were often preceded by a ruse to allow the attacker to close the distance with the suspect prior to overtly beginning the criminal act. Suspects fled with more regularity than in targeted attacks when confronted with forceful resistance. Using this information, I began to see the skills and tactics that increased the odds of prevailing against a criminal attacker. I also noticed some patterns emerge that lead to armed citizens losing these confrontations, and I hope that by learning from the pain of others we can avoid our own pain. Doing so helps make sure the sacrifices of these brave men and women were not in vain.

Names and inconsequential details that do not impact the outcome or lessons learned may be changed to protect the identities of those involved.

One of the first things I noticed in the statistics was roughly 60% of armed citizens who fought back against a single criminal won their fight. I define "win" to mean the armed citizen was not seriously injured and was able to prevent the crime. Roughly 5% tied, meaning both the criminal and the victim were significantly injured or the crime was completed with no significant injury to the criminal. The remaining 35% lost, which unfortunately meant the citizen was seriously injured, victimized by a forcible felony such as rape, or killed. As we dig a little deeper, the differences in tactics of the citizens who won vs. those who lost become apparent.

FACTORS IN LOSING THE FIGHT

A full half of the losses happened when the armed citizen presented a non-working firearm. Generally, this was not a mechanical failure of the weapon, but a user error.

Case #1 was relayed to me by a Sex Crimes detective who was aware of my project. I will refer to the victim as "Jane." Jane lived alone and was awoken by the sounds of someone in her house. She retrieved a handgun prior to the suspect entering her bedroom but was unable to call 911 before being confronted. The suspect charged Jane and she attempted to fire at him but the gun did not fire. The suspect disarmed Jane and then raped her. Jane reported the crime to the police and told the detective she attempted to shoot the suspect but she did not get the thumb safety off and pulled a dead trigger. Jane, to her great credit, vowed to continue to be a fighter and stated she had purchased a striker-fired pistol with no safety.

SHE DID NOT GET THE THUMB SAFETY OFF AND PULLED A DEAD TRIGGER.

I have seen the inability to work the thumb safety under stress come in to play in both self-defense and defense of others. Jane was able to realize her mistake, but due to proximity and physical strength of her attacker she had no time to correct and fire before being disarmed. Others have continued to pull the dead trigger, taking no corrective actions, seemingly stuck in the first phase of the OODA loop (the decision cycle of observe, orient, decide, and act) and not verifying the status of the safety or performing a malfunction drill.

A second lesson we can take from Jane's incident is the layering of security. The suspect was able to gain entry to the home in a relatively quiet manner by removing an air conditioning unit from a window. Had Jane been alerted to the intruder's presence earlier, she would have been in a much better position to both defend herself and to alert authorities. A home alarm, a dog, etc., may have provided that early warning.

Case #2 involved a transaction set up on social media. A young man was going to meet a seller to purchase a video game system, however the sale was a ruse to set up a robbery. The victim arrived and entered an apartment complex. While some of the details are unclear, the evidence indicated he was attacked by two suspects, at least one of which was armed with a handgun. The victim was able to draw a firearm but was shot and killed before firing it. The firearm was determined to contain a loaded magazine but the chamber was empty. We believe he was intentionally carrying on an empty chamber. We do not know if he attempted to rack it or not, but we do know the firearm was not functional as drawn.

The dangers of empty chamber carry are twofold. First, it requires you to rack the slide before the weapon is functional, and if you are set upon before you've completed your draw you may not have both hands available for the task. While it is possible to rack the slide by hooking the rear sight on a belt, shoe, etc. this is a significantly more difficult task while engaged in a hand-to-hand struggle. Second, the status of the firearm is not instinctively known. I have observed shooters on surveillance video ejecting live rounds because, under stress, they cannot recall if they've chambered a cartridge or not. Knowing the firearm is ready to fire from the holster eliminates both of these issues.

THE FIREARM CONTAINED A LOADED MAGAZINE BUT THE CHAMBER WAS EMPTY.

Another factor with the armed citizen's control that contributed to losses was off-body carry.

Case #3 involved a small Mom & Pop retail store. We'll call the proprietors "Bill" and "Wanda." Bill and Wanda had been at a nearby restaurant just prior to the robbery. Bill was approached by an individual in the parking lot who asked him to make change for a $5 so he could use the soda machine. Bill did so, and in the process displayed a roll of money that amounted to approximately $900. Within 15 minutes a female, later discovered to be an accomplice, entered Bill and Wanda's store and briefly scouted it. There were no other customers in the store. Approximately five minutes after the female left, Wanda was preparing to leave with a bank deposit bag. Two male suspects entered the store. One male already had a gun drawn and the other stayed behind him and acted as a lookout, never displaying or implying a weapon. The armed suspect immediately went to Bill and started going through his pockets and verbally demanding his roll of money. He held the gun on Bill but walked passed Wanda and ignored her entirely. Even while patting down Bill, the suspect was looking out the window at the street, likely watching for any potential witnesses entering the store. The unarmed suspect became aware of the bag Wanda was trying to conceal and told the armed suspect to get it from her. Once the armed suspect got the roll of money from Bill, he turned his attention to Wanda.

Wanda was verbally non-compliant, refusing to give the bank bag to him. She edged toward the cash register as the armed suspect continued to shout at her to give him the bag. Once she got to the register she reached under the counter where a handgun was on a shelf and began to swing the handgun toward the armed suspect. The armed suspect fired one shot before Wanda could bring up her own gun, seriously injuring her and causing her to drop the firearm. The suspects began to flee as soon as the shot was fired. Bill picked up the handgun Wanda had dropped and fired at them, striking the lookout in the shoulder.

Wanda was extremely brave and was instrumental in the successful resolution of the investigation. She did, however, make several tactical errors.

The first was off body carry. Both Bill and Wanda had long periods of time where they were not under direct observation by either suspect, but were unable to exploit those openings as they were effectively unarmed. While the armed suspect was patting down Bill, he was blocking the shelf where the firearm was stashed. Only once he moved to approach Wanda was there a path to the weapon. Wanda had to move approximately four feet under direct observation of an increasingly suspicious armed robber who was holding her at gunpoint. Watching the security video, you can see the robber's body language change as he realizes Wanda is noncompliant and he prepares to fight. As she covered the distance he became increasingly agitated, and she attempted to fight when his awareness and preparedness were at their peak. Off-body carry severely hampered her ability to pick her opening.

Neither Bill nor Wanda attempted to distract the suspects. Wanda offered no explanation as to why she was moving and was non-compliant both verbally and physically. Offering an explanation as to why you are taking the actions you are taking sets people at ease. The suspect was expecting compliance, as that's what he'd gotten up to that point. Stating she was going to get the key for the lock on the bag, for example, may have been an effective ruse, as it would appear as ongoing compliance.

The third obstacle to presenting a working firearm was carrying it in a method that essentially made it inaccessible.

> ## [THE FIREARM] WAS CARRIED IN A METHOD THAT ESSENTIALLY MADE IT INACCESSIBLE.

Case #4 involves another transaction set up on an online trading website. A teenager trading sports collectibles arranged a sale in a medium-sized apartment complex. The teenager's father drove him to the apartments to make the transaction, and carried a .380 handgun in his pocket. The father stated he did not normally carry a handgun, but due to hearing so many news stories of robberies that began as an online agreement for a transaction he elected to do so "just in case." The father parked by the curb and his son got out of the SUV and walked toward the building where he was going to meet the buyers. As he approached the building, a masked suspect charged at him from between the buildings with a drawn handgun pointed at him. The suspect closed the distance with the stunned teenager and repeatedly demanded his goods. The teenager was frozen in shock and did not comply with the suspect's demands. The suspect opened fire on him, severely injuring him and creating lasting disabilities. The suspect picked up the dropped goods, got into a parked car, and fled the scene.

The father witnessed the entire incident and never accessed his firearm. Despite taking the firearm specifically in case there was a robbery, he had not actually planned what to do should a robbery occur. His .380 was in his front pants pocket. He was seated, making it difficult to access a pocket carry gun. He had on a long, untucked shirt that covered the pocket, further hampering access. He left his seat belt on, making it difficult to get the shirt out of the way of the pocket opening. His statement was heart-wrenching, as his guilt and pain of not being able to protect his son was palpable. He was only able to exit his SUV and access his gun once the suspect had gotten into a vehicle and left. His panic was so great at that time that he got back into his SUV, drove up to his son, loaded his son in the SUV, and drove several blocks before he realized he did not know where the nearest hospital was and finally called 911.

Particularly in a situation with heightened poten-

> **HE HAD NOT ACTUALLY PLANNED WHAT TO DO SHOULD A ROBBERY OCCUR.**

tial for danger, such as online transaction arrangements, ready access to the weapon, increased situational awareness to note where aggressors could approach from, and pre-contact planning are important elements of successfully repelling a robbery attempt.

Avoiding these errors dramatically increases the odds of the armed citizen prevailing in fighting back against their aggressor. Armed citizens who were faced with only one robber, efficiently deployed a working firearm from on-body carry, and employed a ruse or distraction to create an opening to respond, have won 100% of the time.

Case #5 involved an attempted carjacking of a shopkeeper who had closed up for the night. We'll call the shopkeeper Larry. Larry ran a small specialty store in an L-shaped strip mall. His store was at the corner of the "L" and the parking lot was not well lit in that area, although it was lit significantly better toward either end.

Larry drove a van with a sliding door, and it was parked about 25 yards from his store entrance. He locked up and was walking toward his van with his keys in his hand to activate the remote door locks. As he neared his van, a suspect "appeared out of nowhere" with a handgun pointed at him. The suspect demanded that Larry unlock the sliding door and then get into the driver's seat. Larry complied and the suspect entered the sliding door and sat behind Larry, presumably still holding him at gunpoint. The suspect demanded Larry's wallet and car keys. Larry replied that he could not do so while sitting down as his jeans were too tight to access the pockets while seated. This was not true, but Larry created the ruse on the fly to begin working himself out of the situation he found himself in. The suspect told him to get out of the van.

Larry exited the van, as did the suspect, who was still holding the gun on Larry. Larry told the suspect that he was going to give him his car keys and

READY ACCESS TO THE WEAPON, INCREASED SITUATIONAL AWARENESS, AND PRE-CONTACT PLANNING ARE IMPORTANT ELEMENTS OF SUCCESSFULLY REPELLING A ROBBERY ATTEMPT.

reached into his pocket. Larry reached into his front pants pocket, pulled a small revolver, and fired at the suspect. The suspect immediately began to flee to the back of the van and Larry pursued him. When Larry came around the back of his van he saw the suspect was fleeing across the parking lot. Larry fired two more shots at the suspect as he fled. The suspect was not struck by any of the shots Larry fired.

Reviewing surveillance video and Larry's statement, there are several points to cover as we analyze this incident. The first lesson was Larry's lack of situational awareness. The suspect approached from a well-lit area and would have been in Larry's field of view if Larry were not fixated on his destination, the van. Larry started behind the curve because of this. A scan of his surroundings prior to leaving his business after locking the door, or while walking toward his van, would have alerted him to the presence of the suspect. In the context of the other stores being closed with the windows dark, no other cars in the parking lot in the area, and an unknown male walking directly toward him, he could have reasonably assumed trouble was likely, if not imminent, and began forming a plan at that point.

The second lesson is, by Larry's own admission, he did not have a plan during the initial part of the encounter. He allowed himself to get into an extremely difficult position of being seated with an armed robber behind him because his default reaction was to comply. To Larry's great credit, he thought on his feet and did come up with a ruse to allow him to extricate himself from that position.

The third lesson is that Larry shot at the suspect but did not hit him. Larry admitted this was on purpose with the first shot. He stated he was nervous about the legal ramifications, as well as the emotional toll had he killed the suspect. We do not know why the suspect chose to flee instead of fight, perhaps his gun was not functional or perhaps he was simply frightened away, but what we do know is Larry could not control the suspect's next action. A better

> **JUST AS HE DID NOT HAVE A PLAN TO SHOOT, HE DID NOT HAVE A PLAN TO STOP SHOOTING.**

understanding of his legal justification to use lethal force may have helped Larry maintain the initiative. Larry was also not psychologically prepared to take a life, again per his own words.

Given that information, it may seem illogical that he would chase the fleeing suspect and fire twice more. He could not explain why he then chased the suspect and fired twice more at him. Just as he did not have a plan to shoot, he did not have a plan to stop shooting. When his attacker began to flee, Larry's instinct was to chase him, and with no prior plan on board he followed those instincts. Larry's actions of pursuing and firing at a fleeing suspect who, by his own admission, no longer presented a threat were not legal, but charges were not filed due to the circumstances of no injuries and the other party (the robbery) being unknown. Other jurisdictions may decide differently.

Case #6 was a bad shoot, legally speaking. The victim was open-carrying a handgun while riding a bicycle. We'll call him Frank. Frank stopped at an intersection due to traffic, and while he was waiting for an opening he felt someone tug on his pistol. Frank's holster had a forward cant and the gun grabber was pulling backward, so the gun did not come out. Frank stated he looked down, saw a stranger's hand on his gun, and realized what was happening. He jumped off of his bicycle away from the suspect and used the bicycle as a barricade between them. His movement took the gun out of the reach of the suspect. The suspect was fleeing when Frank completed turning around to face the direction of the gun grabber. Frank drew and fired three shots at the fleeing suspect. Frank's backstop was an apartment complex. Frank did not hit the suspect, nor was any damage found on the apartment buildings, and Frank stated he believed he shot low and hit the dirt behind the suspect.

Frank's statement showed that he let his emotions take over. He did not have a plan for what to do if he was assaulted, and reacted in anger that someone would try to take his gun. He wanted to "teach them a lesson" for attempting to steal from him. When we do not work through scenarios mentally before they happen, when we fail to have a plan onboard, we may revert to these emotion-based responses that can lead to trouble legally and ethically. The prosecutor's office debated charging Frank criminally in this instance. Ultimately, no charges were filed, however it was a very narrow decision and it was made plain to me had he caused any property damage or injured anyone at all he would have faced felony charges.

One of the most important elements of armed citizens defending themselves, particularly against robberies, was biding their time until they could surprise the robber with their resistance. In many instances the robber will become fixated on the item they are taking. They will take their eyes off of the clerk to look into the cash register, for example. In street robberies, the robber will often look around for potential witnesses once they become convinced the victim is compliant. Instead of applying an active ruse like "Larry" did to access his pocket pistol to repel the carjacker, the victims may simply bide their time and wait for such an opening.

> ONE OF THE MOST IMPORTANT ELEMENTS OF ARMED CITIZENS DEFENDING THEMSELVES, PARTICULARLY AGAINST ROBBERIES, WAS BIDING THEIR TIME UNTIL THEY COULD SURPRISE THE ROBBER WITH THEIR RESISTANCE.

Case #7 involved such an instance, and allowed an unarmed victim to overcome and prevail against an armed robber. A physically slight criminal attempted to rob a convenience store where the clerk was built like a heavyweight boxer. We'll call the clerk "Sammy." Sammy was a recent immigrant to the U.S. and his native land was a warzone. He was not a stranger to violence. The robber was a cocaine addict who owed his supplier money. His supplier provided him with a handgun and told him to rob the store to help settle his debt. The robber entered the store and began scanning for other customers. Sammy was alerted by his behavior and stated to me that he initially believed the man was about to shoplift something and run from the store. However, as the man approached him he suspected he was about to be robbed.

The robber pulled a small pistol from his pocket, pointed it at Sammy, and then made his demand for the money. Sammy hit the button to open the cash register and then stepped back with his hands up. He stated he did this so the robber would have to get the cash himself and would no longer watch him. The robber, convinced Sammy was compliant, immediately fixated on the cash drawer and, as he reached across the counter to grab money from the register, his gun tracked with his movement and was no longer pointed at Sammy. Sammy immediately grabbed the robber's forearm and began to pound it against the counter while reaching across with his other hand and tearing the pistol out of the robber's hand. Sammy stated he initially intended to turn the gun on the robber and shoot him, but suddenly remembered he was in America now and wasn't sure if he was legally allowed to shoot robbers. He elected to use his fighting skills instead, realizing he had a significant advantage with the gun out of play, due to his superior size, strength, and skill. Sammy threw the gun down with such force the slide broke off of the frame, and then physically subdued the suspect.

While Sammy did not employ a firearm, his case demonstrates several key aspects of effective resistance. First, he saw trouble coming by being aware of his surroundings and observing the body language and behavior of those entering his store. He also formulated a plan and set up the robber to divert his attention, to "stop watching" him, and intended to begin his resistance at that time. Having that plan formulated, he was able to put it into action so quickly that the robber's thought processes could not catch up and he was disarmed before he realized he was in a fight. In the surveillance video you could see the confusion on the robber's face as he was jerked forward by his forearm, and his confusion quickly became panic. He was disarmed before he stopped looking at the cash register and refocused on Sammy, and from his own admission his only thought from that point forward was escape.

MULTIPLE AGGRESSORS

One of the most difficult situations legally armed citizens can find themselves in is being confronted by multiple aggressors. The difficulty is so great that the success rate dropped to roughly 35% when a single victim was confronted by multiple aggressors. Those who won generally did so because the suspects fled without further aggression once the victim began to resist. Being outnumbered was the single greatest predictor of losing a violent encounter than any other factor I tracked.

Case #8 illustrates some of the difficulties with dealing with multiple suspects. "Robert" was a late night food delivery driver in a rougher area of town. He was sent on a delivery to what turned out to be an abandoned house. The houses in the area were tightly packed and there were thick hedgerows that separated one yard from the next. The street was also quite dark, as many houses were abandoned so no lights were on.

Robert parked at the curb and exited his vehicle. As he reached into his vehicle to get the bags of food, he was confronted by two suspects who were approaching from the direction his vehicle was facing. One was pointing a handgun at him and the other had something in his hand but Robert could not make out what it was. The suspects made a demand for money and continued to approach. Robert drew his handgun and fired at the suspect with the handgun pointed at him, which caused both to turn and flee. However, once Robert had fired three rounds, he was struck by a bullet fired from behind him. The bullet struck him near the spine and temporarily disabled him. Robert never saw who was behind him, but physical evidence indicated the person was likely hiding near the hedgerow of the house behind where Robert parked.

Once he parked his vehicle, Robert's situation was dire. He

THE ONLY SURE WAY FOR ROBERT TO WIN THIS ENCOUNTER WOULD HAVE BEEN TO AVOID IT.

was outnumbered at least three to one. He was unaware of a gunman behind him. While he used his car door for cover against the suspect he could see, his stationary position left him vulnerable from behind. The suspects could cover multiple angles, greatly reducing the benefits of cover for Robert as no matter which way he moved (other than back into his car) exposed him to one side or the other. The suspects he fired at fled, but he was disabled in the time it took him to fire three times at one suspect. He literally could not shoot fast enough to engage all of the targets before he was disabled, even if he had been aware of all of them.

The only sure way for Robert to win this encounter would have been to avoid it. Many delivery driver setups involve an abandoned house, and generally after dark. Driving past the address to verify it was occupied and then parking a bit past the address is one tactic. If the house is dark and appears abandoned, in the age of cell phones it's a simple matter to call the supposed customer and request they turn a porch light on so you can "find the address," which will at least verify the person who called in the order actually lives there and that the house has power.

In contrast to Robert's encounter, another delivery man was able to succeed against multiple attackers by seeing danger signs, forming a plan ahead of time, and utilizing natural barriers so only one suspect at a time could confront him.

Case #9 was very similar to case #8, but the call was to an apartment building. "Shane" the delivery driver had been robbed before and also had successfully defended himself in a prior robbery. He stated he felt like the call could be a setup due to the time, the amount of food ordered, the apparent youth of the caller, etc. When he arrived at the apartment he called the telephone number provided by the "customer" and stated he had not been provided with an apartment number. The "customer" answered and told him the apartment number, which Shane knew to be a basement apartment near the laundry room. He stated his feeling that "something wasn't right" grew stronger, so he put a fixed blade knife in his dominant hand and then picked up the delivery bag. He stated he had done this on many late deliveries when things felt like they might be off. The way he held it, the knife could not be seen by the customer, but he could release the bag and retain the knife by partially opening his hand, making it both hidden and quick to deploy. If the transaction was legitimate, the customer was none the wiser about the knife. If things went wrong, Shane was ready to defend himself.

Shane walked down the stairs, and as he passed the laundry room he observed several males rapidly approaching him. The lead male had a firearm pointed at him and told him to stop. As the lead male entered the laundry room's doorway, Shane dropped his bag and used the knife to slice the suspect's torso deeply enough to expose organs in his abdomen. Shane then fled. The suspect who was cut fell backward into the laundry room after he dropped his weapon and clutched at his wound. Shane retreated to his vehicle and, seeing he was not pursued, contacted 911 to report the incident. The suspect Shane cut was critically injured and was still in the doorway upon officers' arrival.

> **SHANE WAS ABLE TO ACT SO QUICKLY BECAUSE HE SUSPECTED TROUBLE, CREATED A PLAN, AND THEN PUT IT INTO PRACTICE.**

Shane was able to act so quickly because he suspected trouble, created a plan, and then put it into practice. He stated he knew he had to act as the first robber came through the door or he'd have to deal with all of them. Had the robbers remained dedicated to the attack, he had created a significant barrier, both physically and mentally. Seeing the speed and violence of his attack, however, caused those who could still do so to flee, and the fight was over without the suspects' numerical advantage coming in to play.

I cannot say for certain the training levels of most of these individuals. I did not ask the individuals involved about their training, even once I started keeping these stats. This was not the original focus of my project, and also it was not relevant to the investigations, so I believe it would have been inappropriate for someone in my position to do so. No one volunteered any prior training other than military. Some of them asked about local training opportunities and indicated they had not had formal training prior to their incident.

Spencer Blue joined the U.S. Army upon graduation from high school, where he served as a Combat Engineer. He received an Honorable Discharge, returned to his home town, and began pursuing a Bachelor's degree in Criminal Justice. After Sept. 11, 2001, he interrupted his studies and worked Force Protection for military installations in Qatar as a contractor for DynCorp International. Once returning to the U.S., he worked as an armored car guard and as a 911 operator while he sought a sworn law enforcement position. Spencer Blue was hired by a large metropolitan police department, where he has worked for the past 10 years. He started in uniformed patrol in one of the most violent beats in his jurisdiction. He is currently assigned to the Homicide & Robbery office as a Robbery detective. Spencer Blue has investigated hundreds of shootings, stabbings, and robberies as lead or assisting detective.

Chapter 9:

LONE CITIZEN HEROES

BY RON BORSCH

It was an honor to be invited by Massad Ayoob to write a chapter for his new book. Massad's brief criteria were to cover armed and unarmed citizens who have stopped mass murders in progress, single-handedly. Later, I will share more than four dozen examples of these heroes. These initial actors are also what my friend Chris Bird describes in his book, Surviving a Mass Killer Rampage, as "irregular first responders."

The reader should be aware that media reports do not always report the actual sequence of who did what in their efforts to stop rapid mass murder. Real investigative journalists, law enforcement officers, you and I would appreciate those details. Without those details, that leaves us to decide whether some murder stoppages were initiated by lone heroes, or later joined by others, or a group effort. The stories not told here are examples of learned helplessness where many innocents experience "give-up-itus," where they did nothing to stop the murdering.

RESEARCH VERSUS THE POSSE THEORY

Years ago when I was teaching rapid mass murder police response formations, I was a bit disillusioned when it appeared that the "tactical gurus" were not paying attention to what actually worked and what did not in law enforcement responses. Their logic of getting less manpower on scene sooner was certainly a step in the right direction. However, this involved rounding up a posse of four or more officers for some sort of military formation. As time went on and I continued to study current and past events, it became evident to me that when a successful law enforcement response worked, this newer formation concept was nowhere to be found.

About a decade ago, as a relative nobody, my not conforming to the tactical gurus of the day was like trying to swim upstream against the current. Merely documenting the truth and publishing reports on the majority successes of a Single Officers Lifesaving Others (SOLO) earned me arrows in the back from many officers, trainers, SWAT Commanders and even some tactical gurus. Fortunately, there was help coming from enlightened folks who also had the vision to see through the fog of unjustified bias and supported my data-based efforts.

COP WITH A CALCULATOR

Full disclosure would be appropriate here. I am not a trained statistician or researcher. After a well-rounded 47-year law enforcement and training career, I was merely a "cop with a calculator." Of course I am open to any details, as a relevant quote reveals: "Just when we think we're arrived at the 'ultimate solution,' we discover that, as our telescope improves, more stars appear!" (Julian Barnes via John Farnam).

My focus initially was for law enforcement such as my Tactical 1st Responder course (attended by student officers from 10 states). Along the way there were surprises for me! First, the revelation that only about half of rapid mass murders were ever stopped by anyone. This meant of course, that this half of the mass murdering was only stopped when the murderers said it stopped. Then, in the other half when rapid mass murder was stopped by someone, there was my astonishment that about two thirds of that half were stopped by on-site citizens (mostly unarmed) or on-site security, not off-site police officers!

My "Stopwatch of Death" database protocol for rapid mass murder is "within 20 minutes, four or more murdered/attempted at the same time and public place." To establish a database, the focus is aimed toward the more unpredictable random actors that commit rapid mass murder rather than incidents involving criminal gangs, terrorists, spree killers, hostage situations, or domestic violence murders in residences which are not counted. This avoids the oranges versus apples effect, making for an easier-to-manage database for a single uncompensated retiree. It likewise is easier to identify methods of operation that may be helpful in sharing prevention and countermeasure efforts.

After researching these incidents back to 1975 and acquiring almost 200 incidents in my Stopwatch of Death database, my take is that the majority of citizen stoppages of rapid mass murder are initiated primarily by a single lead actor lifesaving others, or single actors lifesaving others acting simultaneously. I have included all of the citizen stoppages that I am aware of so readers can see clearly where a single actor first initiated, where two or more citizens acted singly or were empowered to follow by a single actor or leader. There is no easy way of verifying a sequence. At least one telling is very clear, and has a video link to boot!

TIME AND "NOT MY JOB" DILEMMA

Part of the reason that half of rapid mass murder is not stopped is that many facilities have placed total reliance on off-site police instead of executing plans and countermeasures while they wait. Documented times from first threat to last act are little known or not reported in the media. When the times are known, they are averaging less than six minutes. While six minutes is a relatively short time, it must be understood in context. There is also a delay in notifying police (five to seven minutes per Ed Sanow), which we round to six minutes. Added to that is call taking, dispatching, police response, locating and stopping-the-killer time.

Unfortunately, the reality more often than not is You're On Your Own (YOYO). Thus we can see the value of on-site armed good guys. It's probably normal for those in charge to not want to think about active killers, terrorism, and custodial responsibility for the safety of innocents in their facility. Some would heap great praise and accolades on their local law enforcement, which may be well deserved, but misplaced when used as an excuse to abandon responsibility for taking appropriate safety and security steps.

DANGEROUS CONFRONTATION

Unarmed citizens going up against an active killer with a remote control weapon, such as a firearm, is very dangerous. Many have tried and died despite heroic effort. In non-specific reports, recall that in any surprise attack on untrained persons, people respond differently and rarely function immediately or as fluidly as a well-practiced and experienced team. While most folks are aware of instinctual things like fight or flight, fewer are aware that everyone "freezes" first.

For example, in a surprise life-threatening encounter, we need time to decide what is best, to fight or flee. This freezing could range from a split second to the remainder of an early-terminated life. This is often referred to as "paralysis by analysis." The simplest and best explanation of the mental stages we go through was identified by Col. John Boyd and his "OODA Loop." OODA stands for "observe-orient-decide-act."

In the observe (or perception), orienting, and deciding stages, nothing physical occurs. After this non-action freeze, finally in the last stage, there is initiation of motor action and we begin to do something. Winners and survivors are those who arrive at the act stage before their adversary does. The takeaway here is that no physical action is taken until the mental stages of perception, orienting and deciding are completed.

The OODA loop is cyclical, continuously repeated. While sounding slow, the process can be very fast. Drivers for instance, go through this process every time they see the need to take their foot off of the gas pedal and apply the brakes. For the unprepared, the surprise is greater, as is the processing of denial, the fog of confusion and chaos. The prepared and practiced always act quicker.

TARGETS OF RAPID MASS MURDER

The number one target for rapid mass murder has typically been "laws and facilities that forbid the honest, law abiding, state-vetted and otherwise legal concealed weapon permit holders to have a firearm on their premises." The legal scar here is that criminals and active killers do not recognize such restrictions.

The result is the disarming and victimization of only the innocent and law abiding. With such a legal scar, any pretense of "safety" only favors the health, welfare and safety of the murderous invader. Unless and until our academics and legislators get their head in reality, they are trolling for tragedy and abdicating their custodial responsibility for the safety of innocents in their facilities.

STOPWATCH OF DEATH FACTOR

I created the Stopwatch of Death model and database in order to provide a reliable unit of measurement with which to determine the scale of one active killer incident relative to another. The Stopwatch of Death factor is the number of casualties (murdered and wounded together), divided by the time in minutes.

For instance, the 1999 Columbine High School in Colorado (13 killed, 24 wounded in 13 minutes), gives us a Stopwatch of Death factor of SWD= 2.8

murder attempts per minute. On April 28th, 1996, in a three-event shooting spree at the Broad Arrow Cafe in Tasmania, Australia, an active killer murdered 12 and wounded 10 in a 15 second event. That SWD factor was a shocking 88.0 murder attempts per minute.

Below are examples of both armed and unarmed rapid mass murder stoppages.

(Legend: M= Murdered, W= Wounded, SWD= Stopwatch of Death factor)

030685 **Post Office, Atlanta GA** (M-02, W-01): Male subdued by other workers.

103085 **Springfield Mall, Philadelphia PA** (M-03, W-07): Female disarmed by John Laufer Volunteer Firefighter/EMT shopper as she walked up to him and tried to raise her gun to shoot him. This was a 4-minute event, SWD factor 2.5.

120887 **Post Office, Melbourne Australia** (M-08, W-00): Donald McElroy (already shot once) and Tony Gioia tackled while Frank Carmody, who had been shot several times, wrestled the rifle from the male.

052088 **Hubbard Woods Elementary School, Winnetka IL** (M-01, W-05): A teacher disarmed the shooter, the male shooter left and with a second gun committed suicide off-site.

121688 **Christian School, Virginia Beach VA** (M-01, W-02): Bible teacher Hutch Matson tackled killer when his MK-10 gun jammed. Coward had hundreds of rounds remaining.

082492 **Concordia University, Quebec Canada** (M-04, W-01): Male held a security guard and professor Dr. George Abdou hostage. Murderer briefly put his gun down during a phone call, Abdou kicked it away and the unknown security guard overpowered him.

120793 **Long Island Train, NY** (M-06, W-19): Three passengers – Michael O'Connor, Kevin Blum, and Mark McEntee – tackled the coward and pinned him to one of the train's seats. Several other passengers ran forward to grab his arms and legs and help hold him. This was a 3-minute event, SWD factor 8.3.

111595 **Richland High School, Lynnville TN** (M-02, W-01): Male tackled by a student and coach Ron

Shirey wrestled him to the ground.

020296 **Moses Lake Middle School, WA** (M-05, W-01): Hearing gunshots, teacher-coach Jon Lane entered the classroom to find male holding his students hostage. Lane volunteered as a hostage, and murderer kept him at gunpoint with his rifle while trying to leave. Lane then grabbed the weapon from the coward and wrestled him to the ground.

091796 **Penn State College, PA** (M-01, W-01): The toll might have been higher if not for 21-year-old senior Brendon Malovrh of Downingtown, who tackled female sniper before the high school dropout could finish reloading her rifle.

100197 **High School, Pearl MS** (M-02, W-07): Assistant principal Joel Myrick retrieved a pistol from his truck and, spotting the male attempting to flee the parking lot towards another school after the shooting, shouted for him to stop.

042498 B**anquet facility/school event, Edinboro PA** (M-01, W-03): Owner James Strand intervened and confronted the male with a shotgun, ordering him to drop his weapon.

052198 **School Thurston, Springfield OR** (M-02, W-22): Wounded student Jacob Ryker tackled male and was assisted by several other students. A total of seven students were involved in subduing and disarming the coward who was in possession of another 1100 rounds.

011399 **KSL TV station, Salt Lake City UT** (M-01, W-01): Female opened fire in the lobby of the television station, wounding the building manager and killing another before being tackled by the victim's co-worker.

042899 **W. R. Myers High School, Taber/Alberta High School, Canada** (M-01, W-01): Male with 300 rounds of ammunition and sawed-off .22-caliber rifle fired at three students. Gym coach Cheyno Finnie wrestled coward to the floor.

052199 **Heritage High School, Conyers GA** (M-00, W-06): Male was shooting near the girls' bathroom in the common area. Students first thought it was a prank, then pandemonium. Gunman fired four to six shots into a crowd of students, then cowardly ran out a side door. Assistant Principal Cecil Brinkley talked coward out of suicide then the boy surrendered the gun to him.

091499 **Hospital/Med Center, Anaheim CA** (M-03, W-00): Viet Nam Vet Ronald Robertson, 51, heard the gunfire, rushed to prevent the assailant from reaching the lobby, tackled, grabbed for the gun and, though fatally shot, he and others held the murderer long enough for hospital security to arrive.

120699 **Middle School, Ft. Gibson OK** (M-00, W-04): When his 9mm pistol emptied, the coward was subdued by the school safety officer. He and a teacher held the shooter until police arrived.

060801 **Ikeda Elementary School, Osaka Japan** (M-08, W-15): Adult former employee using a knife started murdering until subdued by two teachers.

042602 **High School, Erfurt Germany** (M-17, W-07): Coward was confronted by teacher, Rainer Heise, who spoke to the male student for a short period of time. He lured the coward, pushed him into an empty room and quickly locked the door. (On-site suicide). This was a 10 minute event, SWD factor 2.4.

011602 **Appalachian Law School, Grundy VA** (M-03, W-03): At the first sound of gunfire, unbeknownst to each other, Tracy Bridges and fellow student Mikael Gross ran to their vehicles to retrieve their personally-owned firearms. Participants and witnesses differ as to the details. According to Ted Besen, a Marine vet and former police officer, he engaged in a physical confrontation with the murderer and knocked him to the ground. Bridges and Gross then arrived from different angles with their guns once the coward was tackled.

070402 **El-Al Airline Airport, Los Angeles CA** (M-02, W-04): After gunman fired 10 bullets at the crowd, a security guard, who was unarmed, managed to knock him down. Meanwhile, El Al's armed security officer, Chaim Sapir, ran to the scene and the assailant stabbed him with a knife. Despite this, Sapir managed to draw his pistol and shoot the gunman in the chest. After he fell, Sapir fired a head shot, killing the coward.

102102 **Melbourne Monash University, Australia**

(M-02, W-05): When the coward stopped shooting and moved to switch weapons, Lee Gordon-Brown, an injured lecturer, grabbed the murderer's hands as he reached into his jacket. Brown and a student in the room, Alastair Boast, a martial artist, tackled him. Bradley Thompson later entered the room and discovered five guns in holsters around Xiang's waist, as well as two magazines near his hip.

071703 **Capital High School, Charleston WV** (M-00, W-01): During a Kanawha County Board of Education meeting, the coward arrived with an AK-47 assault rifle in a black plastic bag and three buckets of gasoline. Splashing two with gas, he tried to ignite the gas with a striker; failing that pulled out the rifle. Jeffery Allred, Bill Courtney and Bill Buchanan seized the attempted arsonist. Unfortunately, as they wrestled, the coward was able to fire three shots, one hitting a librarian.

092403 **Rocori High School, St. Cloud MN** (M-02, W-00): After murdering two, the coward attempted to flee the scene but was confronted by Gym coach Mark Johnson. The coward initially brandished the gun at Johnson who said he raised his hand and shouted "No," and that the assassin then removed the bullets from the weapon and dropped it.

020904 **Columbia High School, East Greenbush NY** (M-00, W-01): A cowardly student opened fire with a pump shotgun firing at least two shells before he was tackled by assistant principal John Shawchuck, who wrestled the attempted killer to the ground. Also responding was Michael Bennett, a special-education teacher who was coming to help when he was shot.

050905 **Conard Community Service Center, San Francisco CA** (M-01, W-00): A recently-fired male employee opened fire with a pistol. The coward dropped the pistol and began to raise a shotgun. Kalifa Coulibaly grabbed him and began struggling for the gun. Owen Spaulding, age 50, sitting on the sidewalk outside the office, saw the pair roll out the front door. Spaulding knew the employee and jumped into the middle of it. Nearby Gregg Wozniak overheard people yelling, "He's got a gun!" so he also jumped in and pried the gun away.

110805 **High School, Campbell County, Jacks-boro TN** (M-01, W-02): A 14-year-old male student opened fire in the office. The gun was wrestled from the teen, but not before he shot three staff members. Principal Gary Seale, one of the administrators who had been shot, managed to get to the school inter-com and order a lockdown. One vice principle was killed and two staff were wounded before an uniden-tified teacher wrestled his weapon away.

031406 **Pine Middle School, Reno NV** (M-00, W-02): Students and teachers heard shots and the gym teacher, Jencie Fagan, approached the coward and challenged him. Fagan managed to convince the male student, 14, to drop his gun and then re-strained him in a "bear hug" until more staff arrived to help

092906 **Weston High School, Cazenovia WI** (M-01, W-00): 14-year-old student entered school with a shotgun and aimed it at a social studies teacher. The school custodian, Dave Thompson, wrestled the shotgun away from the student who then drew a .22 revolver from inside his jacket, Thompson and the teacher ran for cover. Principal John Klang con-fronted the gunman who fired several shots. Fatally wounded, Principal Klang grabbed the coward, wrestled him to the ground and swept away the gun.

060607 **NY/NY Casino, Las Vegas NV** (M-00, W-04): 16 gunshots were mistaken by many for fireworks until people were diving for cover behind slot machines and blackjack tables. The gunman was in the process of a reload when a tourist tackled him for a 38-second stoppage and violent struggle. One man, an unknown off-duty military reservist, wrestled the 9mm pistol free. They estimated he had 100 more rounds. TV and radio reports at the time credited a second man arriving and assisting with a choke-hold, and others also arriving to assist. Spe-cific details as to who did what and when are absent. Credited is Christopher Koenig who ran toward the source of the shots and helped others subdue the alleged gunman. Koenig suffered a broken finger when attempted killer bit his hand. Assisting in the taken down were Justin Lampert, David James, Rob-ert Ura and Paul Ura.

120907 **New Life Church, Colorado Springs CO** (M-02, W-03): A murderer who had already killed two and wounded another two 70 miles away (Youth With A Mission training center in Arvada, Colorado) before escaping to attack a second church with a number of firearms. At New Life Church, he killed two more people and wounded three in the parking lot. No one inside this mega church was harmed due to the courageous action of former police officer Jeanne Assam, a member of the church's safety team. She fatally shot this cowardly murderer several times.

030608 **Mercaz HaRav School, Jerusalem Israel** (M-08, W-11): The lone coward was stopped by long-time Mercaz HaRav student Yitzchak Dadon and off-duty Israel Defense Forces Captain David Shapira who fought back using their personal firearms. Unfortunately, a police patrolman who arrived at the scene before Shapira remained outside in an effort to "freeze the situation" by preventing civilians from entering, instead of making contact and stopping the shooting. Approximate 14-20 minute event, SWD factor 1.4 to 1.0.

072708 **TV Unitarian Universalist Church, Knoxville TN** (M-02, W-07): A performance by 25 children was interrupted by a shotgun-wielding 58-year-old male coward opening fire on the audience. 60-year-old Greg McKendry, an usher who deliberately stood in front of the gunman to protect others, was killed at the scene. The coward was stopped when church members John Bohstedt, Robert Birdwell, Arthur Bolds, and Terry Uselton, along with visitor Jamie Parkey, restrained him.

030809 **First Baptist Church, Maryville IL** (M-01, W-02): During the service, a gunman walked down the aisle and briefly spoke to the Pastor before shooting and killing Rev. Fred Winters. The Pastor used the Bible he was reading from to shield himself from the first round of bullets being pumped at him. The gunman's .45 caliber semi-automatic pistol jammed after the fourth shot was fired. The suicidal coward then started stabbing himself with a four-inch knife when tackled by some of about 150 worshippers. Terry Bullard and Keith Melton were slashed when they tried to subdue him.

022310 **Deer Creek Middle School, Littleton CO** (M-00, W-02): "Sounding like firecrackers," an adult male with a rifle shot a boy and girl. Seventh-grade math teacher David Benke tackled the suspect as he was trying to reload his weapon, he and another man helped hold him until police arrived.

100810 **Carlsbad elementary school playground, San Diego CA** (M-00, W-02): Adult male opened fire with a .357 revolver, wounding two little girls. Three construction workers who saw the shooting acted. Carlos Partida used his pickup truck to knock the coward down. He and co-workers Steven Kane and Mario Contreras then subdued the gunman.

121410 **Bay District School Board meeting, Panama FL** (M-00, W-00): A disgruntled adult fired four shots at six school board members, but missed them all. The coward was then shot several times by retired police officer Mike Jones, the gunman then killed himself with a shot to the head.

010811 **Shopping Center, Tucson AZ** (M-06, W-13): U.S. Representative Gabrielle Giffords and eighteen others were shot during a constituent meeting held in a supermarket parking lot in Casas Adobes, Arizona. A cowardly 22-year-old man who was fixated on Giffords proceeded to fire apparently randomly at other members of the crowd. He stopped to reload, but dropped the loaded magazine from his pocket to the sidewalk, from where bystander Patricia Maisch grabbed it. Another bystander clubbed the back of the assailant's head with a folding chair, and he was tackled to the ground by Bill Badger, a 74-year-old retired United States Army Colonel who had already been wounded. The assassin was further subdued by Maisch and bystanders Roger Sulzgeber and Joseph Zamudio. Zamudio had a weapon on his person, but arrived after the shooting had stopped and did not draw his firearm. This was an approximate 15-second event, SWD factor 76.0.

072411 **Muckleshoot Casino Club Galaxy, Auburn WA** (M-00, W-06): Adult male shot relatives and bystanders until tackled and subdued.

022712 **High School, Chardon OH** (M-03, W-02): Hero Teacher-Coach Frank Hall saw a young man firing into a crowd and charged the coward who pointed the gun at the coach. Hall kept chasing while yelling down the corridor until the coward fled the building. Thereafter, the coward gave himself up to a female driver he flagged down.

081212 **Perry Hall High School, MD** (M-00, W-01): Male, 15-year-old student with a shotgun and 21 rounds randomly opened fire. Students said it sounded like the pop of air that escapes when a bag of air is smashed, or the clap of a door slamming shut. School staff rushed toward the coward. While school counselor Jesse Wasmer struggled to restrain and disarm the coward, another round was fired into the ceiling.

081512 **Christian Family Research Council, Washington DC** (M-00, W-01): 28 -year-old male entered the building with a pistol, two magazines and 50 rounds of ammunition. At the front door the coward shot the building manager acting as an unarmed guard, Leo Johnson, who confronted him. Wounded, he wrestled the gunman to the ground, disarming him. Johnson and others overpowered the gunman at the front door area.

121112 **Clackamas Mall, Portland OR** (M-02, W-01): 22-year-old male coward ran into the shopping center wearing tactical clothing and a hockey mask, firing 17 shots on shoppers and employees with a stolen AR-15. He was unable to reload the rifle at that point. During that time, Nick Meli, a concealed carry permit holder, had drawn his Glock pistol, claimed to have taken aim at the coward, but did not fire since there was a bystander behind him. Meli claims that the coward saw him and that this may have contributed to his decision to commit suicide.

011013 **Taft-Union High School, Taft CA** (M-00, W-02): 16-year-old male student entered a science classroom that morning armed with a 12-gauge shotgun. The coward shot one student before shooting at and missing another. The teacher, who suffered a minor pellet wound to the head, began to evacuate the students out a back door. He and a campus supervisor were able to engage the shooter in conversation and distract him while students evacuated the classroom. The two adults were able to calm the shooter and convince him to put down the gun.

080513 **Municipal Building, Ross Township, Saylorsburg PA** (M-03, W- 04): 15 to 18 people were attending the meeting inside. A 59-year-old coward approached the building armed with a Ruger Mini-14 rifle, began firing 28 times into the building through the windows. He continued firing as he entered and made his way through the building. At some point the coward exited the building, retrieved a .44 Magnum revolver from his vehicle and returned. He was tackled while still shooting. Bernard Kozen and Mark Krashe struggled with him over the gun. They subdued, disarmed and restrained him for police.

082213 **Ronald E. McNair Discovery Learning Elementary Academy, Decatur GA** (M-00, W-00): Armed with multiple guns, an AK-47 and 500 rounds, the 20-year-old coward may have slipped in behind an employee for entry before confronting and holding office staff captive. He fired six shots at officers as they arrived and officers returned fire. Bookkeeper Antoinette Tuff talked the gunman into putting his weapons down and peacefully surrendering while she spoke to him and the 911 operator.

040913 **Lone Star College, Cypress TX** (M-00, W-14): The 20-year-old coward stabbed more than a dozen students, then ran as students pursued. One finally reached him near the parking lot, grabbing the assailant in a bear hug. Ryan Ballard, also closing in, noticed that the attacker was squirming to get his hand into his back pocket, so Ballard knocked both of them to the ground. Coward confessed to police he was "trying to go on a killing spree but the (expletive) blade broke" and that he had fantasies of stabbing people since he was eight years old.

040914 **Franklin Senior High School, Murrysville PA** (M-00, W-22): 16-year-old male student with a pair of 8-inch kitchen knives went on a stabbing spree. This coward was subdued by assistant principal Sam King, with the help of student Ian Griffith, after spotting a school resource officer who was wounded.

060514 **Pacific University, Otto Miller Hall, Seattle WA** (M-01, W-02): Students described the sound as like helium balloons popping after a 26-year-old male student shot three people with a double-barrel shotgun. Seconds after, while the coward was reloading, student-safety monitor Jon Meis, 22, sprayed him in the eyes with OC/Pepper, tackled and disarmed him. Once the killer was down, others assisted. The coward also had extra ammunition and a knife with him. Actual video take-down link: http://www.kiro7.com/news/local/hero-of-spu-shooting-an-example-of-bystander-taking-action/343578948).

072414 **Mercy Fitzgerald Hospital, Darby PA** (M-01, W-01): A female case worker was killed and a doctor wounded. The coward was then shot by the doctor, who returned fire from his own gun.

102214 **Parliament, Ottawa Canada** (M-00, W-01): After shooting a guard in the foot with a rifle, running towards the in-session Parliament, the coward hid from pursuing RCMP officers. Hero Sergeant-at-Arms Kevin Vickers obtained a 9mm handgun from a lock-box, entered the hall where he was advised that the suspect was hiding in the alcove. Vickers immediately ran behind the other side of a nearby column, dove past the column and fired upward, killing the coward.

102414 **Marysville-Pilchuck High School, WA** (M-04, W-01): 15-year-old male student with a handgun. First-year social studies teacher Megan Silberberger tried to apprehend the coward as he may have been attempting to reload, before he fatally shot himself.

061016 **Plaza Live Meet & Greet, Orlando FL** (M-01, W- 01): 27-year-old male was tackled by murder victim's brother Marcus Grimmie. The coward brought two handguns, two magazines and a large knife, and was able to commit suicide on-site.

Ron Borsch manages the PACT Consultant Group. Supported by the seven SEALE Chiefs of Police, he was also the founder and, from 1998 to 2015, manager lead trainer for SEALE Regional Police Training Academy in Bedford, Ohio. Ron built this academy from the seven police department cooperative to eventually serve more than one hundred law enforcement agencies from ten states. Before that, Ron had a three-decade law enforcement career including serving as range master, pistol team captain, defensive tactics instructor, and SWAT. He is also a Viet Nam veteran (1965-66), serving as a U.S. Army Paratrooper with the 101st Airborne. He is on the SchoolGuard.com advisory panel. For the last several years at the International Law Enforcement and Educators Training Association in Chicago IL (ILEETA), Ron has served on two panels of experts annually.

Chapter 10:
CONTACTS WITH THE POLICE

BY **HARVEY HEDDEN**

When we decide to arm ourselves for protection it is important that we not be mistaken for dangerous criminals. You know you are one of the "good guys," but to other "good guys" you might appear to be a "bad guy," as in the case above. There have been numerous cases in which off duty or plainclothes police officers have been mistaken for "a man with a gun" and were killed by uniformed officers. In some cases the officer involved even personally knew the victim but did not recognize him.

> **"** The driver failed to stop for the stop sign, as though she didn't see my marked squad approaching the intersection. So I stopped the late model Ford with lights, no siren, called in my traffic stop and made the approach. As I neared the driver's door she turned away and I glimpsed her handling a small box that looked vaguely familiar. Too late to retreat, I picked up my pace as she now turned towards the open driver's window. I recognized a snubby revolver in her hands being thrust out the window in my general direction. I grasped her hands with my left hand as I drew my weapon with my right, while another part of my mind was trying to understand what she was saying, "I just bought this officer..." I was able to disarm her with my left hand while she continued to say "...for my protection." A moment later she saw my weapon and looked confused, then put everything together and said, 'Oh, you thought I was....oh no!' **"**

When you make the decision to carry a firearm, there are several circumstances in which you may encounter law enforcement, from a simple traffic stop to a shooting, and your goal is to not present yourself as a threat. Police officers, like you, want to go home safely at the end of the workday. Unfortunately, there are criminals who will use every tool – from deception to deadly force – to avoid arrest. Lacking a detector of evil intent, the police officer who stops you doesn't know who you are and must make a threat assessment, based on your demeanor and actions, until they can determine through investigation who and what you are about. They are trained to assume that almost anyone they contact could potentially pose a threat to them. I recall the words of an old veteran when I was only a rookie, "Boot, you must treat everyone you meet with dignity and respect... and have a plan to shoot them." If an officer observes you with a firearm in your possession, you are not innocent until proven guilty. You are a potential threat. Yes, you should expect courtesy, but safety comes first.

Because so many states have concealed carry, more law enforcement agencies are developing training protocols to handle contacts with lawfully armed citizens, whether they are carrying concealed or open. Such initiatives result in safer contacts and fewer complaints from permit holders against officers and agencies. But many agencies lack these protocols or training, and there remains a wide variety of potential responses by law enforcement to contacts with an armed citizen. Some permit holders have found significant variances even within a single police agency. No matter what the training or policy, the person with the badge ultimately is in charge of the contact, and although we may disagree with their conduct it is the best course to follow their instructions and avoid holding court on the street. You can always make a complaint to command at a later time.

THE TRAFFIC STOP

No matter how conscientious you are, it can happen that you will be stopped for a traffic or equipment violation by a police officer. Your vehicle might also be similar to the description of one wanted for a crime or "check the welfare" call. As difficult as it may be, your best response is to not become excited, argumentative or nervous. Take a deep breath, focus on what is happening, listen to any signals or instructions carefully and act slowly and deliberately. At worst the stop may be an inconvenience and you may have to eventually post a bond or pay a fine.

If you are signaled to stop by an officer, decelerate normally and look for a safe place to pull over with a wide shoulder or a parking lot. Officers are killed every year by traffic when out of their squads performing their duties. Turn your engine off. If your driver's license, registration and CCW permit are not immediately accessible, don't start reaching around the interior of the vehicle to locate them after you are stopped or as the officer approaches, as this might be misinterpreted as an attempt to hide something or access a weapon. Turn on your interior lights at night, turn your radio off, put your cellphone down, open your window and place your hands high on the steering wheel and leave them there. Don't turn around or move your mirrors to try to see from where the officer is approaching. Don't try to sneak your seatbelt on or make any other movement that might appear suspicious. If there are passengers in the vehicle, advise them to keep their hands visible, sit still, and let you do the talking unless the officer directly asks them a question.

> **"** In another traffic stop a nervous teen driver put his cigarette in the dash ashtray but then returned his hands to the wheel as I examined his license. Somehow he had forgotten he had stored a few small firecrackers there and somehow the cigarette managed to light their fuse causing them to explode. Fortunately, because his hands were visible to me he avoided being shot. **"**

The officer(s) may or may not initially tell you why you were stopped, but will usually ask for your license and registration. In addition to providing these documents, you may provide your CCW permit to bring that awkward subject into this conversation. If you need to retrieve these from someplace, tell the officer you will obtain them but that you want the officer to know you do have a concealed carry permit valid in the state, and that you are carrying a weapon on you/in the vehicle. This is preferable to the officer seeing your firearm as you reach for your wallet or open your glove box and reveal that hand cannon. Never just blurt out, "I have a gun on me." When officers hear the word "gun," it takes them back to training or street encounters in which a fellow officer found a hidden weapon on a suspect and yelled the warning "gun." Instead use terms like firearm or weapon. Keep your voice calm and your rate of speech slow so that you do not appear to be nervous or agitated.

The officer may ask where the weapon is located. Tell – don't show – the officer where it is. Just because you have told the officer you have a permit and a firearm doesn't mean his guard is down and that you can relax, take your hands off the steering wheel, grab a snack or make a phone call. Don't make idle chatter about the weapon the officer is carrying. Don't expect that since you are a CCW holder the officer views you as a "good guy" and is going to give you a warning instead of a citation.

Note that not all states require you to tell the officer that you are carrying concealed, but it is a strongly recommended practice because if you do not and they do find out through observations or a computer check that you are a CCW permit holder, they will wonder why you did not relate this information to them. Even if you are not carrying a concealed weapon, if you have a permit you should tell the officer that you do but that you are not armed, so that if they run a computer check and learn you have a permit, they won't wonder why you failed to mention it.

From this point the officer may ask you to not make any movement towards the weapon. You might be asked to exit your vehicle. You might be patted down and your weapon taken from you temporarily. You might be asked to turn over the weapon to the officer. In this case, be sure to ask and understand exactly how they want this task completed. Before taking any action, verbally tell the

BEFORE TAKING ANY ACTION, VERBALLY TELL THE OFFICER WHAT YOU ARE GOING TO DO AND GET AN ACKNOWLEDGEMENT THAT THEY AGREE.

officer what you are going to do and get an acknowledgement that they agree. You want to reduce the chance of any confusion wherever possible.

Before turning the weapon over, ask if you may unload the weapon. Whenever handling your weapon always keep the muzzle away from everyone. Make your movement slow and deliberate in a manner that is easy for the officer to observe. You may not like this treatment, but don't argue with the officer. You can always make a complaint later.

It is also possible you weren't stopped for traffic, but because you or your vehicle matches the description of one wanted for a crime. In this case you might be asked to exit the vehicle and may be ordered to the ground and handcuffed at gunpoint. Your best course, again, is to inform the officer verbally and keep your hands visible in front of you and comply with all commands. Do not argue or reach anywhere the officer cannot see. Cellphones or a wallet can appear to be a firearm in reduced light.

PEDESTRIAN STOP

If you are stopped on the street, it might be that you may be a potential witness or suspect (Terry Stop). Use the same cautions about where you place your hands and, before retrieving documents or identification, let the officer know if you have a concealed firearm/permit. Police officers actively look for signs that someone is carrying a concealed firearm and may suspect you are CCW before they even begin a conversation with you. In my own experience, many criminals failed to wear clothing that adequately concealed the weapon, or failed to use a good holster with the consequence that their firearm shifted and caused their clothing to sag or bunch unnaturally. This is another good reason to invest in a quality holster in lieu of the waistband or coat pocket. You don't want to be mistaken for a thug by the police or recognized by a criminal as a source of a free gun.

There are many ordinary tasks that require remastering to carry a concealed firearm, most notably squatting in lieu of bending over. But if you had a lapse and a call went out or an officer saw your weapon, you need to use extreme caution. If a police officer does order you to stop, don't move or turn towards the officer. Keep your hands in plain view and don't reach for your permit. If you are asked to produce it or your identification, repeat the command back to the officer, and then slowly say it again as you perform the action in easy view.

If you are ordered to disarm yourself, ask for details on how the officer wants this accomplished and ask if you can face a direction and or get into a position that is least threatening, such as prone. I caution officers about giving this command because another unit rolling up on the scene could misinterpret the citizen's disarming as drawing the weapon. Do not grip your weapon as you would normally, but use two fingers on the portion of the grip farthest from the trigger. Your other hand should be raised palm facing outward. Some have suggested using the non-gun hand for this action, but my concern would be that the less coordinated hand might drop the weapon and the citizen might try to grab at it. Once the weapon is out of your hands, raise them both; do not move towards your firearm again.

THREATENED USE OF FORCE

Armed citizens use the threat of deadly force with much more frequency than actually firing upon a criminal. Unfortunately, some of those armed citizens decide not to call the police after the incident because they believe that if no actual crime was committed, why make it a police matter? But in many cases citizen witnesses (and in a few others, would-be offenders) have called 911 and described the armed citizen as the bad guy. Law enforcement tends to think of the first involved party that calls as the victim, so it is to your advantage to get your account of an incident heard first.

Assuming the threat is no longer present, re-holster your weapon or otherwise secure it so that you are not visibly armed. Make your hands visible and tell bystanders that you are legally permitted to carry a firearm and that you were concerned for their/ your safety (why you had your weapon in hand). In any scenario, intentional or accidental, in which you believe your weapon may have been observed by someone who would contact the police, you should proactively call 911 to head off a "man with a gun" call. You might still be asked to meet an officer and should use the safety protocols outlined below. Try to stay on the line with the dispatcher until the first responding officers arrive to provide better communication and coordination for a safe response.

EVEN IF YOU CAN, SHOULD YOU?

There are legal considerations in even the threatened use of deadly force. Most importantly, is the threat you are trying to stop one that involves death or great bodily harm, or is it just a property crime? The cost of replacing your wallet or your car, even household possessions, pales in comparison to the costs associated with hiring competent defense counsel for a shooting. Even when you are right, it can cost you dearly to prove it. Typical legal defense costs are around $50K. The cost of George Zimmerman's legal defense was reportedly $2.5 million. If you decide to undertake a citizen's arrest, you will be investing many hours in the subsequent investigation and court appearances. You might be charged or sued for false imprisonment and need to hire counsel to defend your actions. The bottom line is that property is replaceable, people are not.

We tend to imagine a scenario in which a stranger is the attacker, but in fact often this person is known to us or we have had some relationship with that person that may influence how the incident is judged afterwards. After the incident there may be an attempt to paint the incident as an angry reaction or an opportunity for you to settle a score rather than lawful self-defense. In these cases it is preferable that someone else who is unrelated to the offender intervenes, ideally law enforcement. This means you may wish to retreat even if your state laws indicate you are not required to do so.

But there are also important tactical considerations in deciding to use a firearm, such as can I isolate my target if I have to shoot? If I should miss, where might my round end up? Will I put other bystanders at risk if I engage this person in a gunfight, including my own family? But we should also consider the possibility that someone else at the scene might misinterpret your actions and think you are a criminal. Could one of these bystanders be an off duty officer or CCW permit holder?

The police aren't the only side that utilize backup. Could a bystander actually be a covert, armed, seeded backup for the armed suspect you did identify? In Las Vegas, two insane criminals murdered two uniformed officers as they ate lunch, and then fled to a retail store across the street. As panic swept through the store and shoppers and staff tried to flee, a courageous armed civilian prepared to engage one of the shooters but was ambushed by the second and killed. We can take some solace in the fact that other civilians were able to escape while the killers engaged this brave citizen, but it is possible that better tactics might have provided a more satisfactory resolution.

Whether armed or not, the best way to handle an attack is to avoid it altogether. Be aware of potential threats, avoid dangerous environments, and if you get a hunch that something is wrong, believe in it and if possible retreat to a safer area. Often our sub-

WHETHER ARMED OR NOT, THE BEST WAY TO HANDLE AN ATTACK IS TO AVOID IT ALTOGETHER.

conscious mind perceives threats that we are unable to fully conceptualize in our conscious mind until it is too late. This does not mean you should use proactive force based on intuition, only that when you think you might be getting into trouble you may have a limited opportunity to avoid it altogether.

ALL UNITS IN THE AREA, SHOTS FIRED...

In the rare case in which an armed citizen is required to use their weapon to defend their own life or that of another, communicating with responding police is critical. In a perfect scenario, that communication would begin even before the shooting starts. In several cases the 911 recordings even captured the verbal warnings the armed citizen gave to the suspect. In scenarios where the suspect fled the scene, a physical description of the suspect led to their rapid arrest.

Thanks to 911 dispatching with auto location and other advances in technology, such as Shotspotter (http://www.shotspotter.com), police are often able to respond to shootings in urban and suburban areas much more quickly. In some cases the shell casings were still rolling on the pavement when officers arrived. In other cases, particularly more rural jurisdictions, you might wait considerably longer. In either case, contacting law enforcement as soon as possible will expedite their arrival and also begin to provide them with important information to help them determine who are the good guys and who are the bad guys. Never leave the scene (flight = guilt) unless staying in that area would be too dangerous, and then let law enforcement know where you have relocated as soon as possible.

We tend to assume that the police will recognize we are one of the good guys, and this assumption can get us killed. The aftermath of a shooting is sometimes more physically stressful

> WE TEND TO ASSUME THAT THE POLICE WILL RECOGNIZE WE ARE ONE OF THE GOOD GUYS, AND THIS ASSUMPTION CAN GET US KILLED.

than the tactical resolution of the incident itself and could cause you to respond to arriving officers as a new threat. Witnesses who call in a shooting are not always accurate, and responding officers will have to assume anyone they encounter is a potential threat, especially a person with a firearm in hand. In one case, an officer had to remove the service weapon from a brother officer's hands that he had used minutes before to shoot an armed suspect and was still aimed at his body so other officers could safely work the shooting scene. Being aware of these stressors can help you stay alive and protect you legally.

Once it appears there is a pause in the armed confrontation – because the suspect is no longer a threat or has fled the area – take cover, reload, and scan the area to be certain the suspect is not trying to flank you or for other threats like a backup bad guy. Slow your breathing and determine your own status, as you may have been wounded and are not aware of it. Tell anyone in the area that you are a legally armed citizen and that you were attacked and that you are the victim. Ask if any of them were hurt or if they saw the incident.

The body and mind will experience a variety of effects that make us less aware of our surroundings (including tunnel vision and auditory occlusion) making it easy to miss threats. It will also tend to cause diarrhea of the mouth. You should assume that someone has their cellphone video camera rolling and what you say in the heat of this moment will impact whether or not you are prosecuted for this shooting, as well as appear on television.

If the suspect is down, never assume the suspect is out of the fight. Verbally challenge the suspect to give up their weapon and raise their hands. Do not attempt to physically contact the still-armed suspect or chase them if they flee the scene. If you are able, secure their weapon but never assume there is only one. Be cautious when in close proximity to the suspect in case they are faking injury or death to lure you closer or locate you. If circumstances dictate that it is safe to do so, you or someone at the scene might attempt to provide first aid to the suspect within the scope of your/their experience and training, and only after seeing to any innocent injured persons, and only if you are reasonably certain there is no additional threat. Why treat the criminal who tried to hurt you? Because it makes it clear that you used deadly force because you had to, and not because you wanted to murder this person. In cases in which citizens or police officers made such a good faith effort until emergency medical professionals arrived, plaintiff's counsel and prosecutors found it difficult to paint the shooter as a stone cold killer. But you should not risk anyone else's safety or attempt more than very basic first aid without proper training.

INFORMATION FOR RESPONDING AUTHORITIES

Once we have survived the tactical event, we want to be certain we don't create conditions for another one by being misidentified as a threat. This is best achieved in a system that Mas Ayoob calls the three rings of safety. I first heard of this concept in connection with off duty and plainclothes officer involved shootings, but it applies equally well to armed citizens. The three rings of safety that protect the armed citizen include: the message, the welcoming committee, and you. The most critical information that will be repeated in each of these will be the descriptions, location and current status of the armed citizen and the suspect(s) and their weapons and the need for emergency medical response.

The message is communication sent out to law enforcement by someone who will be calm, rational and reliable, which for the reasons stated above might not be you. Ideally someone in authority at this location, like a storeowner, should make the call. Remember that stranger could be a seeded backup. Don't delay this call, as it is possible someone else may have already called 911 and incorrectly identified you as a bad guy. The message should include a description of what has happened, including the elements listed above. Follow up messages can provide updates or more complete information as it becomes available, such as suspect(s) fleeing or hiding in the area. You might consider taking advantage of technology by having someone take photos and or video for the record or to send to the responding officers or dispatch.

If you have any doubts about the ability of the person being tasked to do this important duty, call yourself. The upside of being the caller is that you have more complete information about what is happening and can stay on the line with the dispatcher until the responding officers arrive. The downside is that it distracts you from potential threats still in the area and will be part of the investigative record and possibly replayed by the media. Try not to sound too excited or too calm, as either will be used against you.

The welcoming committee is a reliable person of authority who can meet responding officers, and assume they have none of the information provided to dispatch, and provide the same information to those now on scene just in case they did not receive everything that was provided to the dispatcher or the situation has changed. It is important that they be highly visible and not appear to be a threat. Give this person your cell number in case the officers want to communicate directly with you.

INTERACTION WHEN OFFICERS ARRIVE

You are the final ring of safety in a post-shooting incident. If it is no longer necessary to cover the suspect, depress your muzzle downwards or better yet re-holster and make your hands visible. You might also consider laying your weapon on a nearby object where it is easily accessible. You can then step away from it with your hands visible and direct the officers to its location.

Try to orient yourself in a manner that allows you to see the officers arriving, but not in a manner that it appears you are aiming in their direction. Expect to be surprised by them and that they may yell commands that you are not to move. Do not turn towards the sound of the officers. Make sure you understand and obey their commands. Let them know you are the victim/legally-armed citizen and where the suspect is and what potential threat he is to the officers. If you still have your weapon in hand, the responding officers will likely ask you to holster or put your gun down/away. If you are told to drop the gun, keep the muzzle pointed in a safe direction and try to drop it on its side to reduce any chance of an accidental discharge. They may then ask you to step away from the weapon and into a location and position where you can be searched and possibly even handcuffed until they sort out the scene.

Once the scene is secure, you will want to provide officers information as described above from the message and welcoming committee that helps them capture the suspect if necessary and secure valuable evidence and witnesses. It is best to limit these recollections to things you are certain of and can corroborate with current observations. Never exaggerate or feel the need to say something to fill in gaps in the story. Avoid providing details, because much of what you think you know now will change in 24 to 48 hours. When police officers are involved in shootings, they are not asked for a detailed account for at least 24 hours so that their mind can return to some sense of normalcy (something you may mention to the investigating officers). Conversely, those who tried to fill in the blanks of their memory often had to change their account in light of physical evidence and other witness accounts, which made it look as though they were being deceptive. In my first shooting, I was almost certain I had pulled the trigger on empty chambers in my revolver because I had not heard or felt the .357 magnum discharge, but the next day I had a much better recollection of the event.

WHAT TO SAY

Tell the officers you wish to cooperate with them and will sign a complaint because you are the victim. Use "sir" a lot in speaking with them. Tell them you were in fear for your life or the life of another and had no choice. Don't say you are sorry or that you didn't mean to kill the suspect, just scare them off, or that your gun "went off." If the officer asks for details, state that you are pretty shaken up right now and would like to be able to recover from this traumatic event so that you can provide accurate information, and that you would like to have your attorney present when you do. You may wish to ask to go to the hospital to get checked out because of the stressful event you just experienced, and that you may have health problems that are not immediately visible or recognizable.

In these statements, you have asserted your right to counsel, told the officer that information you provide now could be influenced by the trauma of the shooting (and therefore not accurate), and asked for medical treatment, which if delayed can establish additional trauma and duress during questioning, making your subsequent statements inadmissible in court. Note that if you do go to the hospital, you might ask for a blood test for drugs and alcohol to establish that you were in a proper state of mind at the time of the shooting and that it was not an accident.

But the police want those details and are likely to tell you things like, "If you don't get your side on the record we might have to arrest you and you don't want that," or, "If you're not guilty of anything you have nothing to worry about." They have a job to do and would prefer to complete this investigation rather than have to follow up later. They may downplay the importance of their questions or ask for "yes" or "no" responses to things that "you certainly must know" or offer that telling them about the incident will help you better deal with the trauma. At some time or another I used all these tactics and more to convince people to talk.

You should respond that you appreciate the job they have to do and that you will cooperate once you have had a chance to calm down, just as would be the case if the officer were involved in a shooting, but that you want to have your attorney present before answering any questions. Do not consent to searches of your home, business or vehicle. Anticipate that these may be searched with a warrant and that if you have firearms improperly stored, not only will you be charged but also it will contribute to the picture of you as a reckless gun owner. Expect that you may be arrested, handcuffed, booked, jailed and arraigned. Do not argue or resist the police, but obey all their commands. Technically you have committed a violation of law until some authority determines you have not. Police anticipate that at some point from the arrest but prior to your arraignment, you will insist on speaking with them without your attorney.

YOUR RESPONSE TEAM

If you decide to carry a gun, start your search now for qualified legal counsel with experience in self-defense cases. Don't settle for someone who primarily deals with traffic offenses or car accidents. However, an attorney is only one element in your defense. You may wish to consider hiring a private investigator to look into the background of the suspect and to review the reports of investigating officers for completeness after they are released to your attorney. Your attorney may also seek expert witnesses who can educate a jury or the court about the realities of self-defense.

As we have seen in George Zimmerman and Officer Darren Wilson shootings over the past several years, a lie repeated enough times in the absence of the truth becomes the truth, and can result in a prosecution based more on political correctness than the facts of the case. You may wish to hire a media consultant that, in concert with your attorney, is able to communicate the truth of the event without endangering your defense. Never take on this task yourself as George Zimmerman did by appearing for a TV interview that was subsequently used by the prosecution.

FINAL WORDS

Benjamin Franklin said, "If you fail to plan, you are planning to fail!" Having a plan for a dangerous encounter will reduce your reaction time and make your response more effective. Part of your planning should include mental scrimmages against potential threats. But your planning should also include what you will do if you are contacted by law enforcement, whether it is a traffic stop or the defensive use of your weapon. You want to act in a way that you will be recognized by the police as one of the "good guys" and not put your life or freedom in peril.

ABOUT THE AUTHOR

Harvey Hedden served for 39 years in law enforcement, in roles from patrolman to chief. Most of his career was spent in plainclothes and undercover assignments. He has been a law enforcement trainer for 35 years, specializing in firearms, officer survival, defensive tactics, arrest control, investigations and customer-based policing. He has taught thousands of officers and civilians, authored numerous articles, and created and contributed to a variety of training programs. In 2009 he became the Executive Director of the International Law Enforcement Educators and Trainers Association.

Chapter 11:

THE CRIMINAL TRIAL

BY JIM FLEMING, ESQ.

The prosecution of a criminal defendant involves the application of two overlapping bodies of law. One portion is known as "substantive law," and the other is known as "procedural law." Substantive law is the law that creates, defines, and regulates rights and duties. Procedural law protects the accused from the improper application of criminal laws, and the unlawful treatment of the accused. These laws govern the treatment of criminal suspects, from initial police contact, through arrest, investigation, trial, sentencing, and possible appeal. The Rules of Evidence are essentially procedural rules and principles that govern what evidence a jury or other trier of fact may consider in reaching a verdict during a trial.

A defendant charged with a crime following a self-defense incident will typically be charged by the filing of a complaint which describes the crime the defendant is accused of committing. Each state has its own criminal code, comprising statutes enacted by the state legislatures that define the elements of various crimes and the punishment for violations. Each state also has its own rules of criminal procedure and rules of evidence, enacted by the State Supreme Court. In addition to the criminal statutes or procedural rules, there is also a body of "common law," consisting of appellate court decisions interpreting how the various statutes and rules are to be applied to a given set of facts.

The complaint is prepared by a prosecutor for approval by a judge or magistrate. It identifies the criminal statute the defendant is accused of violating and the basic facts supporting the accusation. The court reviews the complaint to assess whether there is a sufficient legal basis to hold the accused person in custody. This is known as "probable cause." If the court determines that the facts alleged do not establish probable cause, the court must dismiss the complaint and order the release of the accused. The process of preparing the complaint – review by the court, serving it on the accused, and bringing him before the court to answer the accusation – is governed by the Rules of Criminal Procedure. These laws and procedures may vary somewhat from state to state. In other cases, the laws and procedures will be nearly identical from state to state, even if the titles of some of the procedures are different.

It is common for people to believe that private citizens who have been victimized by a crime have the authority to press charges. This is not usually the case. In the majority of jurisdictions, only the prosecuting attorney's office has the authority to file criminal charges. While the police may arrest an individual on specific charges, the police do not file charges, and the booking charges are often later changed by the

IN THE MAJORITY OF JURISDICTIONS, ONLY THE PROSECUTING ATTORNEY'S OFFICE HAS THE AUTHORITY TO FILE CRIMINAL CHARGES.

prosecutor. Usually, the "victim" of a crime does not have much say over the charging decision.

In some cases, the charging decision may be referred to a "grand jury." A grand jury typically consists of between 16 and 23 jurors. The grand jury is not responsible for determining whether a person is guilty of committing a crime. The grand jury is asked to determine whether there is sufficient "probable cause" to pursue criminal charges against an individual. To do that, the grand jury must find that a reasonable suspicion exists that a crime has been committed, and that the individual in question is the person who committed that crime. Grand jury proceedings are much more informal than trial court proceedings. A judge does not preside over the proceedings and usually there are no lawyers present other than the prosecutor. The prosecutor explains the law to the grand jury members and works with them by presenting evidence and the testimony of various witnesses. The written decision of a grand jury is known as an indictment, or "True Bill." If the jury finds that it has heard sufficient evidence from the prosecution to believe that an accused person probably committed a crime and should be indicted, the indictment is sent to the court. If the grand jury returns an indictment, the prosecutor will then charge the defendant.

Once an individual has been charged, the criminal court process consists of a series of hearings required by the Rules of Criminal Procedure, based upon rights found in the United States Constitution and the constitutions of the various states. These hearings may have different names depending upon the jurisdiction, but typically they are known as arraignment, preliminary hearing, pre-trial hearing, and trial. Multiple tasks are accomplished at each stage of the process.

FIRST APPEARANCE/ARRAIGNMENT

The first appearance must be held without undue delay. Most jurisdictions impose a 24-hour limit on initial detention before a first appearance. This limit may be extended to 72 hours if the arrest is made on a Friday. At the first appearance, the judge informs the defendant of the charges described in the complaint. The judge also informs the defendant of his rights, such as the right to remain silent and the right to an attorney. If the defendant cannot afford a private attorney, the court will appoint a public defender. In most jurisdictions, the attorney meets with and represents the defendant at the first appearance.

The court will also set bail at the first appearance. "Bail" refers to the deposit of cash, a bond, or property by the accused with the court. It is imposed as a requirement for the release of the accused from law enforcement custody. The primary purpose of bail is to allow the defendant to remain free until and unless he is convicted of a crime. It serves to protect the right to prepare a defense and also to the presumption of innocence. It is set in an amount high enough to ensure that the defendant will return to court when he is ordered to reappear for other hearings relating to his case, or for trial. If the defendant does not reappear when he is ordered to, the court is authorized to "forfeit" or keep the bail and issue a warrant for the defendant's arrest.

Recently, some states have enacted statutes, modeled on federal law, that permit pretrial detention of persons charged with serious violent offenses, if it can be demonstrated that the defendant is a flight risk or a danger to the community (Fla. Stat. 907.041). Obviously, a criminal homicide will be viewed as a serious violent offense, and it can be easily predicted that a serious assault involving the use of a weapon might be viewed in the same way.

Following arraignment, a preliminary hearing or "omnibus hearing" is held. Before this hearing, the prosecutor and the defense attorney typically discuss the case to see if there is any possibility of a plea agreement or a mutually acceptable resolution of the case. If a deal that is acceptable to the accused can be reached, it is presented to the court for approval at the Preliminary Hearing.

As many as 90% of all criminal cases are settled by plea agreement. Why are plea bargains so popular with both prosecutors and defense attorneys? For prosecutors, it means not having to prosecute the case, which saves time and resources. For defense attorneys, it means reduced risk of conviction on more serious charges, the possibility of decreased jail time, avoiding publicity, and substantially reduced attorney fees.

Plea bargains obviously are not appropriate for all cases. Many experienced criminal defense attorneys have also been confronted with situations where their clients simply refuse to consider the possibility. However, attorneys are sworn to work in the best interests of the client. In some situations, advising the client to accept a plea offer is clearly in the client's best interests. However, it is the client that must make that decision, and the attorney is bound to honor it. The best the attorney can do is to point out the pitfalls of going to trial in a given case, and why he or she is recommending that the client accept the offer. While the facts surrounding the use of deadly force are very clear-cut in some cases, in many others they are not, and can put the client at risk.

> WHILE THE FACTS SURROUNDING THE USE OF DEADLY FORCE ARE VERY CLEAR-CUT IN SOME CASES, IN MANY OTHERS THEY ARE NOT, AND CAN PUT THE CLIENT AT RISK.

PRELIMINARY HEARING

In felony cases, after the arraignment, if the case does not settle or get dismissed the judge holds a preliminary hearing. At this hearing, the accused may challenge the probable cause for the charges or the admissibility of certain evidence alleged to have been collected in violation of the accused's constitutional rights. The procedure used at a preliminary hearing is similar to a trial, except that it is heard by the court instead of by a jury. Unlike the first appearance, the prosecutor relies on witnesses to present the prosecution's evidence, and the defendant may do the same. Both sides are allowed to cross-examine the opposing party's witnesses. After this hearing, the court may dismiss the charges if it finds that they are not supported by adequate evidence. Depending upon the specific issue that is raised, the "burden of production" of evidence is assigned to either the accused, or to the State. If the issue is "probable cause," the State must provide only enough evidence to justify a reasonable belief that a crime occurred and the defendant committed it. This burden is much lower than the burden at trial, where the State must prove guilt of every element of the offense beyond a reasonable doubt.

Although probable cause challenges are sometimes successful, the majority of these challenges are unsuccessful. If the defendant is unsuccessful at the preliminary hearing, it is common practice to enter a plea of not guilty and serve notice on the court and the State of the intent to employ certain affirmative defenses to the charges. Self-defense is an affirmative defense in many jurisdictions. In still others, it is viewed as a justification defense. An affirmative defense to a crime presents facts which, if proven by the defendant, defeat or mitigate the legal consequences of the defendant's conduct which would otherwise be unlawful. A justification defense goes to the elements of the charge itself.

> **AN AFFIRMATIVE DEFENSE TO A CRIME PRESENTS FACTS WHICH, IF PROVEN BY THE DEFENDANT, DEFEAT OR MITIGATE THE LEGAL CONSEQUENCES OF THE DEFENDANT'S CONDUCT WHICH WOULD OTHERWISE BE UNLAWFUL.**

When a defendant claims that he or she acted in self-defense, he or she is admitting one, if not more, of the elements of the charged criminal offenses. For example, assume that John shoots Ted and Ted dies. Depending upon the circumstances, John may be subject to criminal charges, ranging from first-degree murder to involuntary manslaughter. Each of these potential charges have factual elements that must be proven in order to convict a person accused of the crime. Let's say that there is no evidence of premeditation on John's part. John might be charged with involuntary manslaughter. The elements of the offense are:

1. Someone was killed as a result of act by the defendant.

2. The act either was inherently dangerous to others or done with reckless disregard for human life.

3. The defendant knew or should have known his or her conduct was a threat to the lives of others.

By claiming self-defense, John is admitting that someone was killed (Ted) and that he died as a result of the actions of John. He is also admitting that he knew his conduct was a threat to the lives of others. However, he is also claiming that he was justified in using the deadly force that killed Ted. The defendant, in essence, says, "Yes, I shot Ted, and he died as a result. But I did not murder Ted, because, under the circumstances, my acts were legally justifiable." Most criminal defense attorneys know that if they intend to claim self-defense on behalf of their clients, they are required by the Rules of Evidence to provide written notice of the defense to the prosecution. This is usually required prior to a preliminary hearing. In the context of the self-defense case, that is where the issue starts, but it is definitely not where it ends.

WHEN A DEFENDANT PLEADS SELF-DEFENSE, HIS BURDEN IS THE BURDEN OF PRODUCTION. THAT MEANS HE MUST PROVIDE SOME EVIDENCE TO THE COURT TO SUPPORT THE DEFENSE.

When a defendant pleads self-defense, his burden is the burden of production. That means he must provide some evidence to the court to support the defense. Once that threshold showing is met, the burden shifts to the state of disproving the defense beyond a reasonable doubt. Numerous appellate courts have held that the Fourteenth Amendment requires such an allocation of the burdens because the defense is "inextricably bound" to the intent requirement, which the state is required to prove. The more important question is often "how much evidence is enough?"

The handling of this scenario varies widely, depending upon which state is in question. In many jurisdictions, the evidence will be presented to a trial jury and the defendant will have the right to have a self-defense instruction read to the jury. The question of whether a jury accepts the claim of self-defense or rejects it will await the verdict following trial.

Not every state treats self-defense in the same way. In 1997, the Arizona Revised Statutes were amended to include §13-205, which, at that time, placed the burden on the defendant to prove any affirmative defense, including justification defenses, by a preponderance of the evidence. Section 13-205 was amended in 2006 to reflect the current state of the law, which exempts the defendant from proving justification and instead places the burden on the state to prove the lack thereof beyond a reasonable doubt. As a result, self-defense is not seen as an affirmative defense in Arizona. "Justification is not an affirmative defense; instead, if a defendant presents evidence of self-defense, the state must prove "beyond a reasonable doubt that the defendant did not act with justification." (State v. King, 225 Ariz. 87, ¶ 6, 235 P.3d 240, 242 (2010))

In other jurisdictions, specifically those which have enacted what are commonly referred to as "stand your ground" statutes, the procedure is quite different. In Florida, for example, the Legislature enacted the first of the "stand your ground" laws in 2005. The Florida statutes (Florida Statutues, 2015, Title XLVI, Chapter 776, 776.012 to 776.09 et seq.) provide that a person is justified in the use of deadly force and has no duty to retreat if either:

1. The person reasonably believes that such force is necessary to prevent imminent death or great bodily harm to himself or herself or another, or to prevent the imminent commission of a forcible felony; or

2. The person acts under and according to the circumstances set forth in Section 776.013, which relate to the use of force in the context of a home or vehicle invasion.

> ## NOT EVERY STATE TREATS SELF-DEFENSE IN THE SAME WAY.

WHAT IS NEW IN THE FLORIDA STATUTES IS THAT ... A PERSON WHO USES FORCE AS PERMITTED IN SECTION 776.012 OR SECTION 776.013 IS IMMUNE FROM CRIMINAL PROSECUTION AND CIVIL ACTION FOR THE USE OF SUCH FORCE.

Florida's law does not create a new affirmative defense. The principle that a person may use deadly force in self-defense, if he or she reasonably believes that such force is necessary to prevent imminent death or great bodily harm, has been the law in Florida for well over a century. However, what is new in the Florida statutes is that under Section 776.032, a person who uses force as permitted in Section 776.012 or Section 776.013 is immune from criminal prosecution and civil action for the use of such force, although there are certain limited exceptions. This means that, if the defendant can present competent evidence during a pre-trial hearing that his use of deadly force followed the requirements of Section 776.012 or Section 776.013, the state is legally and procedurally barred from pursuing prosecution of the matter. Also, if a civil action is brought against a person who used justifiable deadly force, the court must dismiss the case and award reasonable attorney's fees, court costs, compensation for loss of income, and all expenses incurred in the defense of the case.

Contrary to what is often claimed by opponents of stand your ground laws, this law does not prevent a prosecution from being initiated against the accused. Prosecutors often file charges against defendants, even where there is a clear "stand your ground"

IF THE DEFENDANT CAN PRESENT COMPETENT EVIDENCE DURING A PRE-TRIAL HEARING THAT HIS USE OF DEADLY FORCE FOLLOWED THE REQUIREMENTS OF SECTION 776.012 OR SECTION 776.013, THE STATE IS LEGALLY AND PROCEDURALLY BARRED FROM PURSUING PROSECUTION OF THE MATTER.

defense. In such cases, the prosecutor files charges, and later, at an appropriate stage, the defense attorney will file a "Motion for Declaration of Immunity and Dismissal" (Section 776.032, Florida Statutes (2011), and Rule 3.190(c)(4), Florida Rules of Criminal Procedure). The legal challenge is then heard at a hearing, where the defense must show factual evidence of an entitlement to immunity. The legal standard applied is not, however, "beyond a reasonable doubt," but instead merely proof by a "preponderance of the evidence," a much lower standard. If successful, immunity is granted and the case is dismissed. If unsuccessful, the case continues and it is resolved later, through a trial or a plea of some kind.

At this point in time, 23 states have enacted stand your ground-style laws. (At the time of writing, 23 states have made legislative expansions to the Castle Doctrine: Alabama, Alaska, Arizona, Connecticut, Florida, Georgia, Idaho, Indiana, Kansas, Kentucky, Louisiana, Michigan, Mississippi, Missouri, North Dakota, Oklahoma, South Carolina, South Dakota, Tennessee, Texas, Utah, Wyoming, and West Virginia.) However, don't rely on that statement without further research, since the law in place in any of these states could change at any time.

> ## THE LAW IN PLACE IN ANY OF THESE STATES COULD CHANGE AT ANY TIME.

Other states have similar provisions that are found not in their statutes, but in appellate court case law interpreting their statutes. The remainder tend to be referred to as "duty to retreat" jurisdictions. This is widely misunderstood. In the typical duty to retreat jurisdiction, the individual has a duty, while in a public area, to retreat before employing deadly force if the individual can do so safely. In those jurisdictions, very typically, there is no duty to retreat while inside one's own home. That is because, for many years, the home as been considered the individual's "castle" and at common law there has never been a duty to retreat within one's home. This is frequently referred to as the "castle doctrine" for this very reason, although the mainstream media mischaracterizes this about ninety percent of the time.

Whether applied in a castle doctrine state or a stand your ground state, self-defense remains a defense to a criminal charge stemming from a deadly force encounter. It is often claimed. In some cases, the facts support it. In others they do not. The big difference is what effect the defense has on the burden of proof in further proceedings in the case.

PRE-TRIAL HEARING

The pre-trial hearing is be used for a variety of tasks, including discussion of some type of plea offer. It may also involve arguments relating to the admissibility of evidence, identification of witnesses, and the substance of their expected testimony.

The actual process is fairly uniform across the country. Preliminary trial motions will be argued to the court and rulings made. This may involve questions of law, questions of procedure, issues relating to the admissibility of evidence, preliminary jury instructions, their form and content, and whether witnesses will be allowed to sit in on the trial prior to their testimony, or whether they will be "sequestered," requiring them to remain out away from the trial to prevent their testimony from being contaminated by the testimony of other witnesses and evidence.

THE TRIAL

There is one truth about trials that should not be ignored. A defendant's chances of "winning" are never going to be better than even up, or in other words, 50/50. Cases that are obvious winners and losers get resolved prior to trial. It is the hard-to-read cases, or the cases where the offer of resolution is very one-sided, that end up going to trial.

Every trial attorney who has ever practiced has lost cases they expected to win, and won cases they expected to lose. Its not uncommon for even experienced attorneys to have little idea what the reasons are for the outcome. Judges and their level of experience may play a part. Jurors may hold opinions or beliefs that would prevent them from returning a not guilty verdict, even if they believe that the evidence indicates that a defendant used deadly force in self-defense. Witnesses may or may not impress the jury with their credibility. Any number of small things can add up to an unexpected result.

CASES THAT ARE OBVIOUS WINNERS AND LOSERS GET RESOLVED PRIOR TO TRIAL.

At the beginning of most trials, both the prosecutor and defense counsel are permitted to do a limited questioning of prospective jurors. This is an opportunity to question prospective jurors about their backgrounds, opinions, and beliefs in the hope of revealing bias or some other limitation on the juror's ability to judge the case fairly and impartially. "Voir Dire is the process by which attorneys select, or perhaps more appropriately reject, certain jurors to hear a case." (Cleary, Gordon P.; Tarantino, John A. (2007). Trial Evidence Foundations. Santa Ana, Calif.: James Publishing. Section 201.)

Following jury selection, the jurors are sworn and seated. The judge will then read the preliminary trial instructions. Then the attorneys will be invited to present their opening statements to the jury, outlining their theory of the case, the witnesses to be called, and the evidence to be presented.

Following the opening statements, the State will then proceed to present its case, calling witnesses to testify and using their testimony to authenticate various exhibits. Defense counsel will have the opportunity to object to questions posed by the prosecutor, or witness testimony, if the defense attorney believes they have violated the Rules of Evidence. The defense can also cross-examine State witnesses and challenge the various exhibits. All of this will be conducted under the supervision of the trial judge responsible for rulings on objections, and the admissibility of the testimony and exhibits. Once the State has concluded its case in chief, the State will notify the court that it rests its case. It will not be allowed to put on any new witnesses or introduce new evidence, but may, following the defense case, offer either witnesses or testimony in rebuttal of the evidence presented by the defense. Rebuttal evidence is simply testimony and evidence offered in an attempt to prove that the evidence that was presented by the defense is either inaccurate, or untrue.

Once the State has rested, the defense may bring a motion to dismiss the State's case. The motion argues that insufficient evidence has been presented to prove each element of the crime charged or of a lesser-included offense. This motion is not automatically made in every case. The decision to grant or deny the motion is up to the trial judge. If the motion is denied, the jury will be recalled to give the defense the opportunity to present its case in chief. The defendant is under no legal obligation to prove he or she is not guilty. The burden is on the state to prove the defendant's guilt to the jury beyond a reasonable doubt.

THE DEFENDANT IS UNDER NO LEGAL OBLIGATION TO PROVE HE OR SHE IS NOT GUILTY. THE BURDEN IS ON THE STATE TO PROVE THE DEFENDANT'S GUILT TO THE JURY BEYOND A REASONABLE DOUBT.

If the decision is made to present a defense, witnesses will testify, exhibits offered, objections raised and arguments presented in the same way as during the State's case. Witnesses may include eyewitnesses to the events, and in some cases expert witnesses who will be asked to provide an opinion for the jury on some technical issue or another. What you must keep in mind, concerning the use of expert witnesses, is the question of what they will be allowed to offer opinions about, and what they will not.

In most states, the use of deadly force in self-defense is going to involve consideration by the jury of these questions:

A) Did the defendant have a real apprehension of imminent death or great bodily harm as a result of the actions of the individual upon whom deadly force was used? Did he really believe that it was necessary to use deadly force to avoid death or some serious, crippling injury?

B) Was the judgment of the defendant as to the gravity of the peril to which he was exposed reasonable under the circumstances? Based upon what he was experiencing, would a reasonable person also feel that apprehension?

C) The defendant's election to use deadly force must have been such as a reasonable man would have made in light of the danger to be apprehended. Was the amount of force used by the defendant to protect him/herself reasonable under the circumstances?

Question A is a question of fact, based upon a subjective analysis. What did this defendant believe? An expert witness will not be allowed to answer a question about what the defendant believed. The jury must decide the answer to that question for themselves, based upon the evidence that they see and hear. This prohibition derives from the concept that the jury is the finder of fact. However, questions B and C are objectively based. What would a reasonable person believe, or do in similar circumstances? Here, the expert can offer an opinion, based upon experience, training and knowledge, to aid the trier of fact in understanding the reasonableness of the defendant's beliefs and actions.

When the defense completes its case, the state has the opportunity for the rebuttal previously described. Once the rebuttal has been offered or waived, the court will instruct the jury on the law that they must apply to the evidence in order to render a verdict. The instructions are read to the jury. The jurors in some jurisdictions may be allowed a copy of the instructions in the jury room to refer to if they have questions. In other jurisdictions this is not allowed.

Once the instructions have been read, the attorneys will make their closing arguments. The attorneys are free to discuss the evidence, what it proves and disproves, and why their theory of the case should be accepted by the jurors. There are complex rules as to what an attorney may argue and how that argument may be presented. The state gets to go first, followed by the defense. The state is then allowed one more shot at a rebuttal argument. The jurors then retire to deliberate and return with a verdict. That verdict may be for acquittal ("we find the defendant not guilty") on all counts, acquittal on some of the counts and guilty on others, guilty on all counts, or guilty of a "lesser included offense." A lesser included offense shares some, but not all, of the elements of a greater criminal offense. For example, manslaughter is a lesser included offense of murder. For example, California Penal Code, Section 187(a), defines murder as:

1. An act that resulted in death to another person;

2. Committed with malice aforethought; and

3. Committed without lawful excuse or justification.

Now, look at California Penal Code, Section 192(a), defining voluntary manslaughter:

1. An intentional act that resulted in death to another person;

2. Or, an act performed with a conscious disregard for human life;

3. Committed without lawful excuse or justification.

The element of murder missing in the definition of manslaughter is malice aforethought. So, in a scenario where the State is unable to prove that a defendant's act in killing was committed with malice aforethought, the defendant may still be convicted of manslaughter, the "lesser included offense."

In the event of an acquittal, the case against the defendant is dismissed and the defendant discharged from custody. Although the prosecutor could later bring other, unrelated charges, based upon the same facts, the double jeopardy clause of the Fifth Amendment prohibits retrial on the same charges. (The Double Jeopardy Clause of the Fifth Amendment to the United States Constitution provides: "[N] or shall any person be subject for the same offence to be twice put in jeopardy of life or limb . . . ." This encompasses four essential protections including retrial for the same offense: retrial after an acquittal; retrial after a conviction; retrial after certain mistrials; and multiple punishments for the same offense.)

A not guilty verdict on all charges normally ends a criminal case, because the State cannot appeal an acquittal. A guilty verdict on some or all charges, however, doesn't necessarily mean the case is over. Defendants can move the court requesting that the trial judge overturn the jury's guilty verdict and enter a verdict of not guilty. The defendant

THERE IS NOTHING IN THE LAW THAT GUARANTEES A PERFECT TRIAL.

can also move for a new trial, setting aside the jury's verdict. In some cases, the defendant can also move for mistrial, and seek a new trial. As a last resort, the defendant can appeal, asking an appellate court to reverse a conviction. In the appeal, the defendant can challenge the conviction itself or only the sentence.

The number of cases overturned on appeal is quite low, since the appellate courts provide great leeway for the trial courts to conduct their business. It is really important to remember that there is nothing in the law that guarantees a perfect trial. Therefore, appeals courts will only overturn verdicts that contain clear, serious errors of law, the sorts of errors that have a substantial and detrimental impact upon the outcome of the case.

This is a basic blueprint of the criminal trial process. There are numerous variations that apply in many jurisdictions, and procedures often have names that differ from state to state. However, this general outline describes the process in summary terms that is used uniformly throughout the United States.

ABOUT THE AUTHOR

Attorney Jim Fleming has nearly 30 years of legal experience that can work for the benefit of your case. His background provides unique value to the legal work provided at Fleming Law Offices that you won't find at other law firms. He is a former police investigator and understands the criminal justice system and how it operates.

Chapter 12:
UNDERSTANDING POST-INCIDENT LEGAL ASSISTANCE PLANS

BY MARTY HAYES, J.D.

O n the surface, it seems so straightforward. A person decides their life and their family members' lives are worth defending, so they buy a gun, get a concealed weapon permit (likely going through a state-mandated training course) and then believe they are good to go. Of course, the smart ones also realize that they have not figured out all the nuances of carrying a gun for self-defense, so they seek out legal education and, if they are not skilled with the pistol, pursue additional firearms training, too. But however the path to being an armed citizen in public goes, at some point this person arrives at that moment when getting dressed in the morning means also putting on the gun.

This has been my daily routine for the last 35 years, first as a police officer, then as a private citizen after leaving police work to become a private sector firearms trainer, which I have been

Armed Citizens Legal Defense Network Advisory Board. From left: Marty Hayes, Vincent Schuck, Massad Ayoob, Jim Fleming, Tom Givens, Dennis Tueller, Manny Kapelsohn, and John Farnam. Photo courtesy ACLDN.

doing for 29 years through my training company, The Firearms Academy of Seattle, Inc. It is this experience that led me to realize that there is more to being an armed citizen than just packing a gun and being skilled in its use.

In 1990, I invited Massad Ayoob to the Pacific Northwest to teach one of his Lethal Force Institute's Judicious Use of Deadly Force courses. I was figuratively "blown away" by Ayoob's depth of knowledge and legal experience, revealed in both his classroom presentation on the legalities surrounding self-defense and his expert witness experiences helping defend innocent people being prosecuted for using a firearm in self-defense. Later that year, I made the decision to travel to New Hampshire for two more weeks of training at Ayoob's home range. I subsequently became an adjunct instructor for his training company. Through these experiences, the die was cast and I knew that just teaching how to shoot was not going to be enough for me. I had to get involved in the legal side of the self-defense industry, too.

That was 1990, and in the next ten years I worked as an expert on over a dozen court cases and started thinking about law school. During this time, I saw many, many cases where lawfully-armed citizens used some degree of force in lawful self-defense, but

> **THERE IS MORE TO BEING AN ARMED CITIZEN THAN JUST PACKING A GUN AND BEING SKILLED IN ITS USE.**

were nonetheless prosecuted and many times convicted, or as Jenny Dawson (not her real name) did, take a plea bargain and become a convicted felon, instead of risking trial and conviction.

Her case is typical. Jenny was a lawfully armed citizen who possessed a valid Washington State Concealed Weapons Permit. She kept her .38 revolver at home for self-defense against possible intruders and, as she would explain later, also for protection from her live-in boyfriend. It seems that her boyfriend liked to "hit on her" and as is common in the cases that I have reviewed, the couple was into drugs.

On the night in question, she was home alone and had her revolver hidden in the couch cushions. Her boyfriend and a couple of his friends came home and shortly thereafter, an argument ensued between him and Jenny. He became physically violent and during the physical altercation threw her against the wall and knocked her out. In fact, she hit the wall so hard that her head caved in the sheetrock.

When she came to, her boyfriend and his friends had disappeared. She made her way to her couch and was waiting there with her revolver when the boyfriend showed back up. Pointing the gun at him, she told him to get out. He laughed and asked, "What are you going to do, shoot me?" That is exactly what she did when he came at her with what she believed was intent to take her gun. She only had to shoot him one time, inflicting a through and through wound to his abdomen. He left and got a ride to the hospital from his friends.

Jenny appropriately called 911 and the police arrived and arrested her for attempted murder. Why? Because the boyfriend and his friends told the police a different story. He was about six feet tall and weighed 200 pounds. She was five feet tall and 90 pounds. Disparity of force was certainly present, but still, she was arrested. I have observed that in America, nearly universally, an armed individual who shoots and either wounds or kills an unarmed person is usually prosecuted, or at least arrested pending investigation.

The attorney who brought me in on Jenny's case is both a friend and my student. When he told me about the details of the incident, I agreed to work pro bono on the case as an expert. She had little money to spend on her defense, and to me this was a horrendous travesty of justice. I was prepared to testify at trial that disparity of force was obvious and that it would have been simple for the boyfriend to disarm and kill her. Nonetheless, days before trial the client took a plea to a low level felony and was given credit for time served plus a few more months in jail, as opposed to risking trial and perhaps spending the next 20 years behind bars.

If the person arrested does not have the money to hire his or her own attorney, our system of government provides an attorney. That sounds good, but the courts have determined that the legal defense only has to be a barebones, minimum expense effort. Some courts go the extra mile to make sure the public defender has the resources needed, but that is rare. Typically the defense tends to be less-than-thorough, because money isn't available to hire the experts and consultants that the defense truly needs. To make things worse, public defenders routinely rely upon witness statements and shooting incident reconstruction and analysis from the police investigation instead of doing their own. In my experience, conclusions the police draw and even the scene investigation done by law enforcement can be very wrong. And, lest one gets the wrong impression, I am routinely impressed by the abilities of public defenders. It's just that they are not given the resources to do the job right.

After working this system for years and having made the decision to earn my own law degree, I started thinking about what I would do after graduation to make a positive difference. That was when I hit upon the idea of starting a membership organization that would stand behind any member that needed post-incident support and give them a complete legal defense in court after a self-defense incident.

THE BIRTH OF THE POST-SHOOTING INCIDENT LEGAL DEFENSE INDUSTRY

Up until 2008, with the exception of a couple of

law firms that took retainers and promised to defend the client if they were ever charged after an incident involving use of force in self-defense, no entity existed to help the armed citizen fight a criminal prosecution after self-defense. The closest option was one company selling an insurance policy, which reimbursed your legal fees if you were acquitted after a criminal prosecution. I found the fine print contained in either the retainers or the insurance unacceptable. In the first case, the law firm retainer, I want to be able to control my own legal defense. In the second option, the insurance policy, I recognized that I'd need money up front to fight the criminal charge in order to attain the acquittal required for reimbursement.

With my newly-printed Juris Doctor degree in hand, I started the Armed Citizens' Legal Defense Network with the help of two partners. We knew that if enough trained armed citizens thought membership in the Network was a good idea and paid a reasonable yearly fee, we could grow a legal defense war chest to tap for the legal defense of a member. Interestingly, not only did thousands of armed citizens think the Network was a good idea, so also did a bunch of other people who started businesses mimicking the Network through look-alike plans to assist armed citizens who'd needed to use firearms in self-defense.

Now that you know the history, we can spend the remainder of this chapter discussing the various types of plans available, their advantages and pitfalls.

PRE-PAID LEGAL SCHEMES AND RETAINERS

Many lawyers saw the opportunity to jump on this bandwagon, and now offer enrollment in pre-paid legal plans in which the law firms, in return for payment of a yearly retainer fee, will handle all the legal issues after a self-defense incident. I realize that words like "have an attorney on retainer" create mental pictures of crime bosses giving piles of cash to lawyers who once "on retainer" agree to come to the crime syndicate's aid when trouble arises. While the armed citizen isn't willfully committing crimes, he or she now has the opportunity to have a criminal defense attorney on call to respond after an act of self-defense. And, this type of service may be just what you need. There are, however, some potential problems of which the armed citizen consumer needs to be aware.

Who will be your attorney?

First, you need to find out exactly who will be your attorney. When the Mafioso boss puts an attorney on retainer, he hires a specific person, one who has a proven ability to successfully defend him and his ilk. Are you doing the same thing when you join a pre-paid legal service? Probably not. If the company to which you are sending money is not headquartered in your state, they will need to find an attorney licensed to practice in your area to represent you. How will they do that? Have they already selected an attorney who will represent you? You should find out, unless you are willing to accept anyone the company sends when you call for help.

Attorneys are NOT fungible, by which I mean that while those working in a jurisdiction are licensed there to practice law, most specialize in certain areas of the law. One attorney may be a superior criminal defense attorney who understands the nuances of self-defense law and can to a great job representing you if you are charged with a crime in conjunction with your act of self-defense. But, the next attorney down the street may purport to be a criminal defense attorney, but the closest they ever come to a courtroom is when they send an associate to court to enter a plea on behalf of the client. This concern brings to mind the movie "A Few Good Men." In this classic legal movie, Lt. Kaffee (played by Tom Cruise) was the son of a very well-respected attorney, but he himself had never handled a murder trial until he is assigned by the Judge Advocate General to defend two Marines accused of murdering a fellow Marine. Why was he assigned? Because he was known as the guy who will plea bargain the case and get it settled. Is this going to be your attorney? You had best find out, before you blindly accept the terms and conditions of the lawyer's retainer you sign when you enroll in one of these programs.

Does the plan pay for experts and investigators?

The next big concern I have regarding pre-paid legal plans for armed citizens is whether the program pays for experts and investigators. In many instances, it will be vitally important to have one or more experts working on your case. The lawyers defending George Zimmerman were savvy enough to hire Dr. Vincent DiMaio to testify at trial on behalf of their client. Dr. DiMaio literally wrote the book on gunshot wounds, and his testimony was used very effectively by Zimmerman's legal team to validate the defense narrative that Travon Martin was on top of Zimmerman, bashing Zimmerman's head into the concrete sidewalk when Zimmerman fired his 9mm handgun point blank into Martin's torso. Without this "very expensive" testimony, Zimmerman might very well have been convicted of murder. If the pre-paid legal plan you enroll in does not agree to pay to hire experts, you should be prepared to spend several thousand dollars yourself.

It is of paramount importance for a defense team to hire at least one private investigator, if not more, to interview witnesses. I have seen many cases in which the police account of what a witness said varied widely from what a defense investigator found out from witnesses. In most investigations, the police take written or recorded statements from the witnesses. Incredibly, I have also seen instances where the police officer actually handwrites the statement on behalf of the witness, who then reads and signs it, attesting that the account is accurate. So, if you decide to enroll in one of these plans, you need to make sure that the expense of hiring private investigators is included in the yearly fee, or be prepared to foot that bill yourself, too.

Does the firm have the financial resources to handle your trial?

Another concern that I have about the pre-paid legal plans is how stable and how well funded is the firm or company you are hiring? A criminal case can drag on for two or three years. Will your firm last through a long case like this? Remember, they have taken money from you and many others with the promise to provide a complete legal defense. What do they do with the money they take in on a monthly or yearly basis? Do they set some aside into a trust fund, or do they spend it all on current expenses? I would want assurances that the firm had the financial resources to not only handle the expenses of my criminal trial, but the trials of other plan participants, too, in the same time period. Before signing on the dotted line, ask these questions.

Can you trust them?

My last caveat regarding enrolling in a plan that promises to defend you in court is to check out the principals of the firm. Just who are these attorneys? Google and Yahoo are your friends, but in addition, a private citizen can typically access the disciplinary history of lawyers through the state bar association. Has the attorney ever been disciplined? What for? Now, please understand that just because an attorney has been disciplined by their state bar association, that does not mean that they are incompetent or dishonest. I know attorneys who have been disciplined for some rather meaningless errors, but are very capable advocates. Still, just do your homework before trusting the wrong person.

THE INSURANCE MODEL

Insurance, whether it is a home owners, auto, life or self-defense policy, hinges upon the purchaser (the insured) and the insurance company identifying an occurrence which is outside the control of the purchaser, then the insurer offers to pay money to cover the cost of that occurrence (a claim) in exchange for monthly or yearly payments (premiums) paid by the insured to the insurance company. The insurance company is betting there will be more people willing to pay premiums to cover the cost of any claims and allow the insurance company to operate and make a profit. For example, most everyone has auto insurance. The insurance company collects premiums from all the customers and then pays any claims made by the customers for automobile accidents. Additionally, the incident on which the claim is based must be an accident, not an intentional act. Now, while the car owner may be at fault in the accident, he must not have set out with the intention to wreck the car. The loss has to be outside of your control.

How does that work in the self-defense arena? The insurance policy for armed citizens will typically promise to reimburse the costs of defending yourself in court up to policy limits, IF you are acquitted. You see, the acquittal (or in some instances, the prosecutor's decision to drop the charges) is the incident that is outside your control. Thus, the payoff is subject to acquittal or charges being dropped, and is subject to the limits of the policy. Most policies that I am aware of have a multi-level premium and payoff scheme. You can sign up for $50,000, $100,000, $250,000 or even a million dollars of coverage. And of course, as the limits rise, so do the premiums.

The good news is, if you actually have an insurance policy issued in your name, a host of government regulators are looking out for your interests. State insurance regulators watch insurance companies like hawks, and before the insurance company can sell insurance it must prove that it has the financial backing to reimburse your legal costs if you have a legitimate claim.

Before buying self-defense insurance, you need to understand two separate concerns. First, as I have said, the insurance provider promises to reimburse your legal costs after an acquittal. That means you must come up with the money for the defense. Most people cannot handle a $100,000 legal bill out of pocket, so their defense will be less than the best, simply owing to budgetary limits. Unfortunately, if the defense is lacking, an acquittal is unlikely. Without an acquittal, the insurance company is off the hook. Read the fine print before buying.

> PAYOFF IS SUBJECT TO ACQUITTAL OR CHARGES BEING DROPPED, AND IS SUBJECT TO THE LIMITS OF THE POLICY.

In addition, insurance typically covers a civil claim against you. The policy limits determine how much they will pay out if you are found culpable for wrongful death or battery (the two most common torts resulting from use of force in self-defense). How much money is a wrongful death case worth? Well, that depends on a multitude of variables, but I cannot think of an instance where an individual who took a life and was found culpable for that death would not be facing a million-dollar-plus verdict. So, that means that I would want at least a million dollars of coverage, maybe more. And that million-dollar policy comes with a big price tag.

The good news is that you will not pay out of pocket for the legal defense in the civil lawsuit, because with the insurance company's money on the line, they will hire counsel and defend you. Again though, as is true for pre-paid legal services, you likely do not get to pick your own attorneys. The insurance company will assign lawyers to you. And, if after trial the verdict exceeds the amount of insurance coverage, you will be responsible for the excess.

THE HYBRID MODEL

When we started the Armed Citizens' Legal Defense Network, our sole goal was to help the armed citizen fight that first legal fight, primarily the criminal action, but to also assist with the expenses of defending a civil lawsuit if it came to that. To this day, that is still our driving philosophy. Over the years, newcomers to the post-shooting support industry have offered the pre-paid legal retainer model, or the insurance model, both explained above. But, as we have discussed, each has its shortfalls. So, to fix these problems, many companies have blended both an up-front legal defense benefit with an insurance back-up for civil actions. And, while the blends may still have some of these issues, most have been somewhat mitigated. Fixing those issues comes at a cost, though, and most of these hybrid models have a pretty high price tag for coverage that will actually provide a legitimate defense for the criminal trial, and sufficient civil protection to guard against the civil suit. Do your homework and read the fine print.

THE CO-OP MODEL

The last model of post self-defense legal assistance plans is perhaps best described as a cooperative. In a co-op, a few thousand like-minded people get together under an organization set up just for this purpose and pay yearly dues to be part of a larger group so they don't stand alone at trial. The organization sets aside a portion of the yearly dues in a legal defense fund, and then operates the organization on the remainder of the money. For armed citizens, there is only one such organization currently operating, that being the Armed Citizens' Legal Defense Network, Inc. I run the Network and, in addition to me and my partners, an advisory board consisting of Massad Ayoob, John Farnam, Tom Givens, Dennis Tueller and attorneys Emanuel Kapelsohn and James Fleming guides the Network. The advisory board helps steer the ship so to speak, review and comment on member-involved incidents, and lend credibility to the organization through their support.

RESOURCES NEEDED TO MOUNT A LEGAL DEFENSE

When studying the various plans, you should estimate that it would cost at least $100,000 for a criminal defense, and perhaps much more. For a murder trial, spending less than that will result in a bare-bones defense. Preparation for a murder trial will consist of many months of work by attorneys, investigators and experts who must filter through the evidence and craft the armed citizen's defense. Then when trial arrives, you can plan on at least one week in trial if not two to three weeks, paying for two attorneys and a paralegal, not only for the time in court, but for time before and after trial. It has been my experience working with many attorneys in murder cases that they put in at least 12 hours a day. Let's do the math. 12 hours, times $500, times two attorneys equals $12,000 a day. 10 days times 12 grand equals over $100,000 alone, and you have not yet begun to pay for paralegals, investigators and experts.

When considering what plan to enroll in, make

sure there will be sufficient resources to do the job right for you. If not, you may end up a convicted felon, simply because you ran out of money. For example, consider the David Bennet (not his real name) case, a case of justifiable homicide in my opinion, but one that resulted a conviction, nonetheless.

Mr. Bennet was a firearms enthusiast living in the Southwest, in a conservative state, but one in which the urban areas tended toward liberal politics. Does that sound familiar? Mr. Bennet had a federal firearms license and was trying to build a gunsmithing business at the time of his self-defense shooting. The details of the shooting are this. He had volunteered to help a friend of a friend move some belongings out of her residence before breaking up with her live-in boyfriend. Mr. Bennet had a truck and figured he could help.

While Mr. Bennet was in the house helping the friend gather her things, the boyfriend and two of his buddies showed up and, predictably, a fight occurred. He ended up down on the floor, being hit and kicked by three attackers. When the attack increased to such severity that he believed his life was in grave danger, he took his .40 caliber Springfield XD out of his waistband holster and started shooting. He fired eight shots, striking all three of his attackers, killing one of them. It seemed justified to me, as it likely does to the reader. But, it occurred in a liberal state capital city so he was prosecuted. Driving the prosecution were facts including that he shot unarmed people, and shot the one that died in the back.

I was hired as an expert to make sense of a very poor shooting investigation, one in which the police altered the shooting scene before even photographing it and no scene diagrams or measurements were made.

Mr. Bennet was a young 20-something married man with a wife and child to support, but he had no resources of his own. Enter the parents and the funding for the legal defense. I met his parents a day before I was set to testify at trial. They were the kind of people you would want as a mother and father. They coughed up the money to hire one of the top law firms in the area and had three attorneys at trial, each of which would handle a specific aspect of the two-week trial. While I was not privy to the exact cost of the defense, I would estimate it cost well over $100,000.

Mr. Bennet and his defense team, of which I was part, managed to convince the majority of the jurors in that he was innocent of any criminal act. Unfortunately, a few of the jurors just could not accept idea that shooting someone in the back could be justifiable, and they refused to acquit. The very fair and experienced judge declared a hung jury. Now the prosecution had the choice to either re-file the charges and try again or move on and admit defeat. Did I say this was held in the liberal capital of the state?

Bear also in mind that on retrial the prosecution knows exactly what the defense will be. So, the prosecution filed charges again, and Mr. Bennet was faced with another difficult and costly legal battle. Although he had loving parents, he had used up his parents' discretionary income, and they could no longer afford another legal fight for their son. Consequently, Mr. Bennet was forced to plead guilty to a low-level felony conviction, primarily because he could not afford a do-over. By taking the plea offer, he avoided additional jail/prison time and could move on with his life, although he does so as a convicted felon, denied the right to own guns for self-defense.

When signing up for an aftermath legal plan, ask what happens after a hung jury. Will they cough up another $100,000 for a second trial? You need to know.

APPEALING A GUILTY VERDICT

We have discussed two cases in which lawfully armed citizens entered guilty pleas to avoid the potential consequences of a guilty verdict. But, what happens if you go to trial to fight the charges, fail and are found guilty? In each state in the union, a

> WHEN SIGNING UP FOR AN AFTERMATH LEGAL PLAN, ASK WHAT HAPPENS AFTER A HUNG JURY. WILL THEY COUGH UP ANOTHER $100,000 FOR A SECOND TRIAL?

person has the right to at least one appeal. But you must understand: an appeal does not address the facts of the case. Instead, an appeal scrutinizes the legal process used in reaching the verdict.

The appellate courts give great leeway to trial court decisions over whether or not the facts presented were sufficient to merit a guilty verdict. Consequently, you cannot appeal a bad outcome based on the facts presented to the jury. You are allowed an appeal when the trial judge makes rulings that go against established judicial procedures or protocols, or the judge gives jury instructions that were not warranted. In the vast majority of self-defense cases, the facts are presented clearly and free of incorrect rulings by the judge, and so appeals are generally not successful. Do not count on an appeal, but be ready to fund one if you are found guilty. And, of course, ask in advance whether or not your post incident self-defense plan would fund an appeal for you.

ADDITIONAL BENEFITS OF POST-SHOOTING PLANS

There are a couple additional benefits some plans include of which the armed citizen needs to be aware. These are bail assistance and legal training. Let's discuss bail benefits first.

First, in many states, if a person is charged with first-degree murder, bail is either not allowed or is granted at the discretion of the trial judge. I worked on a case in Pennsylvania where the defendant, an innocent man who was acquitted at trial a year later, spent an entire year in jail before being set free by the trial court. Understand that in many states, you may not even be allowed to try to post bail, but for the purposes of this discussion, let's presume that you were granted bail. What exactly does that mean?

When you go before the judge for the first time and plead not guilty, your attorney should request that you either be released on your own recognizance, or allowed to pay a

> THE DEFENDANT, AN IN- NOCENT MAN WHO WAS ACQUITTED AT TRIAL A YEAR LATER, SPENT AN ENTIRE YEAR IN JAIL BEFORE BEING SET FREE BY THE TRIAL COURT.

low bail. The argument will be that you are a valued member of society, working at a full time job, have family connections and you are a low flight risk. The prosecution will argue that you have the means to flee prosecution because you do have some financial resources, and since you are facing a very serious felony charge, you should be given a very high bail. Typically, the judge will rule somewhere in the middle and grant bail at perhaps $100,000 to $250,000 or maybe more. If the bail is set at $100,000, you then bring 100k in cash to the county clerk and when that money is handed over, you get out of jail. The money serves as collateral to insure that you will come back for trial. After you show up for the trial as you promised in your bail agreement, you will get that money back (less court costs).

If you do not have enough money sitting around or cannot raise funds to pay the bail amount, you may be given the chance to pay a bail bond agent only 10% of the bail. The bail bond agent then guarantees to the court that you will come to trial, or else the agent must pay the total bail. The licensed bail bond agent shoulders this risk for 10% of the bail amount, generally. If you do not show up for trial, in our $100,000 bail example, they will pay the court the entire $100,000.

Sometimes people fail to understand that they will not get back the $10,000 paid to the bail bond agent. That is the fee the agent charges for taking the risk. It may still sound like a pretty good bargain, but you must further understand that the bail bond agent may not only require the 10% fee, but they normally require you to pledge collateral to make up the other $90,000. That means you will need to sign over the titles to your cars, boats, gun collection, retirement funds and perhaps even the deed to your house before the bail bond agent will post the bail. Self-defense legal plans will typically cover the fee to the bail bond agent, but cannot put up the collateral. That remains your responsibility. Many of the available plans advertise a bail assistance program, but you must understand that unless you have the collateral available to guarantee the total amount to the bail bond agent, you will still likely not be released on bail. When you read that a plan pledges to get you out of jail immediately, understand that they are stretching the truth a whole bunch. Don't get sucked in by grandiose claims.

Last, but of greatest importance, is the question of legal education for plan participants. The key to being acquitted is convincing the jury that you used only enough force to stop the assailant from killing or seriously injuring you or other innocent people. You will need to be able to articulate why you felt your life was in danger, and the very best way to do that is documented training.

> ## YOU WILL NEED TO BE ABLE TO ARTICULATE WHY YOU FELT YOUR LIFE WAS IN DANGER, AND THE VERY BEST WAY TO DO THAT IS DOCUMENTED TRAINING.

Documented training means you can re-produce the very same training you underwent in court, if needed. The video you watched, the class handout your instructor used, your training notes, the magazine article or book you read that educated you on how to assess and respond to aggressive acts against you can all be introduced into court and used to educate the jury, under certain circumstances. You see, the jury gets to know what you knew at the time that caused you to legitimately believe your life was in danger. If your legal aftermath plan does not offer an educational component in the form of physical books or videos by legitimate subject matter experts, then you are not getting documentable training. Watching streaming video is not the same as reading a book or watching a physical DVD.

SUMMARY

Over the last eight years, armed citizens have seen both a proliferation of post-incident plans and the maturing of such plans to address many of the questions I have raised in this chapter. It is up to you, the armed citizen consumer, to ask the same questions I have posed to the different companies that offer these plans before you buy. If you get a hard sell approach when you call these companies or you get a runaround, then move on and ask another provider the same questions. The answers to your questions should be given freely and easily without hard sell tactics. But, as affordable as these programs are generally (with some exceptions), you owe it to yourself to participate in some form of post self-defense incident protection. I would encourage you to do a considerable amount of research into all the different types of plans available before signing up.

ABOUT THE AUTHOR

After spending years as a police officer, competitive shooter and police firearms instructor, Marty Hayes, President, Armed Citizens' Legal Defense Network, Inc., started sharing his knowledge of firearms and self-defense-related issues on a professional basis, and in 1990 started the Firearms Academy of Seattle, Inc. For two decades he has been teaching firearms and self-defense to the Seattle/Portland area population, with thousands of satisfied students.

Director Marty Hayes' credentials to teach firearms, self-defense and use of force include certification through the Washington State Criminal Justice Commission as a police firearms instructor; certification through Monadnock PR-24 Training Council as a PR-24 and defensive tactics instructor; certification through National Law Enforcement Training Center as a weapons retention, knife/counter knife, pepper spray and handcuffing instructor; Taser instructor certification, along with multiple certifications from the Lethal Force Institute. He is a staff instructor for the Massad Ayoob Group, and formerly an adjunct instructor for Defense Training International.

He has presented and taught for The American Society of Law Enforcement Trainers, the Washington State Law Enforcement Firearms Instructors Association and the International Law Enforcement Firearms Instructors Association. He also occasionally works as an expert witness/consultant in firearms, deadly force and police use of force cases, and holds a law degree.

MOVING FORWARD

BY MASSAD AYOOB

It has been my privilege to assemble a group of the world's leading subject matter experts to give you their take on their particular provinces in the management of lethal threat. As noted earlier, each element of it is a life study in and of itself. How does an individual who doesn't work in this field assemble a well-rounded skill set (and attitude) that will adequately equip them to deal with such emergencies? And how do we motivate loved ones to be prepared for situations they may not believe will ever happen?

One thing I noticed early when I began training regular citizens in addition to law enforcement was that those who came to the intensive 40-hour classes were strongly motivated. Often, they'd had some precipitating incident that triggered an awareness of danger from violent criminals. Something had happened to them, either an attack or a "near miss," or that had happened to someone close to them. It brought home the reality that violence wasn't just something they saw on TV or read about in the newspapers.

One thing most of us in the self-defense training industry have seen is that from the civilian sector we draw disproportionately from the various medical professions and the practice of law. Interestingly, when lists of concealed carry permit holders have been published, they show the same thing: doctors, nurses, lawyers and judges are very highly represented among those who have permits to carry handguns in public.

The attorneys and judges are the easiest to understand. They are constantly seeing violent criminals in court, and even attorneys in family practice become aware of how often emotionally-disturbed people can depart from normal behavior all the way into criminal violence.

It seems counterintuitive that those who practice the healing arts would be so surprisingly likely to carry guns and take classes in how to use deadly weapons defensively. Once you get down to where the rubber meets the road, it becomes more understandable. The average citizen hears a newscast about last night's home invasion or reads in the newspaper about yesterday's armed robbery or multiple murder of the innocent. The physician, the ER nurse, and the therapist all work regularly with patients who are victims of that sort of violence. They meet the victims. They see the results. This brings the reality home to them in a very personal third dimension. They share firsthand the pain, the crippling, the grief. And they soon come to a conclusion.

"Not me. Not mine!"

Among the docs who have come to me over the decades, the single largest specialty represented is mental health: psychologists and psychiatrists. As one self-styled "shrink" put it to me bluntly, "Mas, by definition, a lot of my patients are crazy." Often, the patient outer-directs his hostility to the caregiver. It's not just that the general public thinks doctors are rich and therefore are fat and juicy targets, or

> THE PHYSICIAN, THE ER NURSE, AND THE THERAPIST ALL WORK REGULARLY WITH PATIENTS WHO ARE VICTIMS OF THAT SORT OF VIOLENCE. THEY MEET THE VICTIMS. THEY SEE THE RESULTS.

that some in the criminal world still think that every physician carries a black bag full of pain-killing drugs to steal.

The self-defense mindset is, in the end, simply one element of a self-reliance mindset. Elsewhere in this book, the point is made that the defensive firearm is an analog to the fire extinguisher and the AED. It should be noted that first aid/trauma management skills are critical for everyone, not just those who carry guns. Any of us, in any walk of life, could be the first or only person present when someone suffers a heart attack, chokes on food, or suffers a traumatic injury. A good person's death or survival may depend on whether we, the best chance they have, know what to do and are equipped to deal with the situation and stave off death until the trained professionals can be summoned and manage to get there. The defensive mindset is exactly the same...and the life the competent self-defender is most likely to save is his or her own.

Approximately 20 years ago, Dave Duffy contacted me to write for his magazine, Backwoods Home, the motto of which was "practical ideas for self-reliant living." He wanted me to do a gun column for the magazine, simply because he considered the firearm to be another tool of that self-reliant lifestyle. Raising one's own food, preparing it, canning it, and harvesting it from nature was an element of that; the magazine's most popular writer, Jackie Clay-Atkinson, uses a Winchester .30-30 rifle every year to bring fresh, organic meat to her family. She also recognized that the same sort of tool could be necessary to save her pets and her livestock from four-legged predators...and her family from the two-legged ones. I've been firearms editor for Backwoods Home ever since. It is significant that the magazine has lost a few readers – and several advertisers – because those people thought self-defense was repugnant and politically incorrect. Yet the publication has flourished because far more people have recognized reality.

LEARNING TO COPE WITH FEAR

Management of any emergency encompasses

management of fear. That element looms particularly large in the area of self-defense. How does the individual learn to cope with fear?

You'll notice that there is no institute of learning called "Courage School." This is because courage is not really something that can be taught, and is probably not transmissible at all except in the rare sense of the inspiring leader on the battlefield. It's questionable whether we who teach survival would want to teach courage. When you think about it, courage is realizing "If I face this thing, it will very likely destroy me," yet facing it anyway out of a sense of duty. Given that so many winners of the Congressional Medal of Honor won it posthumously, that's not exactly survival training.

Most people would take "Gosh, you're fearless!" as a compliment, but the wise person might respond, "You think I'm fearless? Do I look that stupid?"

Never forget that fear is to the mind what pain is to the body. Each is extremely unpleasant, but each also serves as a critical alarm system that tells us, "Something is very seriously wrong here, and if we don't focus on fixing it, we could die from it."

Fear control, on the other hand, is absolutely attainable. Like dealing with any other problem, the best approach is to track its etiology; knowing where it came from is key to being able to manage it.

WE FEAR WHAT WE DO NOT UNDERSTAND, AND WE FEAR WHAT WE CANNOT CONTROL.

Where does fear come from? We humans are the dominant species on this planet, and we only fear two things: we fear what we do not understand, and we fear what we cannot control. Ask yourself if there is anything you're afraid of that doesn't come under one or both of those headings.

If we understand what we're facing and have the mechanisms to control it, can we not manage the fear and take control of the situation?

Education and training are the answer. Professional education and training from proven, competent professionals in the given field is obviously best, but self-education and self-training can suffice, at least sometimes.

In this context, education means cognitive knowledge. How do criminals think? What is their modus operandi? What patterns of crime are being observed in the community where you live? If you have a particular issue – a stalker, let's say – what do we know about the stalker and how he operates?

Training, in this context, refers to a learned physical response. Let's say we are the first to respond to the scene of a motorcycle accident where the victim's leg has been completely, traumatically amputated at the knee. Blood spurts in rhythm with the pulse from the stub of the severed limb. In your pocket is your First Responder card.

Education will have taught you that this hemorrhage will quickly kill the patient if you don't shut it down, and that a tourniquet will be the most efficient way to stop the exsanguination and save the patient's life.

Training will have taught you how to apply that tourniquet.

And, of course, you must have a tourniquet.

The principles are the same in self-defense. Let's leave the scene of the motorcycle accident, and go instead to a crowded shopping area where a man screams out "Allahu Akbar!" and begins to shoot down innocent people. If you have read Ron Borsch's chapter in this book, you know that education, the distilled sum of previous knowledge, teaches that this person will continue to kill and maim until he runs out of ammunition or is physically rendered incapable of continuing his actions. If you are close enough and have been trained in disarming, you may be physically able to get control of his weapon and stop the killing.

But, if you are not close enough to reach him without being murdered yourself, logic tells us that the only thing that is going to stop him is for someone to shoot him decisively enough that he can no longer pull a trigger. Training can develop the skill to place that shot.

However, just as you need to have a tourniquet before you can apply one, you will need to have a gun before you can extinguish a murderous threat with a rescuing bullet of your own.

FINDING THE KNOWLEDGE

I've had the privilege of personally picking the brains of each of the contributors to this book, in most cases spending many hours in their lectures over the years soaking up their knowledge. That's a longer path than most are willing or able to follow, so let's explore some shortcuts.

Dr. Aprill has given you an excellent look at "the mind of the enemy" in this book. To expand on that, start by reading the classic "Inside the Criminal Mind" by Dr. Stanton Samenow. Local colleges and extension universities may be able to enroll you in classes on criminal psychology and deviant human behavior. It's hard to defeat or evade an opponent you don't understand.

In his chapter here, Dr. Semone has given you a no-holds-barred look at the sociological and psychological firestorm that may well follow even the most righteous use of force, particularly deadly force. Dr. Artwohl, in my opinion the leading authority on the topic today, has touched on not only that, but the altered perceptions so often experienced by people in life or death crisis. The better you understand both of those elements, the better you'll be able to deal with them after the fact. Knowing that you might experience tachypsychia ("visual slowdown") and such, as well as knowing how to cope with the worst that society can dump on you and your family after a use-of-force incident, the less likely you will be to hesitate to defend yourself and others with appropriate force if and when it becomes necessary to do so. Dr. Artwohl and her co-author Loren Christensen's book "Deadly Force Encounters" is an excellent starting point. You would also do well to read "Into the Kill Zone" by David Klinger, a cop turned criminal justice professor who has had to kill in the line of duty himself.

There is more useful reading available in the area of survival mindset. High on that list would be "PreFense" by Steve Tarani and "The Gift of Fear" by Gavin de Becker. The author of the latter,

> GAVIN DE BECKER ... DETAILS MANY CASES OF PEOPLE WHO SURVIVED BECAUSE THEY "SENSED DANGER" AND "FOLLOWED THEIR HUNCHES."

an executive protection SME, details many cases of people who survived because they "sensed danger" and "followed their hunches." Those are classic examples of what used to be called "precognition": in a fast-breaking situation, the brain subconsciously correlates clues to recognize danger. When people pushing New Age psychic phenomena theories co-opted the term "precognition" to mean magically seeing the future, most of us reverted to the phrase "subconscious recognition of danger cues" to define this scientific explanation of a hunch.

"Lessons From Armed America" by Kathy Jackson and Mark Walters contains many accounts of ordinary armed citizens who survived deadly encounters with criminals in which they would almost certainly been killed or maimed had they not had their own recourse to a defensive firearm. More can be found in "Thank God I had a Gun" and "Surviving A Mass Killer Rampage," both by Chris Bird. The work of Bird and Jackson/Walters is particularly useful to share with those you care about who find it unimaginable that a criminal would try to harm them or their loved ones, or that an ordinary citizen could fight back against savage, heavily armed criminals and win.

It is important to understand the laws that govern the use of force in general and of lethal force in particular. It is imperative to know the guidelines. For books, I would recommend starting with a couple of mine and one by Andrew Branca. Mine would be "In the Gravest Extreme: the Role of the Firearm in Self Defense" (Police Bookshelf, 1980) and "Deadly Force: Understanding Your Right To Self Defense" (FW Media, 2014). Branca's current (at this writing) third edition of "Law of Self Defense" is his most thorough yet, and strongly recommended. All should be available from Amazon. Andrew and I separately teach courses on this topic at venues around the country: you can find those classes through http://massaday-oobgroup.com (MAG) and lawofselfdefense.com. Also strongly suggested is "Aftermath" by attorney Jim Fleming, an expansion of his chapter here.

Some gun-savvy attorneys have written state-specific gun law books that go deeply into the details of how things are done in that jurisdiction. You can probably find those at your local gun shop. One of the best examples is "Florida Firearms Law, Use, and Ownership" by attorney Jon Gutmacher.

Among the most valuable elements of the book you are reading at the moment are the juxtaposed chapters by Tom Givens and the big city detective who had to use a pseudonym here, "Spencer Blue." Tom focuses on the details of the many successful outcomes his students have had in gunfights with criminals, and "Spencer," on the mostly positive but sometimes negative outcomes of shootings involving mostly untrained armed citizens. For more input on the strategies and training that made winners of so many of Tom's students, read Givens' book "Fighting Smarter" (2015). That book, along with a schedule for Tom's hands-on training around the country, can be found at www.rangemaster.com.

I would be remiss if I didn't mention that our publisher offers a number of other books that might be of interest: http://www.gundigest.com/gun-books .

DEFENSIVE FIREARMS TRAINING

It is said that prior to the Civil War, there were sailles des armes where southern gentlemen could go to learn the weaponcraft necessary for dueling. Not until the legendary Col. Jeff Cooper founded the Gunsite Training Center in Paulden, Arizona in the mid-1970s did serious gunfight training become available for ordinary, law-abiding private citizens. Today, more such training is available, at more venues, than ever.

One must shop carefully to find what is relevant. A class in sniping or house-to-house combat is unlikely to be very relevant to the ordinary citizen worried about mugging or car-jacking. Fortunately, in the time of the Internet, AARs (after action reports) are available on classes offered by all the major instructors. Check them out.

> A CLASS IN SNIPING OR HOUSE-TO-HOUSE COMBAT IS UNLIKELY TO BE VERY RELEVANT TO THE ORDINARY CITIZEN.

Find out what they teach and how they teach it. Ask for a resume, and use it for what a resume is for: do some research and make sure the instructor has been where he says he has been, has done what he says he has done.

There are great self-taught shooting champions such as Dave Sevigny, Jerry Miculek, and Ben Stoeger, but they are few and far between, and even they refined their skills learning from others on the "super squad" when they were on their way up the ladder on the competition circuit. (A class from any of those three grandmasters, by the way, will be of great value to you.) A week invested in a good school will more than pay for itself in time saved "reinventing the wheel" in development of your own skills. If training is not in the cards, a lot can be learned from the best on video. Two gold standard sources are Clint Smith's Thunder Ranch series (https://www.thunderranchinc.com/product-category/training-dvd/) and Panteao Productions (www.panteao.com) . There is a vast amount of material on YouTube, but you need a good grounding in the concepts to be able to separate the wheat from the large amount of chaff.

Many gun-related Internet forums will have up-to-date training calendars. Sources include thehighroad.org, thefiringline.com, glocktalk.com, and pistol-forum.com among others.

LESSER FORCE OPTIONS

Deadly force is the highest and narrowest band in the self-defense spectrum. The defender who has only a gun and nothing to deal with lesser threats is in the position of a nation-state that has nuclear missiles but no conventional forces. That nation will be nibbled to death by ants (read: indigenous guerrilla action), and that person will be unable to properly handle the very common situations where an offending hand needs to be removed from one's person, or a punch or kick needs to be blocked or otherwise forestalled without killing the assailant.

If everyone had time to make martial arts their avocation, there would be a dojo on every corner.

For the great majority who can't devote themselves to weekly training sessions, it is very rewarding to take an intense weekend seminar in basic self-defense techniques. Learn to block or parry a punch or kick, and escape from front or rear strangle, headlock, full Nelson, etc.

An excellent first step is enrolling for a while in a judo dojo. With instructorship rigidly controlled all the way back to the Kodokan in Japan, judo is an art with very few if any phony instructors. Introduction to judo brings two life skills that can be important even if you're never in a fight. One is *ukemi-waza*, the art of breaking one's fall. It works as well in saving you from injury when you slip on an icy sidewalk as it does when an attacker has thrown you to the ground. Another is that from the beginning you'll be grappling with others, and unless the new student is truly phobic he or she will quickly get past fear of physical contact with aggressively-moving human beings. While some judo techniques only work on someone wearing a *gi* (picture pajamas made of canvas-like material), many will work on people in street clothes. You will also learn the extremely useful *shime-waza*, a carotid "choke-out" that does not occlude the airway but can render a much larger, stronger opponent unconscious in seconds.

JUDO BRINGS TWO LIFE SKILLS THAT CAN BE IMPORTANT EVEN IF YOU'RE NEVER IN A FIGHT.

As a member of the local/regional martial arts community, your judo instructor can give you the consumer's guide to the best instructors in other arts, including mixed martial arts that combine grappling with striking.

The best "bang for your buck" in hand-to-hand training for armed citizens can be found in short, training-packed "combatives seminars" that combine bare-handed fighting with the use of weapons. The acknowledged gold standard for this is the ECQC (Extreme Close Quarters Concepts) taught by Craig "Southnarc" Douglas, who wrote a chapter in this book. In the same class are such names as Cecil

Burch and Greg Ellifretz. A search engine can lead you to all of them.

It's also important to consider intermediate force tools. Pepper spray works much better than the Chemical Mace of old, but it's not "the magic spray/ that makes the bad guys go away." You still want a few hours of training with it to learn the accompanying movement patterns, how to minimize the chances of the substance contaminating you as well as the assailant you spray, and whether a fogger, streamer, or foam delivery system will work best for the given individual's particular needs. It is strongly recommended that you take a course where you get sprayed yourself. (Bring a designated driver to get you home.) You will leave with a much more realistic idea of results you can expect, and if you're ever accused of "torturing an unarmed man with sprayed-on hellfire," your instructor can be subpoenaed to testify that what you put your assailant through was nothing you hadn't experienced yourself.

A self-defense tool that has been working remarkably well on the street for forty years now is the Kubotan™ keychain, a 5.5-inch plastic wand that resembles a petrified Tootsie Roll. Handy for pocket or waistband, the Kubotan and the techniques which accompany it are the brainchild of one of the great martial artists of all time, Tak Kubota. In a simple four-hour class, one can learn bear hug releases, choke releases, wrist-lock take-downs, and an assortment of strikes and key-slashes. All the Kubotan techniques can be applied with MagLite's popular Mini-Mag flashlight or equivalent. The Kubotan is legal to carry in public as a rule, though not in courthouses or aboard commercial aircraft, but the Mini-Mag flashlight is allowed in those environments. The Mini-Mag is also allowed in schools, and a handy thing for a latchkey child who might have to walk home from school or library after dark. Amazon.com offers introductory manuals on Kubotan use, but you really want a four-hour hands-on training course to use it effectively.

LIBRARIES

Your public library is likely to have at least some titles on self-defense, and the sports section will have many on martial arts, though you may have to do some sorting to distinguish practical from classical techniques in the latter. You'll find plenty on criminal psychology, and a library could fill a fairly long shelf on body language.

Body language isn't just New Age psychobabble: there's a lot to it. In real life self-defense, it's critical to be able to recognize assaultive behavior indicators for two reasons. One, obviously, is to see the attack coming in time to forestall it or counter it. The other is to be able to convince a jury why you saw a danger signal that impartial eyewitnesses present did not. If you the defendant simply say, "He was gonna hit me," and the witnesses testify "We didn't see anything like that," you may be looking a conviction in the face. But your chances are much better if your attorney can explain to the jury, "My client had been taught to recognize assaultive behavior cues. You heard the witnesses say, when I cross-examined them, that they had no such training or knowledge. When the alleged victim quartered his body to my client, his head forward of his shoulders and his shoulders forward of his hips, his hands rising as he glared at my client with what he was taught to recognize as a target stare, and he saw the man's lips come back from the teeth so far it exposed the canines, my client knew he was in danger. I don't blame the witnesses for not seeing something they weren't looking for, or for not recognizing something they had never learned to recognize."

If you look around, you can probably find an extension university or other source of personal training in body language, preferably with emphasis on recognition of assaultive behavior cues. This would also give you an instructor in your area who could be subpoenaed to come to court as a material witness to testify as to how this all works, and to the fact that he or she did indeed train you to recognize such indicators.

Even if the nearest public library to you is small, it will generally have access to books from larger repositories that your librarian can order for you to check out.

There are also legal libraries, where you can learn more about how your society allows you to respond to criminal attack. While law school libraries are generally open only to their own law students, and law firm libraries open only to their own staff, most people don't realize that most counties maintain legal libraries. They will generally be located in the county seat, at or near the county courthouse, and open to the public whose tax dollars pay for them.

MOST COUNTIES MAINTAIN LEGAL LIBRARIES.

When you go there, bring with you a copy of my book "Deadly Force" and Branca's "Law of Self Defense"; there are things in them that will lead you to the topics you'll want to research at the legal library. Start with what we colloquially call the "black letter law," the Statutes and Criminal or Penal Code of the state in question. Proceed from there to case law; the legal librarian will almost always be happy to show you how to look it up. Next, ask to see the CJS. It stands for "Corpus Juris Secundum," which literally translates to "The Body of the Law." In it you will find excellent explanations of legal principles such as disparity of force and the affirmative defense and more, which are critical to understanding issues in use of force law both criminal and civil. Finally, ask to read your state's recommended jury instructions on all the fine points you'll come across. You'll find no clearer explanation of how legal principles should be applied by the triers of the facts. The recommended jury instructions will also show you the points your side will have to establish to prevail in court should you be wrongly accused in the wake of justifiably defending yourself or other innocent people.

Look into the sort of post-incident support group described by Marty Hayes, the founder of the Armed Citizens Legal Defense Network (armedcitizensnetwork.org) in the chapter on that topic in this book. Dealing with a wrongful accusation after righteous self-defense is an expensive undertaking, and no one should have to go through it alone. That ACLDN website makes its monthly journal available to the public as a public service, and is replete with good information from professionals in the use of force/criminal justice/civil justice fields.

Another treasure trove of valuable information is the website of the Force Science Institute, created by Dr. Bill Lewinsky at the University of Minnesota at Mankato, www.forcescience.org.

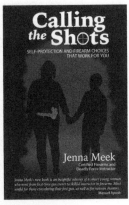

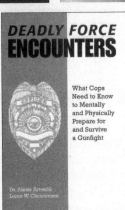

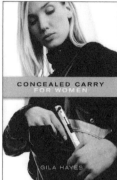

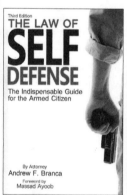

AWAKENING OTHERS

Just as there are people who blissfully ignore health hazards and don't fasten their seat belts because of the dreamy belief "It'll never happen to me," there are altogether too many people who seem to think that violent attacks on individual innocent people just don't happen in their world. Trying to get through to them is as frustrating as a health professional trying to get a chain smoker to quit the habit, but it's worth making the attempt. Just don't be discouraged if you fail to do so. The hard lesson every safety/rescue professional or medical professional learns very early in their career is, "You can't save them all." But it's good to try.

The Bird and Jackson/Walters books mentioned above are good starts. A great read on the topic is the book "The Cornered Cat" by the aforementioned Kathy Jackson, which should be supplemented with her blog of the same name, both available at www.corneredcat.com. Her writing is not only inspirational to newcomers to self-defense but a recharging of the batteries for old hands in the game. While Ms. Jackson's work is of great value to either gender, she is most famous for her all-female classes in self-defense shooting and the feminine side of the armed lifestyle, and her book is nothing less than a manifesto for armed women. More solid reading in that field includes "Personal Defense for Women" and "Concealed Carry For Women," both by Gila Hayes, "Armed and Female" by Paxton Quigley, and "Calling the Shots" by Jenna Meeks. All should be available through Amazon.com. They can prove to be life-saving gifts to people not yet fully informed about self-defense.

A NOTE OF APPRECIATION

I and the publisher want to thank William Aprill, Alexis Artwohl, "Spencer Blue," Ron Borsch, Craig Douglas, Jim Fleming, Tom Givens, Marty Hayes, John Hearne, Harvey Hedden, and Anthony Semone for their contributions, which have made this a one-of-a-kind book. I have learned a great deal from each of them over the years, and now, thanks to their contributions, so have you. I don't miss the chance to train with any of them. Neither should you.

All of us who contributed to this book thank you for reading it. We hope you will share it with others who may benefit from it.

We all want you to stay safe...and to keep your people safe.

ABOUT THE AUTHOR

Massad Ayoob has published thousands of articles in gun magazines, martial arts publications, and law enforcement journals, and authored more than a dozen books on firearms, self-defense, and related topics.

During his distinguished career, Ayoob has won several state and regional handgun shooting championships, appeared as an expert witness for courts in weapons and shooting cases, and currently appears in numerous television shows. He founded the Lethal Force Institute in 1981 and served as its director until 2009, and now trains through Massad Ayoob Group.

Massad Ayoob's recent titles with Gun Digest include:

• Deadly Force: Understanding Your Right to Self Defense

• Gun Digest Book of Concealed Carry 2nd Edition

• Combat Shooting with Massad Ayoob

The following is an excerpt from
Deadly Force: Understanding Your Right to Self Defense
by Massad Ayoob

Available from gundigeststore.com

Debunking Myths of Armed Self-Defense

In April of 2014, the expert testimony of my friend and colleague Bob Smith in Spokane helped win acquittal for Gail Gerlach, who was charged with manslaughter. Gerlach had shot a man who, while stealing his car, had pointed a metallic object at him which appeared to be a gun, and Gerlach had fired one shot, killing the man, who turned out to have been holding shiny keys in the dimly lit vehicle. In the anti-gun Spokane newspaper, internet comments indicated that many people had the clueless idea that Gerlach had shot the man – in the back – to stop the thief from stealing his car. One idiot wrote in defense of doing such, "That 'inert property' as you call it represents a significant part of a man's life. Stealing it is the same as stealing a part of his life. Part of my life is far more important than all of a thief's life."

Analyze that statement. The world revolves around this speaker so much that a bit of his life spent earning an expensive object is worth "all of (another man's) life." Never forget that, in this country, human life is seen by the courts as having a higher value than what those courts call "mere property," even if you're shooting the most incorrigible lifelong thief to keep him from stealing the Hope Diamond. A principle of our law is also that the evil man has the same rights as a good man. Here we have yet another case of a person dangerously confusing "how he thinks things ought to be" with "how things actually are."

As a rule of thumb, American law does not justify the use of deadly force to protect what the courts have called "mere property." In the rare jurisdiction that does appear to allow this, ask yourself how the following words would resonate with a jury when uttered by plaintiff's counsel in closing argument: "Ladies and gentlemen, the defendant has admitted that he killed the deceased over property. How much difference is there in your hearts between the man who kills another to steal that man's property, and one who kills another to maintain possession of his own? Either way, he ended a human life for mere property!"

Why was Gerlach acquitted in this shooting? Because Bob Smith and the rest of the defense team were able to show the jury that he had not shot the man "for stealing his car" at all. As the car thief drove away, he turned in the front seat toward Gerlach and raised a metallic object and pointing it at him. In the prevailing light conditions, it looked like a gun – and Gerlach fired one shot from his 9mm pistol to keep the car thief from shooting him! Since the man was aiming backward at him over his shoulder, the defensively-fired bullet necessarily entered the offender's body behind the lateral midline. At that point, the man stopped pointing the metallic object at him, so Gerlach stopped shooting. It turned out that this object, which Gerlach reasonably presumed to be a gun, was a key holder that resembled one.

Gerlach's belief had been reasonable, and that allowed for the acquittal. It was not a case of a man being acquitted of a homicide charge for shooting "to save mere property."

Let's look at some other common myths which often suffuse discussion of armed citizens' justified use of force.

The "Drag the Corpse Inside and Plant a Knife in His Hand" Myth

The oldest and, sadly, most enduring myth out there is "when you shoot the bad guy on your porch, drag his body inside and put a knife in his hand before you call the police." If I've learned anything in three and a half decades of defending shooters in court, it's that The Truth is their strongest defense, and compromising that truth will kill their case and bring a verdict against them.

The time when someone could actually get away with altering evidence such as this is long gone, destroyed by modern forensic investigation techniques. When a body is moved, something called Locard's Principle comes into play, the principle of "transfer." Evidence from the body – clothing fibers, hair, blood, even skin cells and DNA – will transfer to the surface over which the body is dragged. Simultaneously, dirt or sand or carpet fibers, etc. from the surface will transfer to the body and the clothing of the deceased. The person trying to "cover his tracks" can get on his knees with a bucket of cleanser and scrub the floor "until the cows come home," but he won't get all the evidence off the scene. Much of it will be microscopic: the person who tried to change the evidence won't have a microscope, but the CSI (Crime Scene Investigation) crew most certainly will. The floor can be scrubbed until the naked eye sees no bloodstains, but the investigative technicians need only put down some Luminol, turn on the special lamp, and what their eye could not see before will now glow clearly.

Fingerprint experts are aware of "use patterns," the way human hands grasp certain objects. These fingerprint patterns are distinctly different from what the latent prints look like when a knife or other object is pressed into a dead man's hand. The difference shows up, to them, like a giant red flag.

In short, you could not expect to get away with this stupid "strategy" in this day and age.

Once you were discovered, what criminal charges would you have left yourself open for? Well, let's count...

- Alteration of evidence is a crime in and of itself, sometimes coming under the umbrella of an Obstruction of Justice charge. You may as well plead, because if you've done something this stupid, you're prima facie guilty of that crime.

- Manslaughter is now very much on the table of possible indictments, because what you've done is something the general public, the jury pool from which the Grand Jury is drawn, associates with someone who panicked, shot someone they shouldn't have shot, and is now trying to cover up their guilt.

- Premeditated murder is another possible charge, on the theory that "alteration of evidence may be construed as an indication of prior planning of a crime."

- Perjury, lying under oath, is a felony in most jurisdictions, and is implicit in the incredibly stupid "alter the evidence" meme.

The "Shoot and Scoot" Myth

It's not uncommon to hear, "If you have to shoot someone in self-defense, look both ways for witnesses and if you don't see any, just leave. That way you save all the hassle." I'm told there's a fellow on one of the gun-related Internet boards who claims he's a lawyer (interestingly, without giving his real name) when he posts that stupid advice.

Think about it: The prisons are full of people who looked around for witnesses, and didn't see any until they appeared to testify against them at trial. When an innocent person who did the right thing takes this terrible advice, they fall into an ancient trap called "flight equals guilt." It's the assumption that the cause for leaving the scene was "consciousness of guilt." In the classic US Supreme Court case Illinois v. Wardlow, SCOTUS upheld the actions of police who chased a man, caught him, and found inculpatory evidence upon search. They had chased him solely because he ran when he saw them coming. The majority opinion stated, "Headlong flight–wherever it occurs–is the consummate act of evasion: it is not necessarily indicative of wrongdoing, but it is certainly suggestive of such."

Suppose you are a careful driver, and one night a drunken pedestrian lunges in front of your car faster than it was humanly possible to stop. You remain at the scene and call 9-1-1. You can expect responding and investigating authorities to be sympathetic to you; after all, you went through something horrible that wasn't your fault. But suppose that instead of staying and calling in, you fled the scene. That turns it into "hit and run," and you can expect neither sympathy nor mercy when the weight of the criminal justice system comes down on you full force, soon to be followed by a massive civil suit.

The exact same effect kicks in on the person who leaves the scene without calling the authorities after having had to use a gun in defense of self or others. I've told my students for decades that after their gun comes out, they're in a race to the telephone. The first participant to call in the incident is generally perceived by the justice system as the "Victim/Complainant." The participant who is NOT the first to call in becomes, by default, the "Suspect." Many thugs have been going through the revolving doors of the criminal justice machine since they were juvenile offenders, and know how things work; they'll ditch their weapon, call 9-1-1, and claim that you assaulted them with a gun for no good reason. Your subsequent claim of self-defense will ring hollow in a world where cops and prosecutors alike expect the victim to be the first caller.

Failing to call in immediately, and instead leaving the scene, is the single most common mistake I've seen armed citizens make after they've otherwise properly used their gun to lawfully manage a dangerous incident instigated by a criminal. Once the "flight equals guilt" factor kicks in, you and your attorney will have a very steep uphill fight to prove your innocence.

The "I Can Shoot Anyone I Find in My House" Myth

Yes, there's a legal doctrine that says, "Your home is your castle," but that doesn't include an execution chamber. In virtually every state, the fine print of the law and case law requires that there be a reasonably perceived threat within the totality of the circumstances.

There are any number of situations where you might come home to find someone there whom you do not immediately recognize, even if you live alone. Most people have a key to their home out to someone: a landlord, a cleaning lady, a relative, a friend who comes by to feed the cat when they're gone. Perhaps another member of the family has called a plumber or electrician without bothering to notify you. We see case after case of the trusted person with the key coming unexpectedly to that house when they experience something traumatic at their own home and can't think of anyplace else to go, or the guest who already has a key and arrives unexpectedly early. Such things can make for particularly ugly tragedies if the home defender doesn't take that possibility into consideration when they see an unexpected figure in the shadows.

The "I Was in Fear for My Life" Myth

Opponents of Stand Your Ground laws claimed that they allowed anyone to kill anyone and get away with it by claiming they were in fear for their life. It was blatantly false, but it was claimed so many times in so many newspapers and on so many television programs that some gun owners came to believe it. It's simply not true. As written in Florida at the time of this writing, for example, a successful Stand Your Ground defense requires the shooter to prove that, more likely than not, he or she did indeed fire in self-defense.

Earlier, we mentioned that one Raul Rodriguez strapped on a pistol, shouldered a camcorder, and marched to a nearby home where a neighbor he disliked was holding an outdoor party that was louder than Mr. Rodriguez liked. Walking onto the other man's property and ostentatiously complaining (all the while recording), he started and escalated an argument. When people became angry, and frightened by his gun, he said loudly for the benefit of the camera, "I am in fear of my life" and "I will stand my ground." The situation ended when Rodriguez shot and killed the neighbor he despised, and wounded two other persons present. Charged with murder, he claimed self-defense.

It did him no good. In her opening statement, the prosecutor contemptuously noted that Rodriguez had "used every CHL (concealed handgun license) buzzword in the book." The state presented a damning witness who testified that prior to the shooting, Rodriguez had told her he could kill anyone he wanted and get away with it by uttering the magic words "I was in fear for my life."

There are no magic words, and Raul Rodriguez was convicted of murder and given a long prison sentence.

The "In My State I Can't be Sued for a Self-Defense Shooting" Myth

That's a huge oversimplification. The old saying still pretty much holds true: "anyone can file suit against anyone for anything." As noted elsewhere in the Castle Doctrine/Stand Your Ground chapter, the civil suit preemption provisions found under the umbrella of some SYG laws at most provide for the judge to throw out the case if it has already been determined to be an act of self-defense. However, merely not being criminally charged may not be enough. That's because the decision not to charge may have been motivated by the prosecuting authority's assessment that it could not gain a conviction by proving the act to have been criminal, beyond a reasonable doubt; for a lawsuit, the plaintiff need only meet the much lower standard of preponderance of evidence. The same is true if the defendant in the lawsuit has been tried and acquitted in criminal court. These things fall well short of a "determination" that it was self-defense.

In the states that do have protection against civil suit if the shooting has been ruled to be in self-defense, the question is, who makes that ruling? A ruling by the judge to the effect that the court has determined the act to have been in self-defense may do it. A memorandum of closure by the prosecuting authority specifically stating that their investigation has determined the act to have been in legitimate defense of self or others may do it. The mere fact that the case was not prosecuted, or even a trial that resulted in acquittal in criminal court, may not be enough.

And if the plaintiff's theory of the case is that the incident occurred by accident or through negligence, the protection against lawsuit will most likely be bypassed also.

The defendant's belief that the shooting was justified carries little weight in and of itself.

The "I'm Having a Heart Attack, Call an Ambulance" Myth

The recommendation that the shooter should pretend to be having a heart attack has been propounded widely, sometimes by people who should have been expected to know better. The theory is that the police will stop questioning the shooter for fear of civil liability and rush him to the hospital, where emergency room doctors and nurses won't let an interrogator near them. What's wrong with that theory?

Lots of things.

1. The hospital examination will show that you're not having a heart attack. At best, you are now seen as the panicky sort who exaggerates and overreacts – not at all the profile of the responsible person who effectively and properly managed an emergency. Or, worse, you are recognized as a liar at a time when your credibility will probably be more important than at any other time in your life.

    2. In many jurisdictions, the act of making false pretenses to emergency services personnel (police, fire, emergency medical services) is a crime in and of itself.

    3. Those who judge you will learn that you tied up limited emergency rescue resources that a real heart attack or trauma victim might have needed in a true life-or-death situation. Why? For the shady purpose of misleading and delaying law enforcement investigation of an act for which you are responsible. What sort of impression do you think that will make on judge and/or jury?

    4. Finally, you're going to get a big ambulance/ER bill for no good reason, since you could have forestalled questioning simply by asking for an attorney.

The "Warning Shots Are a Good Idea" Myth

You know a myth is widespread when it emanates from the White House. In 2013 while campaigning for a ban on so-called "assault rifles," Vice-President Joseph Biden told the public he had advised his wife that if there was a home invasion, she was to take a double barrel shotgun and fire both barrels upwards. One can only imagine how the Secret Service Vice-Presidential detail felt when they heard that. I can tell you that across the nation lawyers, cops, and gun-wise people rolled their eyes and shook their heads.

The fact is, warning shots have long been prohibited by most American police departments. This is for several reasons:

    5. What goes up, must come down. The stereotyped warning shot is fired skyward. Shooting live ammunition into the sky is a practice normally associated with Third World countries where respect for human

life is not as great as in the United States. There are many cases on record where such bullets "fell from the sky" and killed innocent people. In one New England case, a man carelessly fired a warning shot upward in the state's largest city; the bullet struck and killed an innocent bystander who was on the upper porch of a tenement building.

6. To fire the warning shot safely, the shooter would have to aim it into something that could safely absorb the projectile. This would force the shooter to take his eyes off of the potentially dangerous criminal opponent he was trying to intimidate – always a poor idea tactically.

7. What appears to be a safe place to plant the warning bullet, may not be. I know a police officer who, trying to break up a riot, fired a warning shot from his 12 gauge shotgun downward from the upper floor walkway of a hotel into what appeared in the dark to be a soft patch of earth. It was, instead, darkened pavement. Double-ought buckshot pellets caromed off the hard surface, one striking a young woman in the eye.

8. Suppose the person who caused you to fire the warning shot runs around a corner. Another gunshot rings out; someone else has shot the man, in a moment when deadly force was not warranted. The bullet goes through and through, fatally, and is not recovered. The man who wrongfully shot him claims that he fired the warning shot, and it was your bullet that caused the wrongful death. It's your word against his...unless you can say, "Officer, you'll find the bullet from MY gun in the friendly oak tree right over there." But it would have been better in these circumstances if you had not fired at all.

9. Warning shots can lead to misunderstandings with deadly unintended consequences. Years ago in the Great Lakes area, two police officers were searching opposite ends of a commercial greenhouse where a burglar alarm had just gone off. One confronted the burglar, who ran. The officer raised his arm skyward for the traditional silver screen warning shot. As is often the case, the blast just made the suspect run faster. On the other end of the building, the brother officer heard the shot and shouted to his partner, asking if he was all right. But the powerful handgun had gone off so close to the first officer's unprotected ear that his ears were ringing, and he didn't hear the shout. The second officer then saw the suspect running. Concluding that the man must have killed the partner who didn't answer, that second officer shot and killed a man who was guilty only of burglary and running from the police.

10. A single gunshot sounds to earwitnesses (and, depending on the circumstances, even eyewitnesses) as if you tried to kill a man you were only trying to warn. Did you yell the standard movie line, "Stop or I'll shoot"? It could sound to an earwitness as if you threatened to kill a man for not obeying you, and then tried to do exactly that. Don't make threats you don't have a right to carry out, and as will be noted elsewhere in this book, the confluence of circumstances that warrants the shooting of a

fleeing felon is extremely rare. (Remember that there are usually more earwitnesses than eyewitnesses; sound generally travels farther than line of sight, especially in the dark. Remember the infamous case of Kitty Genovese, who was murdered as 38 New York witnesses supposedly watched and did nothing. A study of the incident shows that only two of those witnesses actually saw the knife go into her body. However, more than 38 apparently heard her scream, "He stabbed me!")

11. Even if there are no witnesses and the man claims you shot at him and missed, evidence will show that you did fire your gun. If he claims you attempted to murder him, it's his word against yours.

12. Murphy's law is immutable: if your weapon is going to jam, expect it to jam on the warning shot, and leave you helpless when the opponent comes up on you with his gun.

13. The firing of a gun even in the "general direction" of another person is an act of deadly force. If deadly force was warranted, well, "warning shot, hell!" You would have shot directly at him. The warning shot can tell judge and jury that the very fact that you didn't aim the shot at him is a tacit admission that even by your own lights, you knew deadly force was not justified at the time you fired the shot.

14. If the man turns on you in the next moment and you do have to shoot him or die, you've wasted precious ammunition. With the still-popular five-shot revolver, you've just thrown away 20% of your potentially life-saving firepower. In one case in the Philippines, a man went berserk in a crowded open-air market and began stabbing and slashing people with a knife in each hand. In a nearby home, an off-duty Filipino police officer heard the screams, grabbed his six-shot service revolver (with no spare ammunition), and ran to the scene. When he confronted the madman, the latter turned on him. The officer fired three warning shots into the air, sending half of all he had to protect himself and the public into the stratosphere. He turned and ran, trying to shoot over his shoulder, and missed with his last three shots. He tripped and fell, and the pursuing knife-wielder literally ripped him apart. Responding officers shot and killed the madman, but their off-duty brother was already dead by then.

A subset of the warning shot is what I've come to call the "chaser shot." This is the sort of warning shot that sends the message, "and keep running and don't come back!" This too can backfire in multiple ways. I worked on one case where a retired physician was attacked by a burglar, and fired a shot at him and missed. The criminal turned and ran. In the grip of fear, untrained, the physician fired a "chaser shot"; he didn't intend for it to hit the suspect, but it did. The criminal ran a considerable distance and then collapsed, dying, from the wound. The doctor was charged with manslaughter. His lawyer was able to keep him out of jail, but it took a lot of legal fees to do that. I consulted in another where a man was attacked by multiple people in a driveway. He shot and killed his primary assailant, and then drove away. As he did so, he raised his .38 and fired one shot over the heads of the attacker's accomplices to keep them from running toward his vehicle and dragging him out. The bullet went harmlessly over their heads and buried itself in a roof. The jury acquitted him entirely on the homicide charge, understanding that it was self-defense, but due to an obscure law in that state intended to combat drive-by shootings, convicted him on the lesser included charge of firing a gun from a moving vehicle. It was a felony level conviction, and he ended up serving prison time for it.

It is clear why most law enforcement agencies forbid warning shots, and why most private sector instructors including this writer recommend against firing them. For many years, however, I have taught Ayoob's Law of Necessary Hypocrisy, which holds this: "If I have told you, 'Do not do this, it is incredibly stupid,' and you have replied, 'Well, I might be in some situation you haven't foreseen where I may feel a need to do it anyway,' I want you to know the least incredibly stupid way of doing the incredibly stupid thing." That applies to things like trying to do a building search alone, for example. Applied to the warning shot, if I felt some unique set of circumstances fit the doctrine of competing harms and compelled me to fire a warning shot, I would shout "Final warning!" (not "Stop or I'll shoot"), and would take care to fire the bullet into something that could safely and retrievably absorb the projectile. Safely, for all the reasons stated above, and retrievably because if someone else was doing some shooting, I'd want to be able to prove that my warning shot wasn't the one that caused death or crippling injury.

But, clearly, the take-away lesson is **DON'T FIRE WARNING SHOTS!**

The "Make Sure Your Opponent is Dead" Myth

This is the theory which says that if you ever have to shoot someone, make sure he's dead before you call the police. It's born in the public fear of liars and lawyers and of a legal system most people don't fully understand. It's the old "dead men tell no tales" theory. If he's dead, he can't lie, right?

There is a great deal wrong with that sort of thinking. We shoot to stop, not to kill; if he drops his weapon and ceases hostility after a minor wound, he has been stopped. Hell, if you shoot at him and miss and he throws his weapon away and screams, "I give up," your right to shoot any more has just come to a screeching halt.

Can he lie? Sure. But just as smart homicide detectives and forensic pathologists can truly reconstruct events from their examination of the scene and the silent dead, a cunning and unscrupulous lawyer can craft a "theory of the case" around a criminal's corpse better than he could from the testimony of a wounded member of the underworld.

Why? Because Mark Twain was absolutely right when he said that the best thing about telling the truth was that it's easy to remember. If it was me and not fate determining whether or not my opponent died from my gunfire, I'd rather he survive. Not only because it spares his innocent family grief, but because the decades have shown me that the criminal himself can usually be caught in his lies. Caught by good detectives, and caught by your attorney. If he's dead, though, a crafty attorney who has put his ethics in his wallet can come up with any BS theory he wants, and be much harder to trip up than a live criminal. On the other hand, if your opponent has survived to give false testimony as to what happened, skilled questioning by everyone from police detectives to your defense lawyer can reveal him for the lying SOB he is.

Finally, the "make sure he's dead" meme implies that you can look at an opponent who's now out of the fight, hors de combat, and execute him to keep him from lying about you. There's a word for that: Murder.

Anyone who thinks he can do that, I'd rather not be reading one of my books. I'd rather he take his eyes off this page, instead, and go look in a mirror, and ask himself what kind of human being he has become.

Given the advanced state of evidence analysis and homicide investigation today, I can tell you what kind of person he is going to become: a convicted murderer, spending his life in prison.

The "You'll Never Have to Take the Stand" Myth

This is one that actually comes from the lawyers. It's no big secret that the great majority of people who are charged with criminal offenses are in fact guilty, either of the crime with which they are charged or at least, some lesser included offense. These people become the mainstream, meat-and-potatoes clientele of defense lawyers. If guilty men get on the stand under oath, one of two things will happen during competent cross-examination by skilled prosecutors: they will tell the truth and absolutely convict themselves, or they will lie and get caught in the lie, and still convict themselves. If they choose the latter path, the defense attorney is in the line of fire for an accusation that he suborned their client's perjury: a low-level felony in and of itself in certain jurisdictions, and certainly grounds for the attorney to be disbarred. Therefore, it's not surprising that they advise their clients not to take the stand.

This is a classic example of why the strategies defense lawyers employ, to guard the Constitutional rights of their often-guilty clients, do not work for the innocent person who has been falsely accused. If it was indeed self-defense, you'll be employing the affirmative defense discussed at length elsewhere in this book. You'll be stipulating that you did indeed fire the shot(s) that killed the deceased, but that you acted correctly in doing so.

The prosecution has the burden of establishing mens rea, literally "the guilty mind." They have to show that you either intended to commit a crime, or acted with negligence so gross that it rose to a culpable standard. Your only defense against that is your "mind-set": what was in your mind when you took that action. Why did you do it?

If you don't go on the witness stand to testify to why you did it, who else on earth can?

Oh, sure, your attorney can state in opening argument that you did it in lawful defense of self or other innocent parties...but whatever your lawyer says has to be backed up by facts, evidence, and testimony. The key testimony will be yours.

I've had a few cases where we simply couldn't put the defendant on the stand. In one, the defendant's doctor flatly told the lawyer that if he went on the stand, he'd win the case but lose the patient, because the defendant's heart condition was so precarious the physician didn't think he would survive the stress of the experience. Fortunately, the evidence in favor of self-defense was so strong that the attorney – Jeff Weiner, who wrote the foreword for this book – was able to make it clear to judge and prosecution alike before trial. The result was a withhold of adjudication, meaning essentially that if the defendant kept his nose clean for a certain period of time, the charge would go away. He did and it did, and the client was a free man who soon had his concealed carry permit back.

Another was a battered woman so beaten down throughout her life, we knew she'd be putty in the hands of an alpha male lawyer cross-examining her. Mark Seiden tried the case brilliantly without putting her on the stand, and the evidence and testimony of other witnesses was so strong that the jury "got it." They acquitted her on all charges after about two hours of deliberation.

Those were exceptions, in my experience. The "keep the defendant off the stand" strategy is used primarily for guilty clients. One of what I whimsically call "Ayoob's Laws" is this one: "If you hire a guilty man's lawyer who gives you a guilty man's defense, you can expect a guilty man's verdict."

Think about it. Why would your attorney tell you not to take the stand?

Perhaps he thinks you're guilty, like so many of the rest of his clients. If you are truly innocent, do you really want your life in the hands of someone who thinks you're guilty?

Maybe he thinks you're so stupid that you can be easily led down the primrose path in cross-examination by opposing counsel. Maybe he thinks you're too weak to withstand cross examination. Maybe he thinks you're a lunatic gun nut who will say something stupid on the witness stand and turn the jury against you.

Whatever his rationale, I can only tell you this: If I was the defendant in a righteous shooting case that had turned into a false accusation, and my lawyer told me, "Don't worry, you'll never have to take the stand," I know what I would do.

I would ask that lawyer, "How much do I owe you for your time so far?" I would then write a check for that amount, put it on his or her desk, and say, "You're fired."

Because that lawyer will have just told me that he or she has no clue how to deliver an affirmative defense for a person who has used a weapon in honest defense of self or other innocents.